Anonymous

Money Growers Manual

Anonymous

Money Growers Manual

ISBN/EAN: 9783744785174

Printed in Europe, USA, Canada, Australia, Japan

Cover: Foto ©Lupo / pixelio.de

More available books at **www.hansebooks.com**

Johnson & Stokes 1892

Money Growers Manual

Why?

THERE are *reasons* why sensible people should buy their seeds of JOHNSON & STOKES. More than one hundred thousand such people have found by experience what these reasons are; but many thousands of new customers, who are seeking such a house, ought to know, too.

Growing seeds of the right sort is a difficult business. It requires rare facilities and experience just to grow good seeds. But we undertake more than this. The best sort of a seed business must be carried on doubly, so to speak,—it must grow plants, and it must grow seeds. It must grow the plants first, to find out whether the seeds of those plants are worth growing.

Few seed houses will take the trouble to do this. We make it a chief feature of our business. What we do is not merely to grow seeds: it is to grow the *right seeds*, from *tested stocks*. Our customers get not merely seeds that will grow: they get seeds that it will *pay* them to grow.

We are constantly working at the problem of *what to plant*, and what *not to plant*. We have a perfect system of trials and seed tests. Our business is not with unsophisticated amateurs and fancy farmers: it is chiefly with experienced planters and market gardeners, who cultivate for profit. Their requirements are exacting. They demand not only seeds that will grow, but seeds that will *pay*. We must furnish them. *We do furnish them.*

Attentive readers of our MANUAL will notice two peculiarities: first, it omits much that other lists contain; second, it contains much that other lists omit. We give you *cream* only. Our extended trials and experience enable us to weed out many varieties that are unworthy of cultivation; and they also enable us to introduce *tested* novelties and specialties of great value, many of which can be had only of us. Our customers have thus a double advantage.

Our Great Double Seed Warehouses, the largest in the East, are arranged expressly for the seed business.

Every letter and order has our personal attention, being read by one of our firm.

Our force of employees have most of them devoted a lifetime to the business. Like our Seeds, they are TESTED.

Our prices are always as low as those of any reliable house; but never too low to pay for *the best seeds that it is possible to produce.*

We want YOUR custom.

Respectfully,

JOHNSON & STOKES,
Philadelphia, Pa.

217 AND 219 MARKET ST.
206 AND 208 CHURCH ST.

FROM ACTUAL PHOTOGRAPHS. NOVELTIES AND SPECIALTIES

THE tendency to exaggerate illustrations in seed catalogues has become so great that we have decided to offer in future our novelties and leading specialties from actual copies of photographs taken during growth and those for 1892 will be found illustrated in this way on the first sixteen pages of this book. While experienced gardeners can distinguish these greatly exaggerated cuts, that appear each season in so many catalogues, as readily as a bank clerk can counterfeit money, yet there are, no doubt, some inexperienced amateurs who are humbugged and deceived by them. We have always deplored and discouraged such quackery and deception by instructing our engravers to follow nature as closely as possible in making all our cuts, therefore those that appear on all our pages may be depended upon as being as accurate as it is possible to engrave them.

GOLDEN-EYED BUTTER WAX BEAN—Photograph of an average plant.

NEW GOLDEN-EYED BUTTER WAX BEAN.
THE EARLIEST AND BEST WAX BEAN FOR BOTH THE HOME AND MARKET GARDEN.

This fine new variety, which we offered last spring for the first time, is pronounced by leading gardeners who have grown it, the **earliest and most salable** of any they have ever had. It is earlier than the popular Wardwell's Kidney Wax and Golden Wax sorts. The vine grows vigorously about one and a half feet, holding the great profusion of handsome pods well off the ground, thus keeping them clean and attractive. The pods are flat, larger and handsomer than Golden Wax and remarkably free from blight and rust. It will pay every market or family gardener to plant a considerable portion of his crops in it this season, **as in quality, appearance and size it leaves nothing to be desired.** Pkt., 10c.; pint, 35c.; qt., 60c., post-paid; qt., 45c.; peck. $2.25; bush., $8.00, by freight or express.

OUR FREE PREMIUMS FOR 1892—BOOKS AND SEEDS.

We have several **valuable novelties** and **new and improved varieties** in vegetables, which have never been offered for sale and will not under any circumstances be sold this season. We shall be glad, however, to add one or more liberal seed packages **free for trial** to all customers whose orders indicate an interest in new sorts. We also publish on page 21 a complete list of the leading agricultural and horticultural books, any of which can be had free with your vegetable and flower seed orders, as per offers. The selection of any of these **books as premiums** does not prevent the selection of seeds to the value of $1.25 for each $1.00 sent us for seeds in packets, as per offer on page 22.

AN EXACT PHOTOGRAPHIC REPRODUCTION OF A PLANT OF DREER'S BUSH LIMA BEAN, BEARING ONE HUNDRED AND EIGHTY-FIVE PODS.

DREER'S ⁂ BUSH ⁂ LARGE ⁂ LIMA ⁂ BEAN,
THE BEST OF ALL THE DWARF OR BUSH LIMAS.

This remarkable bean was distributed to a very limited extent last year and has in the past season's trials fully confirmed our good opinion of its merits. It is a true Bush variety of **Dreer's Improved Large Lima**, possessing all the good qualities of that excellent and well-known sort. The plants grow from one and a half to two feet high, of vigorous bushy habit, showing no disposition whatever to run, producing pods in great abundance. The beans grow close together in the pods, are very thick, sweet and succulent, and ripen fully ten days earlier than any of the Pole Limas.

The following notes are taken from trials last summer:

First planting made May 4th, matured August 3d, ninety-one days from planting. During growing period the weather was wet and unfavorable. The beans were well set, however, and matured eight days before any of the Pole Limas. The pods of the Bush variety were equally as large and full.

Second planting made on same soil May 19th, matured August 13th, eighty-six days; ten days ahead of Dreer's Improved Pole Lima. The beans were better set owing to a longer period of dry weather. Many of the pods contained five beans, and nearly one half had four in a pod. Where this Bush variety is planted on light, rich soil, it shows an increase in crop and less growth of plant.

As examples of the productiveness of this bean, we have received many specimens from gardeners who have grown it on trial, bearing from one hundred to one hundred and eighty-five pods.

With two such varieties as **Dreer's Bush Large Lima Bean** and **Henderson's Bush Lima**, which is the Bush form of the Small or Sieva Lima (see page 25), no garden need be without a supply of the truly luscious Lima Bean, and free from the unsightly poles necessary to grow the Pole varieties.

The supply of seed of **Dreer's New Bush Large Lima Bean** is so limited this year that we can only offer it in sealed packages at the price of 20c. per packet, 3 packets for 50c., or 7 packets for $1.00. Nor can we sell more than seven packets to any one person.

NEW AND DESIRABLE BEETS.

An exact Photographic Copy from Nature of two entirely new Beets, now offered for the first time.

JOHNSON & STOKES' NEW SURPRISE BEET.

See also Colored Illustration painted from Nature, on back of this book.

In offering this unparalleled new and distinct variety we can assure our customers that we not only have a great "**Surprise**" for them, but a genuine prize. After an exhaustive trial for the past three seasons on our Bucks County farm, where it was originated, and also from the unqualified recommendations of several of our Philadelphia truckers, to whom we gave the seed for trial, we pronounce it without exception the **Earliest Beet** ever produced. Its table qualities are much superior to any variety with which we are familiar, the flesh being unusually sweet, fine grained and tender, retaining its fine blood-red color when cooked. It has the very small top of the well-known Egyptian variety, which admirably fits it for growing under glass, as well as in the open ground, but unlike the latter, it retains its **faultless quality**, even after it has lost its leaves from age. While the Egyptian has heretofore been about the earliest sort obtainable, it is a well-known fact that its poor quality often rendered it undesirable, and that it is not marketable at all in its middle and later stage of growth, owing to its tasteless, hard, woody nature, and disposition to crack open. These defects, as well as all others, are entirely absent in the **New Surprise.** It will prove a "**Money Grower**" to every market or private gardener who plants it. Pkt., 10c.; oz., 20c.; ¼ lb., 60c.; lb., $2.00.

FORD'S PERFECTED HALF-LONG BEET.

This new variety is the result of many years careful selection by Mr. James Ford, one of the oldest and most successful of Philadelphia market gardeners, and who is well-known to most of our customers as the originator of the now celebrated **Ford's Mammoth Podded Lima Bean.** It has many valuable and distinct points of merit not possessed by any other existing sort. The color is several shades darker red than the well-known Philadelphia Perfection and Bastian Half-Long sorts, while it is so uniformly thoroughbred that the beets are almost exact duplicates of one another in color, shape and size. It is also earlier than any other Half-Long sort, being ready to market a few days after the Early Turnip varieties, while as a **fall and winter beet it has no equal,** as none other can approach it in keeping qualities. We offer seed grown by the originator. Pkt., 10c.; oz., 20c.; ¼ lb., 50c.; lb., $1.50.

THE : MONEY : GROWERS' : CABBAGES.

A PHOTOGRAPH TAKEN IN OUR FIELD OF JOHNSON & STOKES' EARLIEST CABBAGE GROWING FOR SEED.

JOHNSON & STOKES' EARLIEST CABBAGE.

No words of praise can be written that would recommend this most desirable cabbage too highly. Now in the **seventh year of its great popularity,** with demand greater than ever before. We have supplied it to more than 5,000 market gardeners, among them some of the largest growers of cabbage in the United States, and have received hundreds of testimonial letters from all sections of the country, pronouncing it the best and most profitable cabbage they have ever grown.

It is **ten days earlier** than Early Jersey Wakefield and is **unsurpassed in fine quality, great beauty and vigor of growth.** The heads are slightly conical, **remarkably large, solid and uniform in growth and of the finest quality.** Pkt., 10c.; oz., 30c.; 2 oz., 75c.; ¼ lb., $1.25; lb., $4.00, post-paid.

JOHNSON & STOKES' NEW WONDERFUL CABBAGE.

When we introduced our now famous **Johnson & Stokes' Earliest Cabbage** some years ago, we thought we had reached the top of the ladder of **extreme earliness** in the cabbage family. Encouraged by the phenomenal success of that variety, our motto always being "**onward,**" induced us to try again, and by persistent selection for several years of the very earliest heads of that variety, we have produced a new and improved strain of our celebrated cabbage, which produces **fair-sized, good marketable heads in seventy-five to eighty days from sowing the seed,** and outdoes it in earliness by six to ten days. This makes our **New Wonderful Cabbage** more than **two weeks ahead** of any known variety, except **Johnson & Stokes' Earliest.** It does not, of course, form quite so large a head as our **Earliest,** but in all other respects it **fully equals it.** It has few loose outer leaves, and every plant forms a good head. It will produce a larger crop than any other variety, as it can readily be planted as close as fifteen to sixteen inches apart each way, or about 15,000 to the acre. Pkt., 10c.; oz., 30c.; ¼ lb., $1.25; lb., $4.00.

JOHNSON & STOKES'
Hard - Heading - Savoy - Cabbage.

This variety is the result of many years careful selection, and in it we have certainly reached perfection in the Savoys. It is unquestionably the best and most profitable strain for the market gardener to grow, being far superior to the ordinary Imported Drumhead Savoy, as generally sold by seedsmen, the seed of which can be supplied at less than half the price. The heads are large, very uniform, solid and hard, of a deep green color, very curly and sure to head, keeps well and retains its color until very late in the season. It is also the best for home use, owing to its unexceptionally fine quality, possessing the rich, sweet flavor of the cauliflower when cooked. Grow it once and you will grow it always. Pkt., 10c.; oz., 30c.; ¼ lb., $1.00; lb., $4.00.

JOHNSON & STOKES' HARD HEADING SAVOY.
Photograph taken in the field while growing.

∴ NOVELTIES ∴ AND ∴ SPECIALTIES ∴

Section of field of Johnson & Stokes' Market Gardeners' Cabbage, No. 2. Photographed during growth. The plants in this field were set in three foot rows, eighteen inches apart, giving 9,680 to the acre or fully one thousand more heads to an acre than can be obtained from any other large heading variety and proving it certainly the most compact of all large cabbages.

JOHNSON & STOKES' MARKET GARDENERS' CABBAGE, NO. 2.

This very valuable new variety is decidedly the **Earliest and most compact of all large cabbages**. It was offered by us for the first time in the spring of 1889, and has given unbounded satisfaction in all sections. It is pronounced by many prominent gardeners who are now growing it almost exclusively, the **very best of all cabbages as a second early and summer market sort**.

The originator had for several years sold the seed to cabbage growers in Northern New Jersey at $2.00 per ounce until we purchased the variety and his entire crop of seed in 1888. In it we have a cabbage so **hardy** and **vigorous** that it can be set much **earlier than Jersey Wakefield** or **Early Summer** and will produce fine solid marketable heads, more than **twice as large as Jersey Wakefield** and one-half again as large as **Early Summer**, and come in as **early as the Wakefield**, and two weeks earlier than Early Summer or any other round or flat-headed variety. Could anything more be wished for in an early market cabbage? On the other hand, when planted for a fall or winter crop, there is no other cabbage which will withstand the summer sun so well, and is so sure to form **large, deep solid heads**, the quality of which is equal to the best, and when stored for winter will keep perfectly until very late in the spring, coming out in fine salable condition.

Such a cabbage is Johnson & Stokes' Market Gardeners' Cabbage, No. 2, and all who have not yet given it a trial, will, after growing it, be as enthusiastic in its praise as we are. **Try some of the best seed of the very best cabbage in cultivation.** Pkt., 15c.; oz., 65c.; ¼ lb., $1.75 ; lb., $6.50.

C. H. Metcalf, Milford, Mass., Feb. 2, 1891, writes: "Your J. & S. Market Gardeners' Cabbage, No. 2 is away ahead of all others in earliness, size and fine quality. My crop last season was all heads, eight of which would, on an average, fill a barrel plump full."

B. Bruemmer, Springfield, Ohio, Oct. 17, 1890, writes: "Your J. & S. Market Gardeners' Cabbage, No. 2, is pronounced by all the finest ever grown around here. I had it in market on the third day of July and it eclipsed all others. Our gardens here are not complete without Johnson & Stokes' seeds."

Dr. J. Z. Taylor, Deals Island, Md., June 15, 1891, writes: "I have grown them all but can find nothing equal in any respect to your J. & S. Market Gardeners' Cabbage, No. 2."

A. Miller, Albion, N. Y., Sept. 29, 1891, writes: "Your Market Gardeners' Cabbage, No. 2, is considered here as simply a wonder. It took first premium over seven others at the county fair. Your J. & S. Earliest is more than you claim for it."

Geraty & Towles, the largest cabbage growers of South Carolina, June 7, 1891, write: "Your J. & S. Earliest Cabbage is the earliest and finest stock we ever saw."

E. B. Warcener, Brooksville, Fla., March 16, 1891, writes: "Your J. & S. Earliest Cabbage is pronounced by truckers, the finest ever grown in Hernando County. By far the earliest, heads large, solid and of the finest quality for market and shipping."

H. F. Boley, Hillsdale, Mich., writes: "J. & S. Wonderful Cabbages are wonderful indeed. Earliest and best in market."

W. L. Owens, Jarvesburg, N. C., writes: "Johnson & Stokes' Earliest Cabbage stands at the head of the list. I have planted no other for three years; they are extra keepers, and form a very large solid head in about eighty-two days from sowing."

MASTIFF · GOLDEN · POD POLE BEAN.

NEW MASTIFF GOLDEN POD POLE BEAN.

This magnificent new Pole Bean, which we introduce this season to the public, under the above deserving name, we feel sure will prove the most valuable variety ever offered. For three years we have made comparative tests on our Trial Grounds, with other most excellent sorts and each season it has proven to be by far the largest and most productive of all. In size and appearance of pod it bears the same relation to other pole varieties as the Yosemite Mammoth Wax does to the Dwarf sorts. The accompanying photograph, made during growth, while it gives a fair idea of its wonderful productiveness, does not do complete justice to their enormous size, having been taken before maturity. The pods are remarkably handsome and fleshy, attaining a length of from ten to fourteen inches and of rich buttery flavor when cooked. The beans when dry are of a light yellow, almost the color of the pod itself when fit for use as a string bean. We believe it certain to become the leading Wax Pole Bean and every garden should contain it. Our stock has been worked up from a small package sent us three years ago by a customer and is so limited this season that we can only offer it in sealed packages. We are sure, however, all who try it will return for seed next season, when we hope to be able to offer it in quantity. Prices for 1892: Pkt., 15c.; 4 pkts., 50c.; 10 pkts., $1.00, postpaid.

New Customers.

As this catalogue will reach many who have never had our seeds, we would urge such to send us a **trial order**, no matter how small, and, although you may be satisfied with seeds bought elsewhere, we believe our **special strains** of many of the newer varieties will make them as profitable to you as they have been to thousands of others who are now regular customers.

LOUDERBACK'S ALL YEAR ROUND CABBAGE.

We feel a pride in having been the first seedsmen to offer to the public a variety of cabbage with so many valuable points as **Louderback's All Year Round**. This cabbage originated with Daniel Louderback, one of the oldest and most successful of Philadelphia market gardeners, and has had a great local reputation among his neighbors for several years. It is not only the finest Early Drumhead in cultivation, but is equally as good for **second and third early, intermediate or late**. It heads large, compact and solid, with very short stem and few outer leaves, unflagging under the hottest sun or heaviest frost and may be sown successively and continuously during all periods when cabbage is planted. It is a very rapid grower and while it will well repay good treatment, yet it does not require special culture to develop. As an all round cabbage nothing that we have ever seen approaches it. The seed we offer was grown by Daniel Louderback, the originator. We recommend it to all desiring something very choice, and want a variety from which they can have cabbage every month in the year, as it is a splendid keeper. Pkt., 10c.; oz., 45c.; 2 oz., 80c.; ¼ lb., $1.25; lb., $4.00.

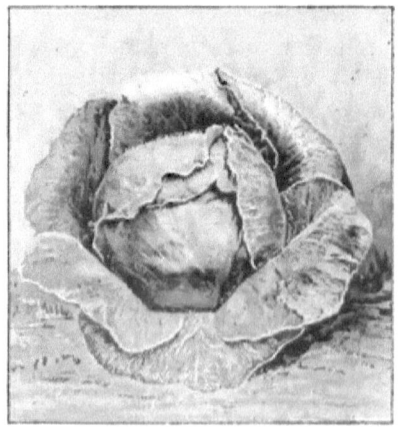

PHOTO OF LOUDERBACK'S ALL YEAR ROUND CABBAGE.

∴ NOVELTIES ∴ AND ∴ SPECIALTIES ∴

One of our market garden customers in Manitoba was so delighted with his crop of Early Alabaster Cauliflower that he had a large photograph made and sent to us, of which the above is an exact copy, reduced in size. He writes: "The seed was sown April 18th, transplanted June 1st, cauliflowers such as were never before seen in that northern latitude were cut for market July 14th."

JOHNSON & STOKES' EARLY ALABASTER CAULIFLOWER.

THE EARLIEST OF ALL.   THE EASIEST GROWN.   THE SUREST HEADER.

The Early Alabaster is an entirely new and distinct sort, of American origin. It was originally a sport from the finest German strain of the selected Dwarf Erfurt, one **extra** fine **head** appearing some **ten days in advance** of any other in the crop of one of the largest and most expert cauliflower growers on Long Island in 1881. The seed of this was carefully saved by him, and from it our stock has been brought up. Careful selections have been made each year, the type is fixed, and we confidently recommend this as **the earliest and best cauliflower in the world** and it is so pronounced by all growers who have had it. It is suited for forcing as well as for growing in open ground, being of very dwarf erect habit, with short outer leaves. It can be planted less than two feet apart each way. It is a **sure header**, every plant forming a large, solid and perfect head of remarkably pure snowy-white color, of the finest table quality. All market and family gardeners who have failed in growing this delicious vegetable may rest assured that the trouble has come from either inferior or imported unacclimated seed, and should bear in mind that our seed of the **Early Alabaster is American-grown**, and from it a crop of cauliflower can be grown as easily as a crop of cabbage, and with greater profit, as one ounce of cauliflower seed will produce about 2,500 plants, the crop of which would usually bring in this market $300 to $400. **Pkt., 25c.; 5 pkts., $1.00; ⅛ oz., $1.50; ½ oz., $3.00; oz., $6.00; ¼ lb., $20.00.**

New Cabbage, Carolina Hard Header.

This entirely new and distinct late cabbage was originated in Buncombe County, North Carolina, where it has had a great local reputation for a few years past, the seed frequently being sold by local gardeners who were fortunate enough to have it, at the rate of $1.00 per ounce. An old gardener in describing this cabbage says: "*It heads as sure as the sun rises.*" It grows good sized flat and very hard heads, averaging fifteen to twenty-five pounds each, very short stock or stem, and darker green in color than any other cabbage of its class; earlier than the best strains of Late Flat Dutch, and while it is the most reliable hard-heading cabbage for the South we find it equally valuable for the North, having tested it for three successive seasons on our Trial Grounds. The seed we offer, now for the first time, is also grown on our Pennsylvania farm. *Money growers will make no mistake in planting it largely.* Pkt., 10c.; oz., 40c.; 2 oz., 75c.; ¼ lb., $1.25; lb., $4.00.

Photograph of the New Cabbage, Carolina Hard-Header.

Johnson & Stokes' Golden Self-Blanching Celery.

A VARIETY WHICH EVERY FAMILY AND MARKET GARDENER SHOULD GROW.

The **Golden Self-Blanching Celery** we first introduced to the American public in 1883, since which time it has been pronounced by hundreds of our market garden patrons, who have grown it on our recommendation, the **very best and most profitable celery in cultivation.** Our illustration above was photographed from an average bunch as it appeared in Philadelphia markets on September 1st, and will give some idea of its very **handsome form** and even growth, reaching a very large size, but very stocky and robust. The stalks grow vigorously, with large ribs, very thickly and closely set. It is very early and **entirely self-blanching**, without any banking up or covering whatever, even the outer ribs assuming a yellowish-white color of a very fresh and pleasing appearance. The heart is of a **beautiful golden-yellow color, very large, crisp and solid,** and **unsurpassed in delicious quality and flavor.** It is unequalled in striking appearance on the table or market stall, and decidedly the **best keeper** of all the Self-Blanching varieties. Many of our largest celery growers are now planting their entire crops in this variety. It is such a shy seeder that the genuine seed can never be sold at a less price than we offer it this season. By planting a large acreage, we are glad to state, we have been successful in growing the best supply we have ever had, and hope to be able to fill all orders at our very reasonable prices. Each **package** contains our trade label. Pkt., 15c.; oz., 40c.; ¼ lb., $1.10; lb., $4.00; 2 lbs., $7.50.

NOVELTIES AND SPECIALTIES

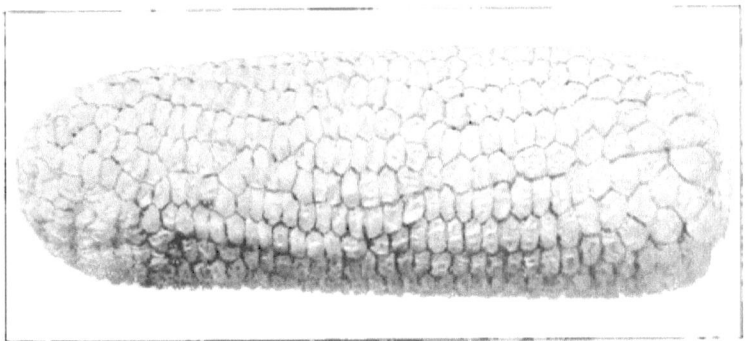

• • EARLY DAWN SWEET CORN. • •

From our own trials and hundreds of reports received, we believe this new and distinct sugar corn to be the **most valuable introduction** since the Burlington Hybrid and Cory. The originator, a gardener in Northern Vermont, in sending us the seed for trial, claimed it to be the only large-eared variety, the seed of which could be ripened in that northern latitude. It is unquestionably the **Largest-eared White-cobbed Early Sweet Corn**, with rich, creamy-white kernels, so large, plump and deep, that the shell or hull so prominent in most varieties is reduced to a minimum. The ears, in many instances, having sixteen to twenty-two rows. We believe it to be the best early genuine Sweet or Sugar Corn grown. Try it. Pkt., 15c.; pint 30c., qt., 50c., post-paid; qt., 35c.; 4 qts., $1.00; peck, $1.75; bush., $6.00, by freight or express.

Burlington Hybrid Sweet Corn

There is nothing in this catalogue more worthy of the careful consideration of gardeners than this new corn, and we felt highly gratified in having been the first seedsmen to offer it to the public in the spring of 1889. It is not an untried novelty, having been grown for several years with great profit by a few truckers of Burlington County, N. J., who have kept the stock closely guarded among themselves, they positively refusing to sell seed to any one, and also by many of our own patrons, on our recommendation, many of whom write us it gives them entire control of the early markets, proving extremely profitable. It is a cross between Adams' Extra Early and some large-eared productive variety of sugar corn. Its great market value can be readily seen from the fact that it **is as early as the Adams'**, with an ear **fully as large as Stowell's Evergreen** and more **productive** than either, producing equal to the most prolific field corn, it having frequently produced over one hundred bushels to the acre grown for a field crop. Although not legitimately a sugar corn, yet the husks, blades and ear in a green state exactly resemble the sugar varieties, and it sells readily in market as a sweet or sugar corn. It is, however, of much better eating quality than the Adams'. When dry the grain is smooth and of a creamy-white color. The stalks grow to a height of about five feet and very compact, admitting of closer planting than any other variety; the ears begin to set low down and are borne three to four to a stalk. Pkt., 10c.; pint, 25c.; qt., 45c., post paid; qt., 30c.; peck, $1.25, bush., $4.30, by freight.

Photograph of three average ears Burlington Hybrid,¹ natural size.

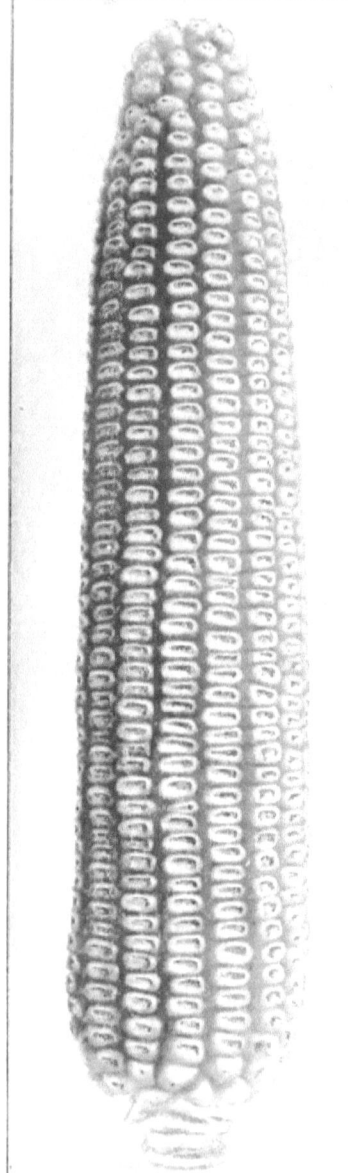

Photo of an average ear of Peach Blossom Mammoth. ½ natural size.

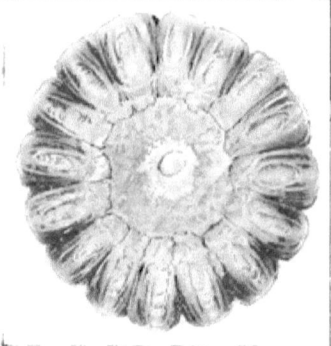

Section of ear of Peach Blossom Mammoth, ½ natural size.

A NEW FIELD CORN
Peach Blossom Mammoth.

This valuable new and distinct variety of field corn, which is now offered for sale for the first time, is a cross between the celebrated **Chester County Mammoth and Ohio Red**, brought to its present standard by careful selection made by Mr. Wm. Peck, who with a few of his neighbors, residing in the great corn growing district of Chester County, Pa., will grow no other sort, owing to its **many superior qualities** over all other varieties of field corn. It is without doubt the **most productive corn** in cultivation, as from our own experience with it, on our Chester County farm, as well as that of the farmers who are now growing it, it is indeed a rare and unfavorable season when it does not yield over one hundred bushels to the acre. It grows vigorously to a height of ten to twelve feet, **withstanding drought** better than any other corn known, ripens in good season, but not early, hence we do not recommend it for latitudes north of Central Pennsylvania. As will be seen from the photograph above of an average ear broken in half, the cob is very small for so large an ear, grain very deep and broad, of a beautiful golden color, handsomely tinted, and striped on the outside with light pink, hence the name given it by the originator, "Peach Blossom." **Fifty-five to sixty ears will shell a bushel.** It is softer, even when ground on the cob, sweeter and more nutritious for feeding than other sorts, making the finest meal. If you want to grow one of the **best field corns** in this country **try Peach Blossom**. Prices for 1892. Pkt., 15c.; ear, 25c.; lb., 40c.; 3 lbs., $1.00, post-paid by mail. By express or freight, shelled, peck, $1.00; bush., $3.00; sack of 2 bush., $5.00; on ear, wrapped, 25 ears, $2.00; 50 ears, $3.50; 100 ears, $6.00.

☞ For all other varieties of **Field Corn**, see Farm Seeds, page 76.

∴ NOVELTIES ∴ AND ∴ SPECIALTIES ∴

Photograph of specimens of Jersey Belle taken from field on our New Jersey Farm June 11, 1891, five days before any New Jersey grown Muskmelons were received in Philadelphia markets.

JERSEY ∶ BELLE ∶ MUSKMELON.

A NEW EXTRA EARLY VARIETY NOW OFFERED FOR THE FIRST TIME.

Notwithstanding we have never before offered this new Cantaloupe for sale, we have for the past few months been overwhelmed with inquiries and orders for the seed, this demand having been created by the fact that we last season distributed several thousand packages labelled New Muskmelon, No. 100, free for trial among our customers, the inquiries for the seed coming from them and their neighbors and friends who saw the melons during growth. We have received hundreds of acknowledgments and unsolicited testimonials similar to those published at the bottom of this page, and regret we have not room to publish more of them.

Notwithstanding we have had this very valuable variety under test for two years this is the first season, owing to its very shy seeding property, that we have been able to offer the seed for sale. In our trials it has always been the **first to ripen** and what is more remarkable it has proven the **largest of all the first early sorts**, grown alongside of them and under the same conditions. Unlike our **Extra Early Prize** and other very early sorts it does best on light soils, and will even develop perfectly on white sand. As shown in our photograph above it is flattened on the ends, deeply ribbed and heavily netted, indicating by its outward appearance the **exquisite quality** of the beautiful green flesh within.

In our patch of two and a half acres, this season, we were unable to find a poor-flavored melon, all we tested being uniformly rich and lusciously sweet. **The Jersey Belle**, when known, will rapidly popularize itself as the best of all extra early cantaloupes for either home use, market or shipping. With two such melons as **Jersey Belle and Johnson & Stokes' Superb** (the finest late variety in existence), all who plant them can have a feast of this most enjoyable and wholesome vegetable fruit the entire season. The supply of seed of **Jersey Belle** is so limited this season that we can only offer it in sealed packages at the following prices. Per pkt., 15c.; 4 pkt., 50c.; 10 pkts., $1.00.

A FEW SAMPLES OF EXPRESSIONS OF ALL REPORTS RECEIVED.

C. P. Sconso, Afton, N. J., Sept. 21, 1891. "Muskmelon, No. 100, proved to be the largest extra early variety, the most delicious and productive of any I have ever cultivated; indeed, enough cannot be said in its praise."

Tuto, J. Cooper, Shawneetown, Ill., Oct. 18, 1891, writes: "Your New Muskmelon, No. 100, yielded a most productive crop. It is the earliest and best melon I ever grew, surpassing all others in flavor and quality."

J. O. Darby, Birmingham, Ala., Sept. 15, 1891: "The New Muskmelon, No. 100, is simply splendid, the very earliest and most productive of all. Too much cannot be said in its praise."

R. B. Hogg, Ordinary, Va., Oct. 16, 1891, writes: "The New Muskmelon, No. 100, is the most productive and delicious in quality. They somewhat resemble the Jenny Lind in shape, but are of larger size and much earlier."

A PHOTOGRAPH OF THE GRAND NEW CANTALOUPE, OR MUSKMELON, JOHNSON & STOKES' SUPERB.

NEW MUSKMELON, JOHNSON & STOKES' SUPERB.

This is without question the handsomest late melon and most luscious of all the green-fleshed sorts. In describing its handsome shape and beautiful netted appearance, we cannot do better than to refer to the photograph above, made from an ordinary specimen taken from our patch. In a test with forty other green-fleshed varieties, it surpassed them all in growth, thickness of flesh and rich, delicious flavor. It attains a very large size, and its shipping and market qualities are superior to the well-known Montreal, Hackensack and other large market melons, while in quality and fine appearance they cannot even compare with the "**Superb.**" All who want the most profitable for late market, or those who want the best for the home garden, need seek no further. Pkt., 10c.; oz., 40c.; ¼ lb., $1.00; lb., $3.75.

PHOTO OF HENDERSON'S SUCCESSION, TAKEN DURING GROWTH.

HENDERSON'S
✻ SUCCESSION CABBAGE ✻

Attention was first called to this new cabbage by Mr. Van Sielen, of Long Island, who originated the well-known Early Summer Cabbage. It was first offered for sale three years since by our friends, Peter Henderson & Co., and has given satisfaction wherever planted. It follows ten days after Early Summer, comes off with much larger and heavier heads, and is very valuable for mid-summer use. It grows so compactly that notwithstanding its large size, it can readily be planted almost as close as Early Summer. In a large field which we grew for seed this season, every plant formed large head of as perfect and uniform shape as that shown in our photograph opposite. Pkt., 10c.; oz., 30c.; ¼ lb., 85c., lb., $3.00.

NOVELTIES AND SPECIALTIES

OUR PEDIGREE ONION SEED

No one can appreciate the value of **reliable seeds** better than those who have been **once disappointed**, and too much care cannot be exercised in selecting your supply. There is no vegetable where the quality of the seed exerts a greater influence upon the crop than in onions. Our stock is all grown from **choice bulbs selected carefully by hand, and is unsurpassed in this country.** During our whole business career as seedsmen, it has always been our aim to make **quality a first consideration**, price afterwards, and in no one crop have we met with greater reward for our efforts than in onions, the demand for our seed having increased so rapidly that we have been obliged to **double our facilities** for growing every year for several years past.

PHOTOGRAPH OF A GROWING CROP OF OUR PEDIGREE ONION SEED, ON OUR PENNSYLVANIA FARM.

PHILADELPHIA-GROWN SEED, or such raised in that portion of Pennsylvania, is unquestionably earlier than New England seed, and still more so as compared with Western seed. This is an important feature as the early marketed onions always bring the highest prices. The growth conclusively proves the assertion, Philadelphia seed making bulbs of better quality for keeping or immediate use either as sets or full-sized onions, long before seed from any other locality. Large, full-sized onions can be grown from our seed the first season in any section of the United States, both North and South, at no greater cost than carrots, parsnips, beets, ruta-bagas, or the onion sets themselves, while the net return per acre will be from two to five times as great. Five pounds of seed will sow an acre for this purpose. To grow small sets, fifty to sixty pounds to the acre is required.

- - THE SHORT CROPS OF 1891. - -

Owing to the scarcity and high prices of onions in the spring of 1891, the acreage planted for seed purposes throughout the United States was, from the best information obtainable, less than one-half that of 1889 and 1890. The yield of seed too in many sections has been very light and the total crops are much shorter than for several years past. As under these circumstances prices must advance very materially with the season, we advise all who want to take advantage of the prices offered below to order early. Write for special prices on larger lots. For prices by mail, postage paid, see pages 56-60.

Onion Seed by Freight or Express.	5 lb. Lots. Per lb.	10 lb. Lots. Per lb.	Onion Seed by Freight or Express.	5 lb. Lots. Per lb.	10 lb. Lots. Per lb.
Early Round Yellow Danvers,	$1 75	$1 70	Extra Large Red Wethersfield,	$1 70	$1 65
Philadelphia Yellow Globe Danvers,	2 10	2 00	Philadelphia Extra Early Red,	1 70	1 65
			Southport Red Globe,	1 85	1 80
Philadelphia Yellow Dutch or Strasburg,	1 85	1 80	American Extra Early Pearl,	4 85	4 75
			New Ivory Ball,	3 35	3 25
Southport Yellow Globe,	1 85	1 80	White Portugal or Silver Skin,	3 10	3 00
New Golden Ball,	2 60	2 50	Large White Globe,	2 85	2 75

Johnson & Stokes' Champion Spring and Summer Lettuce.

This new variety was offered for sale for the first time last spring, and, from the number of favorable reports, it has certainly proven a boon to every market and family gardener who planted it. It is certainly one of the **most valuable and distinct varieties in existence.** The photograph above hardly does it justice, as it would be impossible to portray on paper its beautiful **bright golden color and flaky light appearance,** in which it is unapproached by any other lettuce. It is not only one of the best early lettuces for spring planting, forming good solid heads before half grown, but alike valuable for growing during the hottest summer months, being one of the slowest to shoot to seed. The quality and flavor are simply perfect, surpassing all other varieties of cabbage lettuce. The seed is also very distinct from any known lettuce, being a brownish yellow in color. The testimonials below speak for themselves, we have enough similar ones on file in our office to fill several pages of this book. All are unanimous in giving Champion Spring and Summer the highest praise. Pkt., 15c.; oz., 45c.; ¼ lb., $1.25; lb., $4.00.

"Champion Spring and Summer Lettuce cannot be beat. It knocks out anything in this section of the country. It is earlier than Salamander by ten days and makes much larger and handsomer heads in June. Its equal certainly does not exist."—J. W. FISHER, Springfield, N. Y.

"Your seeds have given the greatest satisfaction here. The new lettuce, Champion Spring and Summer, proved the very best of all sorts. It stays in its headed state longer than any other variety we have ever grown. It simply can't be beat."—JOHN P. WILLIAMS, Anna, Ill.

"We were delighted with the Champion Spring and Summer Lettuce. It is three times as large as the Boston Market or White-Seeded Tennis Ball, at the same time being equally as tender and as quick in growth. In appearance and in all other respects it is far superior to any we have ever seen or grown, and too much cannot be said in its favor. The Cumberland Red Tomato is superior to any we have ever raised. All the other seeds purchased of you are the finest and best we ever had."—C. H. METCALF & SONS, Milford, Maine.

THORBURN'S LONG KEEPER TOMATO.

PHOTO OF A BASKET OF THORBURN'S LONGKEEPER, FROM OUR TRIAL GROUNDS.

We tested this new tomato on our Trial Grounds the past season and find all the claims made by the originator, E. S. Carman, editor of the *Rural New Yorker*, fully substantiated. Mr. Carman wrote last year the following letter, giving its origin and history:

About thirteen years ago I raised all the kinds of tomatoes popular at that time. Six of each were selected the same day, of apparently the same stage of maturity, and of a bright red color, as well as of the large size and shapeliest form. These were kept in a darkened room until all were more or less decayed.

From the first one to decay I selected seeds, which were planted the next year. Careful selections have been made every year since, always with a view to increasing their long-keeping qualities, uniformity in shape, earliness in ripening, as well as the productiveness of the vines.

This is the origin of this tomato, which has been named "Thorburn's Long-Keeper," and which is now offered to the public for the first time.

Signed. E. S. CARMAN.

We recommend this tomato strongly to all growers with whom keeping is a desideratum. Pkt., 10c.; oz., 35c.; ¼ lb., $1.00.

∴ NOVELTIES ∴ AND ∴ SPECIALTIES ∴ 15

PHOTOGRAPH OF AN AVERAGE SPECIMEN OF THE NEW SQUASH, ISLAND PRIZE.

THE ISLAND PRIZE SQUASH.

The above photograph will give some idea of the **handsome shape and size** of this valuable new fall and winter squash. The seed was first sent us by a lady customer in California, the only history of it she could give being that "it was brought to San Francisco from one of the Pacific Islands." We were struck with the very distinct appearance of the seed, and divided it between two veteran squash growers, one in New Jersey, and the other in Nebraska, both of whom agreed in pronouncing it a most valuable acquisition and upon whose testimony we first offered it for sale last spring. Hundreds of reports from customers who purchased the seed then, proclaim it as the very best and most productive squash they have ever grown, being **the dryest and sweetest of all squashes**, and growing so rapidly that the striped bug can get no chance to injure it. The outside skin is a bright, creamy-yellow faintly and beautifully netted, while the flesh is very thick, and of a deep orange-yellow, and as we said before, remarkably sweet and **rich in saccharine.** The shape and size are excellent and most convenient for either home use or market. It is also a wonderful keeper, we having kept specimens on exhibition in our office until last June. All who want something really choice and fine in squashes should try the **Island Prize.** Seed scarce. Per Pkt., 15c.; 2 pkts., 25c.; 5 pkts., 60c.; 10 pkts., $1.00, post-paid.

THE SWEET NUT SQUASH.

PHOTOGRAPH OF THE NEW SWEET NUT SQUASH.

This new squash originated with Mr. Paynter Frame, of Delaware, who has been instrumental in getting up many valuable new varieties. Mr. Frame says it is the only squash that is absolutely **borer proof,** the squash borer having never been known to touch it even when all other varieties were affected. The accompanying photograph fairly represents its fine medium size and form. When only half grown and cooked green, as summer squashes, they are dry, fine flavored and most delicious eating. Cut in slices and fried like egg-plants, they can hardly be distinguished from that excellent vegetable, but their **greatest value consists in being used as a winter squash.** When pulled before frost, laid away in a dry room or cellar, they will keep sound and sweet the whole winter through. For making pies, custards, etc., their beautiful yellow flesh possesses a dry, rich, sweet flavor, even without the use of sugar and fully equal to a good sweet potato. It is also enormously productive, as many as eight perfect squashes having been grown on a single vine. Stock of seed this season is small. Pkt., 10c.; 3 pkts., 25c.; oz., 50c.; 4 oz., $1.50.

16 :·: JOHNSON ·:· & ·:· STOKES ·:· PHILADELPHIA ·:·

Pkt., 15c.; 2 pkts., 25c.; oz., 60c.; 2 oz., $1.00; ¼ lb., $1.75; lb., $6.00.

THE CUMBERLAND RED TOMATO.

· LARGEST AND HANDSOMEST OF ALL ·

As will be remembered, this magnificent tomato was first offered for sale last spring, being made the subject of a beautiful colored plate in our 1891 catalogue. No other tomato we ever offered has met with so large a sale and been so generally commended in all sections of the country. We have received hundreds of unsolicited testimonials similar to those published on the margin alongside this page. The photograph above of an average specimen taken from our patch, will give an idea of their enormous size and **handsome smooth shape.** They originated a few years ago in Cumberland Co., N. J., where they have been grown with great profit by a few truckers, from the fact that they have always commanded very high prices when shipped to Philadelphia markets; and it was only after great persuasion and at high cost that we were able to obtain from the originator a few ounces of his **selected stock seed** to grow from. The vines grow vigorously and produce abundantly until killed by frost. Foliage a very dark green. The skin is remarkably tough, and the tomatoes keep a long time after being pulled, making them an excellent market and shipping variety. We have in the past few years introduced several new and very valuable tomatoes, but think the **Cumberland Red eclipses them all** in its magnificent color and form, solidity, weight, and **extraordinary large size.**

Prices for 1892: Pkt., 15c.; 2 pkts., 25c.; oz., 60c.; 2 oz., $1.00; ¼ lb., $1.75; lb., $6.00, post-paid.

What Others Say.

ISAAC STEEN, Dobbins, N. J., Oct. 19, 1891, writes: "Your Cumberland Red Tomato is more than you claim for it. They are the best I ever grew; ahead of all others in size, fine quality and quantity produced. They yield me over 100 baskets to an acre."

A. A. McQUEEN, Weatherford, Texas, Feb. 21, 1891, writes: "The Cumberland Red Tomato proved the finest I ever grew. They stood the drought when all other kinds failed, and bore until frost. No others can equal them."

THOS. H. BUXTON, Chadd's Ford, Pa., the great tomato specialist, writes: "Cumberland Red is the best tomato out of 51 varieties tested. It ripened 4 days after Dwarf Champion—June 30th. One specimen weighed by me turned the scale at 2¾ ounces. Smooth as an apple."

JOHN W. SCHLAFLY, Beidler, Ohio, April 4, 1891, writes: "The Cumberland Red is superior to any by far the largest of any tomato I ever had. It is also the finest flavored, has very few seeds, and its flesh the most solid and juicy."

S. C. HAGER, Senights, Pa., writes: "The Cumberland Red Tomato is the finest I ever saw; I had some that weighed over two pounds."

∴ NOVELTIES ∴ AND ∴ SPECIALTIES ∴

Read the Verdict.

C. K. BALLARD, Milwaukee, Oregon, Sept. 27, 1891, writes: "Sensation Lettuce is entitled to the blue ribbon, and is indeed a sensation here. It is by far the best ever grown for family use or market, grows vigorously, every plant a perfect head, and maintains its tender and delicious quality throughout the entire season."

J. B. BUTTS, Americus, Ga., Oct. 15, 1891, writes: "The Sensation is decidedly the best lettuce I ever planted; it well deserves the name."

J. S. GIBSON, Brentwood, N. Y., Sept. 7, 1891, writes: "You have a gem in the new Sensation lettuce. I am a large grower of lettuce and for the past thirty years have been growing all the most noted varieties, but yours is an improvement on them all."

ALBERT CRIST, Stafford, Kansas, Oct. 1, 1891, writes: "Sensation Lettuce is the very finest of all. Very large and beautiful remaining tender and sweet longer than any other kind known here."

WM. H. PURDIE, Columbus, N. Y., Aug. 20, 1891, writes: "Your rightly named lettuce—the Sensation—is the finest I ever saw; it is the very best in quality, and in my opinion no gardener can afford to be without it."

J. FULLER, Leominster, Mass., Aug. 24, 1891, writes: "The new Sensation Lettuce is the best I ever had anything to do with. It seems to melt in the mouth."

E. L. SHAFTO, Hamilton, N. J., Oct. 11, 1891, writes: "I gave your Sensation Lettuce a trial alongside three other kinds and found it the best. Heads large as Early Cabbage and does not shoot to seed."

THE SENSATION LETTUCE.

This remarkable new candidate from France appeals not only to the shrewd market gardener but to every owner of a home garden who may desire something extra choice in quality. It is now creating a great **sensation** among Paris market gardeners, where more lettuce is probably grown than any other place in the world; the French being fine judges and great lovers of lettuce. Last year we imported, direct from the originator, sufficient seed to put up several thousand small packets, which we distributed free for trial among our customers. We have received many hundred letters from both market and family gardeners, who all agree in pronouncing it the best lettuce they have ever grown for forcing, and equally valuable for growing in open ground during the hottest summer months. It is a beautiful light yellowish-green color, leaves much blistered on the surface, and of very superior even quality. It has the peculiarity of forming a solid head, even before half grown. It is the shyest seeder of any lettuce we have ever grown, and is necessarily high in price. We offer American seed of our own growing. Large pkt., 20c.; oz., 50c.; ¼ lb., $1.50; lb., $5.00.

✦ DONALD'S ELMIRA ASPARAGUS. ✦

For some years past the city of Elmira, New York, has had the reputation of having on sale the finest and largest asparagus grown in the State. This asparagus has attracted much attention from dealers and commission merchants generally throughout the State, all anxious to get it. Upon inquiry we found this asparagus was grown entirely by one prominent market gardener, Mr. A. Donald, who had become noted as growing this asparagus for which he realized handsome prices and although a large grower, was unable to supply half the demand. Mr. Donald being an old customer of ours, by paying a high price we induced him, last fall a year, to save us some seed from one of his choicest beds and from which we have grown and offer for sale this season splendid and strong one-year-old roots. The color is notably different from either the famous Barr's Philadelphia Mammoth or Palmetto, while the stalks are more tender and succulent. Its mammoth size can be realized from the fact that in whole crops five stalks will average a pound in weight. Mr. Donald has been offered fifty cents a pound for his asparagus to ship to New York City, but the dealers in Elmira would not allow him to ship it even at such figures. We have on file in our office testimonials from the leading produce merchants of Elmira fully substantiating all claims made for Donald's Elmira Asparagus. Prices of seed: Pkt., 10c.; oz., 25c.; ¼ lb., 75c.; lb., $2.50, strong roots, $1.75 per 100 ($2.00 per 100, post-paid); $6.00 for 500; $10.00 per 1,000.

Johnson's Dixie Watermelon - -

See colored illustration painted from nature on back of this book.

The Great New Watermelon, Surpassing the Famous Kolb Gem as a Shipper and Without a Peer in Fine Quality and Productiveness.

$100 CASH PRIZES FOR THE HEAVIEST JOHNSON'S DIXIES GROWN IN 1892.

$50 to the grower of the heaviest, $30 for Second heaviest, $20 for Third heaviest. Conditions of competition accompany all orders for seed.

NOTHING we have ever introduced has met with such large sale and brought us so many strong recommendations from truckers and melon growers in all sections of the country. **Johnson's Dixie** was the only watermelon that was in demand **at good prices** and realized **profit** to the growers on New York, Philadelphia and Boston markets the past summer.

Our attention was first attracted to this melon by a few appearing on our markets in the summer of 1889, and selling rapidly at double the price of Kolb Gem, or any other variety, owing to their large size, very distinct and handsome fresh appearance and fine quality. It is a cross between the **Kolb Gem** and **Old Fashioned Mountain Sweet**, made by one of the largest truck and melon growers of North Carolina, surpassing the former in shipping qualities and fully equalling the latter in fine eating quality and flavor, being a week to **ten days earlier** than either, with a remarkably thin rind, almost impenetrable, which preserves it for a great length of time, keeping three times as long as either before showing decay. Its great productiveness is shown from the fact that the past two seasons they matured from **six to eight large melons** to the vine, while Kolb Gem rarely produced more than two or three. The vines grow strong and rapidly with more laterals than any other melon and have the singular and very valuable quality of **rooting from every joint**, adding greatly to the productiveness and life of the vines. The meat is more scarlet, finer and of much better quality. These strong claims have been more than verified by ourselves and hundreds of other growers the past two seasons.

FROM THE LARGEST MELON GROWER OF FLORIDA AND THE SOUTH.

WM. M. GIRARDEAU, who is well known as the largest melon grower in Florida and the South, Sept. 1, 1891, writes: "Seeing Johnson's Dixie watermelon so highly recommended, and being much interested as a large melon grower in anything new in my line, I decided to try a few acres of this variety. I planted twelve acres in them and must say was very agreeably surprised. I had a splendid yield of very large melons, in every way superior to the Kolb Gem, both as to shipping and table qualities. I found them to ripen out to within one-fourth inch of inside of rind, and although full ripe the center rind was even tougher than the Kolb Gem, and bore transportation much better, besides it overran to the greatest advantage I ever had to Kolb in its shape. The 'Dixie' is what we call a long melon and shows up so much better in a car, and much more easily packed. It will certainly supersede Kolb Gem and all others as a shipper."

FROM THE LARGEST MELON GROWER OF NEW JERSEY.

ISRAEL L. BLACK, Gloucester Co., N. J., Oct. 20, 1891, writes: "The only melon that would sell in Philadelphia and New York markets this season was Johnson's Dixie. It netted me three times the price of Kolb Gem and other varieties. Kolb Gems were shipped back to many growers; no sale alongside Dixies. From their good eating and shipping qualities this must become the coming melon in all other markets as they are now in Philadelphia, New York, Chester and other places. It is the only watermelon grown near us this section, worthy of cultivation, and I shall plant no other the coming season. I have grown melons all my life and have never seen one equal Johnson's Dixie."

FROM THE LARGEST MELON GROWER OF NEBRASKA.

CHAUNCEY P. COY, of Nebraska, a good authority, and who is probably the largest melon grower in the United States, his annual plantings amounting to several hundred acres, writes: "I have carefully noted the new melon, Johnson's Dixie, and had it set work much superior in all respects to Kolb Gem, the color is noticeably different, being a much darker green and meat is initially striped, giving one the thought of a little distance off the bloom on a green gage plum. The form is longer while the quality is away ahead. Kolb is in flesh rose color, while Johnson's Dixie is extremely sweet, juicy and tender."

Johnson's Dixie is, without doubt, the most important novelty in melons ever introduced and like all good things is being counterfeited, beware of spurious seed offered at low prices.

Prices for 1892. Seed of our own growing from stock seed selected by the originator. Per pkt., 10c.; oz., 25c.; ¼ lb., 70c.; lb., $2.25, post-paid; 5 lbs and over, by freight or express, $2 00 per lb.

We have many hundred testimonials of just such as are published below, and regret our limited space forbids the publication of more of them. As will be noticed, they come from well-known growers.

A. J. CLAYTON, Red Valley, N. J., Sept. 30, 1891, writes: "I have raised watermelons for over twenty years, but have never yet found a variety equal to Johnson's Dixie."

J. B. BUTTS, Americus, Ga., Oct. 15, 1891, writes: "Johnson's Dixie is the best melon of the age. It is the hardiest and most prolific I ever grew."

AARON PAUL, a well known and extensive melon grower at Sewell, N. J., says: "Johnson's Dixie is the best, hardiest and most productive melon I have ever seen or grown. My patch was a sight to behold, averaging seven to eight fine, large melons to the vine, while its eating quality is unequalled by any other variety known to me. Its fine appearance and shipping qualities are to my mind so much superior to Kolb Gem as to place it beyond comparison. Its extreme hardiness to both cold and wet weather is simply wonderful, and I doubt if its equal exists."

Jos B. CLEMENTS & Co., Commission Merchants, Dock St., Philadelphia, says: "The Dixie is the coming melon. Brought half again as much as other kinds. In quality equal to Old Mountain Sweet. Best in this market for twenty years."

PHILLAND TITUS, Pedricktown, N. J., Sept. 10, 1891, writes: "Johnson's Dixie is the finest melon ever grown here, best in quality and outyielded all others. They will entirely take the place of Kolb Gem and all others. The only melon that yielded any profit to growers this season."

J. F. VANLANDING, Drayton Island, Fla., writes: "Dixie melon very fine, I got $50 to $90 per hundred for all I shipped and could not begin to supply the demand."

W. W. MORGAN, Pine River, Wis., March 2, 1891, writes: "Johnson's Dixie watermelon is the earliest and best I have ever raised or seen."

∴ NOVELTIES ∴ AND ∴ SPECIALTIES ∴

Felton's Model White Box Radish.

No radish we have ever introduced has given such general satisfaction to growers as the **Philadelphia White Box,** first named and introduced by us in 1888. Our customers were, however, no doubt, gratified and surprised to find we offered last season a **still better and more desirable radish,** selected and improved by the well-known Philadelphia market gardener whose name it bears. It possesses all the excellent qualities of the now popular **Philadelphia White Box,** and is superior in the following respects. In the first place the shape is rounder and much handsomer, as shown in the accompanying cut. It is also earlier, with fewer and shorter leaves; hence it can be sown more thickly in the row, enabling the grower to raise, at least, one-third more radishes in the same space, whether under glass, in frames or boxes, or in squares or borders in open ground. It is indeed, a model, **perfect in all respects,** being solid, juicy and unsurpassed in flavor in all stages of growth and equally valuable for the home or market garden. Pkt., 10c.; oz., 15c.; ¼ lb., 35c.; lb., $1.25.

The Startle, or Twenty-Day Forcing Radish.

A new and distinct type of the well-known olive shaped radish, selected by a Philadelphia market gardener. It is undoubtedly the earliest and finest forcing half-long or olive-shaped variety known, maturing in about twenty days. Color, brilliant red; flesh, pure white, crisp, sweet and fresh to the taste. It has a very small, short top, and is alike valuable for forcing or open ground. Pkt., 5c.; oz., 10c.; ¼ lb., 30c.; lb. $1.00.

Myer's Purple Top Beauty Ruta-Baga.

This new variety is purely of American origin, and is so far removed by careful selection and breeding from the old forms of Ruta-baga, that it appears almost a plant of distinct family. It is undoubtedly the finest Swede to be obtained, whether wanted for market garden or stock feeding purposes. The root is smooth and beautiful. Its handsome shape and purple crown are well shown in the accompanying cut. The flesh is golden-yellow, fine grained, solid, sweet, fine flavored and very nutritious. It is extremely hardy, and earlier to mature than any other form of Ruta-baga, and will produce nearly twice the weight per acre more than any other variety. Pkt., 5c.; oz., 10c.; ¼ lb., 25c.; lb., 75c., post-paid; 5 lbs. and over, 6cc. per lb., by freight or express.

The New Vegetable Fruit.

We distributed several thousand packages of this small round fruit last season, free for trial among our customers. While some do not seem satisfied with it, a large number of our lady customers write they are greatly delighted with it, and pronounce it a most valuable acquisition for preserving and excellent as a substitute for apples for pies, etc. Leaving the question of its usefulness to our lady friends, we can only add that it is one of the most beautiful of vine fruits, of bright yellow color irregularly striped and splashed with beautiful dark mahogany, and so fragrant that a single specimen will perfume a room. Should be planted four by four feet and two plants allowed to grow to a hill. Pkt., 10c.; 3 pkts., 25c.

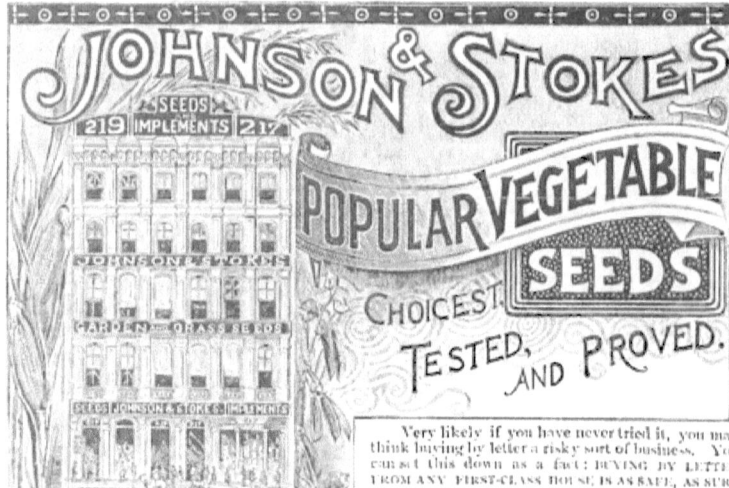

JOHNSON & STOKES

219 SEEDS IMPLEMENTS 217

POPULAR VEGETABLE SEEDS

CHOICEST, TESTED, AND PROVED.

THE LARGEST SEED WAREHOUSE IN THE EAST.

Very likely if you have never tried it, you may think buying by letter a risky sort of business. You can set this down as a fact: BUYING BY LETTER FROM ANY FIRST-CLASS HOUSE IS AS SAFE, AS SURE AND YOU WILL BE AS HONESTLY TREATED AS IF YOU STOOD BY THE COUNTER AND PAID SPOT CASH. You can find many such houses in the U. S. Of course, some establishments have greater facilities than others; and also give more attention to such trade. There is a *choice* in almost everything. As good a question as you can ask about any store is: "How does it prosper?" A look outside or better a look inside answers the question for ours. No business will go on growing and growing unless it *deserves* to grow. There must be downright merit to bring success.

Could anything be easier than to make a test?

SEEDS FREE BY MAIL

WE PAY THE POSTAGE

All **Vegetable and Flower Seeds** by the packet, ounce, pound, pint or quart, will be delivered by us **postage paid, and free of all expense**, to any post office in the United States. Thus, you have only to enclose with the order the cost of the seeds as given in this catalogue (either by P. O. order, express money order, postal note, draft, cash or stamps), and they will be safely delivered, neatly packed, without extra charge. Purchasers of seeds, in large or small quantities, cannot fail to see the great advantages to them of this offer, as it places our store at your very door, and enables customers thousands of miles away to obtain their supplies as cheaply as if they called in person at our store.

CUSTOMERS ORDERING TO BE SENT BY FREIGHT OR EXPRESS

may deduct postage at the rate of eight cents per pound, or fifteen cents per quart from our prices. When sent in this way the purchaser pays the transportation charges on receipt of seed. Freight rates from Philadelphia to all points are very low.

HOW TO SEND MONEY.

Cash should always accompany the order. We will be responsible for money sent to us by **P. O. Order**, **Express Money Order**, **Bank Draft**, **Express** or by **Registered Letter**. Every postmaster is required to register any letter on payment of ten cents extra postage. The cost of remitting may, on all orders over $1.00, be deducted from the amount sent. Amounts of $1.00 or less may be sent by ordinary letter.

POSTAGE STAMPS THE SAME AS CASH.

When notes are not obtainable, or to make proper change, we accept postage stamps the same as cash (two-cent stamps preferred).

C. O. D. Orders exceeding ten dollars can be sent C. O. D. by express, when twenty-five per cent. of the amount accompanies the order. We are obliged to add the extra express charges for the return of money on all C. O. D. orders. It is, therefore, less expense to the purchaser to forward full amount of money with order. Plants cannot be sent C. O. D., neither can goods be sent C. O. D. by freight.

WE GUARANTEE ALL SHIPMENTS of Seeds, Bulbs, Plants, Implements, Live Stock, etc., shall reach the purchaser safely and in good condition.

NEW SEEDS FREE — $100 FOR THEIR NAMES

The Four Remarkable New Varieties described below may be had free by all purchasers from this catalogue who order to the amount of $2.00 and over, with the privilege of competing for $100 CASH PRIZES ($25 for each variety) for the best and most appropriate names given them.

NEW BEET NO. 25

Originated by a successful Philadelphia Market Gardener, who has kept it entirely in his own hands until the past season, when we secured his entire stock of seed at a fabulous price. It is the handsomest in form and best in quality of any Deep Blood Turnip Beet ever seen in Philadelphia markets. Although moderately early, it is not the earliest, but has many important advantages over all known varieties, which will rapidly popularize it as the very best for summer, autumn and winter use for both market and private planters.

NEW WINTER CABBAGE NO. 31

Since our introduction a few years since of our famous MATCHLESS LATE FLAT DUTCH and the new popular DIAMOND WINTER and LOUDERBACK'S ALL YEAR ROUND cabbages, we have tested many new and highly recommended Main Crop or Winter Cabbages, and not until the past year have we found one that would at all compete with these splendid varieties. In the NEW WINTER CABBAGE NO. 31, however, we believe they have a successful rival. This cabbage, the seed of which has never been offered for sale by any seedsman, is being sold now (January 1st) in our Philadelphia markets at $6.00 per 100, while ordinary varieties are bringing $3.00 to $4.00 per 100. It is of perfect shape, head very deep, and so hard and solid that there is absolutely no waste at all in preparing it. It is also the surest heading variety we ever saw.

NEW CELERY NO. 42

This celery was first sent us by one of our Market Garden customers in England, who claimed it to be the best white celery grown on the British Isles and the longest keeper of any known there. In our tests the past two seasons we found it fully equal, in all respects, to our best American varieties, which is saying a great deal for it, as the strains now grown and offered by us on pages 4 and 37 of this catalogue are hard to beat. It will surely prove a valuable addition to our list of fine celeries when fully introduced in America.

NEW ONION NO. 56

Had we the naming of this magnificent new onion we would probably call it the WHITE PRIZE TAKER, but having left the naming of these new sorts entirely with our customers, we believe even a better name than this will be given it. In magnificent shape and enormous size it resembles our celebrated PRIZE TAKER, OR SPANISH KING, the seed of which we are now growing here in America, differing only in its pure white skin. Nothing equal to it, in the onion line, has ever been seen in America.

We Want Names WORTHY OF EACH OF THESE SPLENDID NEW VARIETIES and will pay $100 for them

CONDITIONS OF COMPETITION. Customers who order seeds from this catalogue to the amount of $2.00 and over, can select free a packet of any of the above new varieties and suggest one name for that variety. Those who order $3.00 and over, can select free any two varieties and suggest one name for each variety selected. Those ordering $4.00 and over, can select free any three varieties and suggest one name for each. Those ordering $5.00 and over, are entitled to all four varieties with privilege of suggesting names for all four.

The names can be sent in with your order, or at any time before September 1, 1892, at which time they will be carefully considered by an impartial disinterested committee of three, whose decision shall be final and the prize money forwarded to the successful competitors.

These free seeds may be selected by pasting them on the order sheet with your order, or on the coupon below, writing the names suggested opposite the varieties selected.

COUPON — TO CUT OFF

To JOHNSON & STOKES, Philadelphia, Pa.:

Please send me with my order enclosed, free seeds as offered in your special circular.

Names of Seeds Selected Free With Order.	Names suggested in competition for cash prizes offered.

Name of Competitor, _____ Post-Office, _____ State, _____

NOTE.—Should you prefer Flower Seeds to Vegetable Seeds, you may instead of these, select from our Superb Asters offered on the next page of this circular, one or more packets to the amount of 25 cts. for each $2.00 sent us.

Please remember that these Special Premiums are entirely free and do not prevent the selection of our book premiums offered on page 23, or of the liberal premiums on seeds in packets as on page 22.

SUPERB ASTERS.

Not only the most popular, but the most effective in the entire list. While most easy of culture, there is no flower which combines so much beauty and variety of color and shape and habit as the modern Aster. For a late summer or fall display they have no successful rival. Give them a rich soil, and in hot, dry weather they should be mulched and well watered.

Truffaut's Pæony Perfection Aster. A very favorite type. Thrifty, upright plants; large fine flowers, with long incurved petals. The florists' Aster and one of the finest.

Per Pkt.
320. A. Pæony Perfection. Finest mixed; all colors... 10
321. A. Pæony Perfection. Satin-white,...... 10
322. " " Crimson,........ 10
323. " " Dark blue,....... 10
324. " " Violet with white, 10
325. " " Rose............. 10
326. " " White with carmine, 10

DWARF CHRYSANTHEMUM-FLOWERED ASTERS.

Plants only ten to twelve inches high; producing flowers of the largest size and choicest colors.
327. A. Chrysanthemum-Flowered, Mixed.. 10
328. " " Pure white 10

VICTORIA ASTERS.

A magnificent race of Asters. The colors include many delicate and some gorgeous shades; flowers very double and four inches across and from twenty to thirty in a single plant; fifteen to eighteen inches high.
329. A. Victoria. Choice mixed,............ 15
330. " Pure white,............... 15

GERMAN QUILLED ASTER.

Flowers composed of tube or quilled-shape petals. Very beautiful, with a great variety of colors.
331. German Quilled. (Betteridge's Prize). Mixed, 10
332. German Quilled. Pure white,......... 10

DEEP SCARLET TRIUMPH ASTER.

333. This is undoubtedly the most beautiful and perfect of all dwarf Asters. Each plant forms an elegant bouquet of itself; seven to eight inches high. The flowers measure from two and one-half to three inches across, of faultless form. The color is rich brilliant scarlet; each plant bears at least thirty to forty flowers of exquisite beauty,................... 25

COMET ASTER.

334. Its long wavy and twisted petals are formed into a loose yet dense half-globe, resembling the Japanese Chrysanthemums; flowers three and one-half to four and one-half inches across. Each petal a delicate pink, margined with white.................... 20

TRUFFAUT'S PÆONY PERFECTION ASTER.

NEW PEARL ASTER.

This entirely new and distinct class of Asters is superior to most other types. The plants form handsome pyramids about fifteen inches high and are literally covered with a mass of the most perfect flowers, round in shape and three and one-half to four inches in diameter, finely and fully imbricated, and borne on long stems. They are most admirably adapted for pots and borders and especially valuable for cut-flowers.

337. New Pearl Mixed, . . 25
338. " " Pure White,........... 25

COMET ASTER.

NEW QUEEN ASTER.
The Finest Dwarf Aster in Cultivation.

This splendid Aster makes dwarf bushy plants about ten inches high, of compact habit of growth, producing a great number of double flowers, which resemble in shape and size the Victoria Aster. It is excellent for pot culture and for bedding. As yet there are only two colors distinct enough to be worthy of introduction.
335. Satin White Queen,............................... 20
336. Crimson Queen,................................. 20

CROWN ASTER.

NEW PEARL ASTER.

339. The centre of each flower is white, surrounded by a broad margin of color, such as crimson, rose, violet, etc.; flowers large and freely produced; height, eighteen inches to two feet. 10

OUR FREE BOOK PREMIUMS FOR 1892.

The most complete list of Standard Books ever offered, written by acknowledged authorities on the subjects of which they treat. We will send them post-paid, on receipt of price, or **they will be sent free as Premiums** with all vegetable and flower seed orders from this catalogue, as follows:

Those ordering **$2.00 and over**, may select free any book priced at 30c. or less.
Those ordering **$3.00 and upwards**, may select free any book priced at 50c. or less.
Those ordering **$6.00 and upwards**, may select free any book priced at $1.00 or less.
Those ordering **$8.00 and upwards**, may select free any book or books, the total price of which is $1.50 or less.
Those ordering **$10.00 and upwards**, may select free one or more books, the total price of which is $2.00 or less.
Those ordering **$12.00 and upwards**, may select free one or more books, the total price of which is $2.50 or less.
Those ordering **$20.00 and upwards**, may select free one or more books, the total price of which is $4.00 or less.

Please remember these Premiums apply only to Vegetable and Flower Seeds and cannot be allowed on Seed Potatoes, Farm or Grass Seeds, Implements, Garden Tools, Fertilizers and Live Stock.

On Vegetable Culture.

Asparagus Culture. Best methods employed in England and France, by Barnes & Robinson	$0 50
Broom Corn and Brooms, Cloth	50
Cabbages—How to Grow Them, Gregory. Paper	30
Cranberry Culture, White. Cloth	1 25
Cauliflowers and how to Grow Them, Brill	20
Hop Culture. 40 engravings	30
Kalamazoo Celery, Kedzie	50
Mushroom Culture, Vilmorin. Paper Circular	10
Mushrooms—How to Grow Them. The most complete work published on the subject, giving minute details and illustrations. Cloth	1 50
New Onion Culture—How to grow 2,000 bushels to the acre, T. Greiner	50
The Peanut Plant, B. W. Jones	50
New Potato Culture, as developed by the French system and the use of chemical fertilizers, Carmen	50
Squashes—How to Grow Them, Gregory	30
Sweet Potato Culture, Fitz	60
Tobacco Culture. Full practical details	25

On Floriculture.

Practical Floriculture. A Book for Florists, Henderson	1 50
Horticulturist Rule Book, Bailey	1 00
The Window Garden	10
Landscape Gardening. A collection of Plans illustrating the improvement of home grounds, etc., Long	50
How to Destroy Insects on Plants and Flowers, Barnard	30
My Handkerchief Garden, Barnard	25
Handbook of Plants. A very valuable book of reference, containing everything relating to general Horticulture, and with plain directions for the Cultivation of Vegetables, Fruits and Flowers; 800 illustrations. Henderson	4 00
The Rose, Ellwanger	1 25
Hints on Cacti, Blanc	10
The Garden's Story. The pleasures and trials of an amateur gardener, Ellwanger	50
Graperies and Horticultural Buildings, Woodward	1 00

On Live Stock.

Profits in Poultry. Useful and ornamental Breeds and their profitable management	1 00
An Egg Farm, Stoddard	50
Duck Culture, Rankin	50
Pleasures of a Pigeon Fancier, Lucas	1 50
A. B. C. of Bee Culture, A. I. Root	1 25
The Dairyman's Manual, Stewart	2 00
The Shepherd's Manual, Stewart	1 50
The Modern Horse Doctor, Dodd	1 50
The Pig. A complete manual on the subject, Joseph Harris	1 50
Training of Shepherd Dogs, Wickham	50
Dog Training. Full directions how to train Hunting and Pet Dogs	1 00
Diseases of Dogs, Dalziel	80
The Collie. Its history, points and breeding, Dalziel	1 00
How to Rid Buildings and Farms of Rats, Picket	20
Hunter and Trapper, Thrasher	75

On Farm and Garden Topics.

$100 Prize Essays. Valuable essays by practical growers on the following subjects: How and What to Grow in the South for Northern Markets," "Culture of Cabbage and Onions, with Hints for Storing and Marketing," "The Family Vegetable Garden," Johnson & Stokes." Paper	$0 30
Practical Farm Chemistry, T. Greiner	1 00
Gardening for Profit, Henderson	2 00
Gardening for Pleasure, Henderson	2 00
How the Farm Pays, Henderson and Crozier	2 50
Play and Profit in my Garden. In this are combined rare literary taste and skill, with agricultural experience and good sense. E. P. Roe	1 50
How Crops Grow. A treatise on the chemical composition, structure and life of the plant, Johnson	2 00
How Crops Feed. A treatise on the atmosphere and the soil as related to the nutrition of plants, Johnson	2 00
Silos, Ensilage and Silage, Miles	50
Irrigation, Stewart	1 50
Draining for Profit and Health, Waring	1 50
Land Measurer for Farmers, Boddie	60

On Fruit.

The Fruit Garden, Barry	2 00
The Nursery Book. A complete guide to propagation and pollenation, Bailey	1 00
Fungus Diseases of the grape and other plants and their treatment. A complete Work, F. Lamson, Scribner. Cloth	75
Grape Culturist, Fuller	1 50
Strawberry Culturist, Fuller	25

Magazines.

Farm Poultry. A Monthly Magazine devoted to Poultry Raising, will be found a wonderful guide and help to every one who attempts to raise a chicken. Yearly subscription	50
Orchard and Garden. A Monthly Journal devoted to the interest of the Orchard, Vineyard, Fruit, Vegetable and Flower Garden. Yearly Subscription	50
Housekeepers' Weekly. This charming paper, the only WEEKLY household journal, is a great favorite with women. "Better than a dozen monthlies." Yearly Subscription	1 00
Farm Journal. A Monthly Journal of the Farm. The brightest, spiciest farm paper published. Yearly Subscription	50

ALL THOSE WHO PASS THROUGH THE DOOR OF SUCCESS FIND IT LABELLED "PUSH."

VEGETABLE SEEDS
General List

IN the following pages we have endeavored to list the cream of all varieties known in America that are really worthy of cultivation, weeding out many varieties that are still catalogued by other seedsmen, but which our extended trials and experience have proven to us are unworthy of further cultivation. We take great pains each season to inform ourselves fully as to the true character of everything offered as new or superior, either in this country or in Europe; and our customers may rest assured that, if they fail to find in our Manual any much lauded variety, the probability is much greater that we have tested it and found it of little or no value, than that it is unknown to us. It is our constant aim to gain and hold the confidence of all customers and assure them from disappointment. Under this head we also illustrate and describe many of our choice Specialties; among them will be found many valuable novelties recently introduced, to the growing of which we have given special attention. The varieties which we have printed in CAPITALS are highly recommended, many of them being improved sorts of great merit.

LIBERAL PREMIUMS ON SEEDS IN PACKETS.
As an inducement to our customers to get their neighbors and friends to club with them in sending their orders, we will allow each purchaser of seeds in packets, to select 25 cents' worth extra for each $1.00 sent us. Thus, **purchasers remitting $1.00 may select seeds, in packets only, to the amount of $1.25; those remitting $2.00, to the amount of $2.50; those remitting $3.00, to the amount of $3.75, and so on.** In addition, every purchaser of $2.00 and over, in one order, is entitled to select a book premium as offered on page 21.

ASPARAGUS.

Asparagus is one of the earliest spring vegetables, and would be in matters of use were it not for the prevalent idea that it is difficult to grow it. We think this is a mistake, and that it can be as easily and as cheaply and easily as this. Directions for planting and culture will be found in our book of $100 Prize Essays, which may be selected for a book premium with all orders of $2 and over from this catalogue. A bed 12 x 40 feet, requiring about 100 roots or plants, should give an abundant supply for an ordinary family. One ounce seed will sow forty feet of row; 7,500 seeds will plant an acre.

DONALD'S ELMIRA ASPARAGUS. A magnificent new asparagus now offered for the first time. See Novelties, page 17.

CONOVER'S COLOSSAL. A well-known, good standard variety. Seed: Pkt., 5c.; oz., 10c.; ¼ lb., 20c.; lb., 50c. Roots, 1 year old, 75c. per 100 by mail, post-paid, $1.15 per 1,000, $4.50 per 1,000, 2 years old, $1.00 per 100, $5.00 per 1,000, by express or freight.

NEW PALMETTO ASPARAGUS. Attention was first called to this new asparagus by Mr. John Nix, a large vegetable grower of South Carolina, where it is supposed to have originated. It is now quite extensively grown by a few Southern gardeners for New York and Philadelphia markets, where it sells at very high prices, owing to its mammoth size, evenness and regularity in growth and appearance. An average bunch of fifteen shoots will measure thirteen to fourteen inches in circumference. For the past four seasons this asparagus is received in Northern markets ten days ahead of all other varieties and sold at fabulous prices, even in after other varieties had come in. Although of Southern origin, it is equally well adapted to both North and South. Price of seed: Pkt., 5c.; oz., 10c.; ¼ lb., 20c.; lb., $1.00. Splendid strong roots, $1.50 per 100 by mail, $1.25 per 100; $7.50 per 1,000 Thousands of 1,000 rate.)

ASPARAGUS CULTURE—Best Methods, By Jas. Barnes and William Robinson. Price, 50c., or may be had free. See book premiums, preceding page.

BARR'S PHILADELPHIA MAMMOTH ASPARAGUS
EARLIEST AND LARGEST IN CULTIVATION

BARR'S PHILADELPHIA MAMMOTH. The grand variety originated some years ago with Crawford Barr, of Montgomery County, Pa., a prominent market gardener. It was side by side with the Conover's Colossal, and subject to the same treatment, it comes in earlier and grows more than twice as large. It is very productive, throwing up great numbers of strong, well-developed shoots throughout the entire season. It is tender to the stem end of its lowest tier, which, together with the fact that it requires much less labor in cutting and bunching, thus lessening the expense of marketing, makes it the most desirable of any kind yet introduced for the market gardener. It has attracted much attention in Philadelphia markets, where it is much sought after and sells at double the price of any other sort. Price of seed: Pkt., 5c.; oz., 15c.; ¼ lb., 40c.; lb., $1.25. Price of good, strong roots, 1 year old, $1.25 per bunch in mail, $1.50 per 100; $6.00 per 1,000, 2 years old, $1.50 per 100, $7.00 per 1,000. (50 roots at 1,000 rate.)

ARTICHOKE.

Large Green Globe. Pkt., 10c.; oz., 25c.; lb., $2.50.
ARTICHOKE ROOTS for hog feed will be found under Farm Seeds. Peck, $1.00; bush., $3.00; bbl., $7.50.

BEANS. Dwarf Green Podded Sorts.
LARGE PACKETS OF ANY VARIETY 10c. EACH, POST-PAID.

One quart will plant one hundred feet of drill, two bushels will plant an acre in drills.

> Please remember that our prices on all Beans by the pint or quart include prepayment of postage by us. If ordered to be sent by express or freight, 8c. per pint or 15c. per quart may be deducted.

Early Red Speckled Valentine. The well-known old standard sort. Pint, 20c.; qt., 40c., post-paid; peck, $1.25; bush., $4.75.

EMPEROR WILLIAM. A new extra early variety with large green flat pods of fine quality. It is very productive and valuable for either family use or market. Can also be used as a White Shell Bean when dry. Pkt., 10c.; pint, 25c.; qt., 45c.; peck, $1.30; bush., $5.50.

Hampus, or First of All. One of the earliest green podded sorts, very desirable when young. Pint, 20c.; qt., 40c.

Early Mohawk. The hardiest of the early varieties, and will endure a light frost; largely planted in the South. Pint, 20c.; qt., 35c.; peck, $1.00; bush., $3.75.

Refugee, or Brown Valentine. Very productive and will stand a slight frost; a fine string or pickling bean. Pint, 20c.; qt., 40c.; peck, $1.25; bush., $4.75.

NE PLUS ULTRA. This bean differs from all the other varieties in both seed and habit of growth. It is very early, growing very dwarf and compact, and producing its magnificent long pods in such great profusion as to completely hide the bush. It is very hardy, of fine delicate flavor, most productive and excellent for forcing. Pint, 25c.; qt., 60c.

Early Long Yellow Six Weeks. Hardy, prolific and of good quality. Pint, 20c.; qt., 40c.; peck, $1.25; bush., $4.25.

NEW EXTRA EARLY REFUGEE BEAN. 10 DAYS EARLIER THAN THE "OLD" REFUGEE.

NEW EXTRA EARLY REFUGEE. This entirely distinct new bush bean has all the first-rate qualities of the well-known Refugee, but will be ready for the market or table at least ten days earlier. One of our most extensive market gardeners near New York City says he has planted it in the spring, gathered the ripe crop, and again planted it in time for fall pickling. It is an immense yielder and sure to produce a crop in either a wet or dry season. Pkt., 10c.; pint, 25c.; qt., 45c.; peck, $1.50; bush., $5.50.

NEW UNION WHITE VALENTINE. Perhaps no greater improvement in dwarf beans has ever been accomplished than in this variety. It originated in Jefferson County, N. Y., with one of our largest bean growers, and, as its name implies, is a complete union of all good qualities necessary to make a dwarf green-pod bean perfect. It is much earlier and of a dwarfer habit than the old White Valentine, the pods being rounder, smoother, plumper and more meaty and entirely stringless. Among many others it possesses the peculiar and valuable quality of remaining in a tender cooking condition longer than any other green-podded variety. This, together with its extreme earliness—being fit to pork in thirty days from time of germination—makes it an exceedingly valuable sort for spring or fall planting. The beans, when ripe, are pure white, thus enabling the grower to sell them as shelled beans at a profitable figure in case he cannot sell them in the green state. Pkt., 10c.; pint, 25c.; qt., 45c.; peck, $1.50; bush., $5.50.

Early China Red Eye. Of good quality, used as a string or shell bean. Pint, 20c.; qt., 40c.

BEST OF ALL. This newly introduced dwarf bean is, as its name indicates, one of the best. It originated in Germany, with long glossy pods about twice as long as those of the Valentine, very tender and succulent and an enormous producer, very popular in the South. Pint, 25c.; qt., 45c.; peck, $1.40; bush., $5.00.

Broad Windsor. An English bean, valuable from its habit of ripening unequally, some pods being full while others are in various stages of filling. Pint, 35c.

BEANS.—Dwarf Wax Sorts.
LARGE PACKETS, 10c. EACH, POST-PAID.

NEW GOLDEN-EYED BUTTER WAX. One of the earliest and best Dwarf Wax Beans for either market or family garden. See Novelties, page 1. Pkt., 10c.; pint, 35c.; qt., 60c.

NEW EXTRA EARLY REFUGEE WAX. This new variety, now offered by us for the first time, is one of the earliest beans grown. It is a perfect Refugee with wax pods that are long, round and of a golden yellow color. It is suitable for early or late sowing, and for a wet or dry season. If sown in spring, it will give seed in time for a second crop in fall. Is an immense yielder. Pkt., 10c.; pint, 35c.; qt., 60c.

NEW SPECKLED WAX. The best late wax podded bean. Its long, cylindrical, waxy yellow pods are tender, crisp, and of the best quality when in condition to use for snaps, while as a green shelled bean the variety has no superior. For those who wish to plant but one variety, this is the best. Pkt., 10c.; pint, 30c.; qt., 50c.

IMPROVED ROUND POD EXTRA EARLY VALENTINE BEAN.

NEW IMPROVED ROUND POD EXTRA EARLY RED VALENTINE. This is unquestionably the very best and earliest green snap-short bean. It is at least ten days earlier than the Early Red Valentine, and is usually ready to pick thirty-five to forty days from the time of planting. The habit of the vine is dwarf, the pods are smooth, round, stringless and very thickly set, remaining green and tender a long time after they are fit to pull. The strain we offer will be found unusually prolific, and to hold the pods well up from the ground. Vines very uniform, making little or no top growth, setting its fruit all low on the bush, ripening very uniformly, and producing enormously. Pkt., 10c.; pint, 20c.; qt., 45c., post-paid. By freight or express, pint, 17c.; qt., 30c.; peck, $1.50; bush., $5.50.

"YOUR IMPROVED ROUND POD VALENTINE ARE DECIDEDLY THE EARLIEST AND BEST EVER OFFERED IN THIS MARKET." W. M. OLDHAM, DENISON, TEXAS.

NEW SADDLE-BACK WAX. This new bean is so named from the peculiar form of pods, which on the back are very broad, flat and indented with a crease, giving them a decidedly novel shape, not found in any other bean. Extremely hardy and productive. Pkt., 10c.; pint, 30c.; qt. 60c.

YOSEMITE MAMMOTH WAX. This splendid new bean has been so named on account of its enormous size. The pods frequently attain a length of ten inches, with the thickness of a man's finger. The pods are nearly all solid pulp, the seeds being very small, when the pods are fit for use. Pods are a rich golden color and absolutely stringless, cooking tender and delicious. It is enormously productive, as many as fifty of its monster pods having been counted on one bush. Pkt., 10c.; pint., 40c.; qt., 75c.

SCARLET AND VIOLET FLAGEOLET OR PERFECTION WAX BEANS. These varieties were brought from Germany several years since. In character of growth of vine and pods they do not differ very materially. Both have very vigorous, strong-growing vines, bearing very large, long, flat and tender wax-like pods. The Scarlet Flageolet is a little the earlier, but the Violet has larger pods. We recommend both as among the largest and most showy dwarf wax beans in cultivation.

SCARLET FLAGEOLET WAX. Pkt., 10c., pint, 25c.; qt., 50c., postpaid; peck, $1.75; bush., $6.50.

VIOLET OR PERFECTION WAX. Pkt., 10c.; pint, 25c.; qt., 50c., postpaid; peck, $1.70; bush., $6.25.

GERMAN BLACK WAX. A well-known and popular variety; pods when fit for use are waxy yellow, tender and productive. Pint, 25c.; qt., 4oc.; peck, $1.25; bush., $4.75.

GOLDEN WAX. This variety is a few days earlier than the old German Black Wax; pods long, brittle, entirely stringless, of a rich golden color; as a snap, it excels in rich buttery flavor, while as a bean for winter use, it has few equals. Pint, 25c.; qt., 40c., peck, $1.25; bush., $4.75.

WARDWELL'S KIDNEY WAX BEAN
HARDIEST AND MOST PRODUCTIVE

WARDWELL'S EARLY DWARF KIDNEY WAX. This new variety introduced by us four years ago, has more than exceeded our most sanguine expectations, and has given unbounded satisfaction wherever tried. Leading market gardeners are unanimous in saying it is the earliest, hardiest, most productive and saleable yellow wax bean they ever grew.

The most valuable point, however, is in its favor is that it has not yet shown the slightest indication of rust or spot, no matter where or under what condition grown. It is greatly superior to the well-known Dwarf German Black Wax or Golden Wax sorts in every respect, being nearly a week earlier and yielding a third greater. The vines are remarkably vigorous, hardy and productive; the pods are very large, smooth, showy, tender, perfectly stringless and of unusually fine quality. The entire pod assumes a rich golden color at a very early stage of growth, a very important feature which no other sort does. The dry beans are white, with two slashes of reddish purple more or less visible and a distinct kidney shape. Prepared for the table it has a fine buttery flavor, and is destined to become the leading snap bean, as well as a strongly endorsed winter shelled sort. Pkt., 10c.; pint, 25c.; qt., 50c., postpaid; peck, $1.75; bush., $6.50.

NEW BLACK-EYE WAX. This is one of the earliest wax beans we have tested. It is a cross between the Golden and Dwarf Black Wax. Vines medium size, erect, bearing its pods near the centre. Leaves large, thin, quite dark green in color. Pods long, straight, round or of a lighter color than those of the Golden Wax. They cook quickly both as snap and shell bean. Dry beans, medium size long, round, white, with black spot around the eye. Pkt., 10c.; pint, 25c.; qt., 75c.; peck, $1.50; bush., $5.50.

NEW PROLIFIC GERMAN, or CYLINDER BLACK WAX. This is an entirely new and improved strain of the old favorite German or Black Wax bean, originated by a large bean grower of Genesee County, N. Y. We find it very superior to the old strain, being much straighter and more than twice as productive. Pods perfectly round, straighter, longer and of an even, rich golden color. Our stock is grown for us by the originator, and is entirely pure and thoroughbred. Pkt., 10c.; pint, 30c.; qt., 50c., postpaid; qt., 35c.; peck, $1.50; bush., $5.75, by freight.

GRISWOLD'S EVERBEARING WAX. In this new bean, which we introduced two years since, we believe we have on offer one of the most valuable dwarf wax varieties for the family garden ever offered. It originated with Thomas Griswold, the well-known Connecticut seed grower. The pods are thick, fleshy, entirely stringless, growing six to seven inches in length, and exceedingly rich, buttery and fine flavored when cooked. Their great feature of value, however, is in their continuing character, beginning to bear early and continuing to produce their magnificent pods in great abundance throughout the entire season, and long after all other varieties are done. We counted this season in my single vines with eighty to ninety pods ready for picking, and a mass of blossoms on the same vine at the same time. The stalk is stiffer and branches out more than any other bean, hence they should never be planted less than ten inches apart in the rows. The beans are a fine kidney shape and very distinctly marked. Pkt., 10c.; pint, 30c.; qt., 75c.; postpaid; peck, $2.50.

Dwarf White Wax. Similar to Black Wax except in color of seed. Pint, 3oc.; qt., 5oc.; peck, $1.50.

Improved Rust-Proof Golden Wax.
GRENNELL'S STRAIN. **WILLIAMS' STRAIN.**

We offer two strains of these beans, both originated in Jefferson County, N. Y., by two celebrated bean growers. Both are great improvements and when fully introduced will entirely take the place of the old Golden Wax, which has for so many years been a favorite. Both are entirely rust-proof and extremely hardy and every claim made for them has been fully substantiated the past two seasons, not only in our own trials, but by a number of our best gardeners who have grown them. Grennell's strain is the earliest, while Williams' strain has the largest and the best pods. Pkt., 10c., pint, 25c.; qt., 50c.; peck, $1.70; bush., $6.25.

THERE HAS NEVER BEEN A TIME IN THE HISTORY OF AGRICULTURE WHEN IF YOU MAKE AN ACRE OF LAND PRODUCE ALL IT OUGHT TO, AND USE SENSE AND SKILL IN MARKETING THE PRODUCTS, AGRICULTURE WAS MORE PROFITABLE THAN IT IS NOW.

VARIETIES FOR SHELL BEANS.
Large packets, 10c. each, post-paid.

Henderson's New Bush Lima Bean.

Previous to the introduction of this valuable variety, three years since, thousands were deterred from cultivating the most delicious of vegetables—the Lima Bean—from the great trouble and expense of procuring poles on which to grow them. This is now a thing of the past, as the *New Bush Lima* grows without the aid of stakes or poles, in compact bush form, from fifteen to eighteen inches high, and produces enormous crops of delicious Lima Beans, which can be as easily gathered as the common garden bush beans. It is at least two weeks *earlier* than any of the climbing Limas and produces a continuous crop from the time it comes into bearing until frost, and being enormously productive, 371 pods having been counted on a single plant. A very small patch will keep a family supplied throughout the season. The beans are of the size of the Sieva or Southern Lima and, as before stated, of delicious quality. Pkt., 10c.; pint, 45c.; qt., 75c., post-paid. Peck, $4.75; bush., $14.00.

NEW SNOWFLAKE FIELD. This valuable new variety, introduced three years since, has given wonderful results. It has proven very much *earlier* and more *prolific* than either the common standard Pea Bean, or Prolific Tree Bean, which it resembles somewhat in appearance. The plant grows upright, holding its pods well up from the ground. They are borne in thick clusters, and ripen all at once, as many as eighty well-filled pods appearing on a single vine. The leaves fall off earlier than with other varieties, thus opening the pods to the sun. We believe it will eventually supplant all other varieties of White Pea Beans. Pkt., 10c.; pint, 25c.; qt., 45c.; peck, $1.25; bush., $4.50.

HENDERSON'S NEW BUSH LIMA BEAN.

Pkt., 10c.; pint, 40c.; qt., 75c., post-paid.

BURLINGAME MEDIUMS. This is the leading field bean grown in Central New York. Many thousand bushels are grown each season on the Genesee Flats, and fifty bushels to the acre is not an uncommon yield. The beans are pearly white in color and do not rust or spot. Burlingame Mediums are much sought after by dealers everywhere, and always command top-notch market prices. Pkt., 10c.; pint, 20c.; qt., 3½c.; peck, $1.00; bush., $3.75.

PROLIFIC TREE. A valuable variety for field culture, growing about twenty inches in height, branching out in all directions, bearing its pods so high that they do not touch the ground. They have yielded at the rate of nearly one hundred bushels to the acre. They resemble the common Navy Bean, more rounded at the ends and very white, cooking in less time. Pint, 20c.; qt., 30c.; peck, $1.00; bush., $3.75.

Dwarf Horticultural. A dwarf variety of the Horticultural Pole Bean. Pint, 20c.; qt., 35c.

Royal Dwarf, or White Kidney. Among the best as a winter bean. Pint, 20c.; qt., 35c.; peck, $1.00; bush., $3.75.

White Marrowfat. Extensively grown for sale as a dry bean for winter use; excellent shelled, either green or dry. Pint, 20c.; qt., 35c.; peck, $1.00; bush., $3.75.

White Navy, or Pea Bean. A well-known standard sort for field culture. Seed white, nearly round. Very productive. Pint, 20c.; qt., 30c.; peck, $1.00; bush., $3.75.

POLE, OR RUNNING BEANS.

☞ Bear in mind that our prices on beans by the pint and quart include postage. Customers who order them sent by freight or express can deduct 8c. per pint or 15c. per quart from these prices.

LAZY WIFE'S POLE. This fine pole bean, introduced by us a few years since, has become a great favorite. The pods grow from four to six inches long, entirely stringless, and of a rich buttery flavor when cooked. The pods remain green, and retain their tender, rich, stringless flavor until nearly ripe. The beans are white, and are unsurpassed as shell beans for winter use. They are pronounced by all who have grown them the best green podded snapshort Pole Bean in cultivation. We cannot commend this bean too highly. Pkt., 10c.; pint, 35c.; qt., 60c., post-paid; qt., 45c.; 4 qts., $1.50; peck, $2.75, by express.

CREASE-BACK, OR BEST OF ALL POLE. A well-known and highly esteemed Southern variety. Very early and productive. Forms very full, round pods, distinctly creased along back, hence its name. Pint, 30c.; qt., 60c.

NEW GOLDEN WAX FLAGEOLET. This magnificent New Wax Pole Bean, from Germany, is also very early in ripening. It is entirely stringless, the pods growing seven to eight inches long, round, fleshy, and of the finest quality, being exceedingly tender and succulent. The vine begins to bear when quite young, continuing to grow and bear most profusely the entire season. It is worthy of the highest praise, and we hope every customer who orders beans will include at least a packet of this new variety, as it is sure to please. Pkt., 10c.; pint, 30c.; qt., 60c., post-paid; qt., 45c.; 4 qts., $1.50; peck, $2.50, by express.

EXTRA EARLY GREEN CLUSTER. This new bean is almost as early as the Bush varieties. The beans are nearly as large as the Lima, and when cooked possess the rich flavor of that variety to such an extent that it is difficult to distinguish them from Limas. They are frequently fit for the table before Lima Beans commence to blossom. They are very productive and continue in bearing a long time. Do not confound this variety with the Early Golden Cluster Wax Pole Bean, which is used as a snapshort. Pkt., 10c.; pint, 30c.; qt., 35c.

LAZY WIFE'S POLE BEAN.

"ALL THE SEED GOT OF YOU DID FINE. THE FORD MAMMOTH LIMA BEANS AND CHIRK CASTLE MANGEL WERE PERFECT WONDERS. NOTHING BETTER COULD BE WISHED FOR."
J. D. EMERSLEY, DOS CABEZOS, ARIZONA.

JOHNSON & STOKES

THE CREAM OF THE LIMA BEANS
FORD'S NEW MAMMOTH PODDED LIMA

This grand new Lima Bean, first introduced by us, is the result of over twenty years' selection by one of the oldest and most successful market gardeners around Philadelphia, whose name is Ford. No novelty we have ever offered cost us so much money to obtain seed stock, and even at the fabulous price offered Mr. Ford for his entire stock, he hesitated before selling, but finally accepted our offer. Its great value can be realized when we say from our own personal knowledge, it far surpasses in mammoth size, great productiveness and fine quality such excellent varieties as the King of the Garden, Salem Improved and other fine sorts. The pods grow to an average length of eight inches, as shown in the accompanying engraving made from nature, and are produced in immense clusters, containing from five to seven large beans per pod, of the most excellent quality, for using either in the green or dry state. The vines grow vigorously, setting the beans early at the bottom of the pods, and continue in bearing right up to frost. **Ford's Mammoth Podded** is absolutely, without exception, the largest podded, finest flavored and most productive of all Lima Beans. Pkt., 10c.; pint, 65c.; qt., 75c., post-paid; by freight or express, qt., 65c.; 4 qts., $2.25; peck, $1.60.

STOKES' EVERGREEN LIMA BEAN.

In this new Lima, offered last Spring for the first time, we have the result of several years' patient selection from our Salem Mammoth, which, as is well known, is the largest in size of bean of all other Limas. The **Stokes' Evergreen** not only holds the full size (double that of any other Lima) and great productiveness of the **Salem Mammoth**, but has the very remarkable additional quality of holding entirely the **deep green color** of the unripe or green state in all stages of growth and even **when dry and shelled**, thus giving the dry beans when cooked for use during the winter and spring months not only the entire green appearance but also the delicious flavor of beans just pulled or fresh from the vine. This very valuable evergreen quality is now entirely fixed and thoroughbred in this variety, as in the product of our own field of four acres this season there was not a bean that showed the least whiteness when threshed out, all retaining their beautiful deep green color and superb flavor when cooked. Could a more valuable acquisition in Lima Beans be wished for? Seed scarce. Pkt., 15c.; pint, 60c.; qt., $1.00, post-paid; qt., 85c.; 4 qts., $3.00, by freight or express.

JERSEY EXTRA EARLY LIMA.

Four years' careful comparative tests by several of our most prominent Lima Bean growers has proved this selection to be fully ten **days or two weeks earlier** than any other. The pods are large and numerous, invariably having from four to five beans of a pleasant shade of green in each pod. These beans for the past few seasons have appeared in Philadelphia markets about two weeks ahead of all other Limas, selling at from $3.00 to $4.00 per bu-hel of pods. We advise all our customers who grow for market and want a "profitable thing" in Lima Beans to plant this sort largely. Pkt., 10c.; pint, 35c.; qt., 60c., postpaid; qt., 45c.; 4 qts., $1.50; peck, $2.75; bush., $10.00, by express or freight.

KING OF THE GARDEN LIMA.

This new Lima Bean has fully sustained the strong claims made for it. They are vigorous growers, setting their beans early at bottom of pods, producing continuously to the end of the season. They are more prolific than the ordinary Lima, bearing their pods five to seven inches long in clusters of four and five, with five to six beans in a pod. Pkt., 10c.; pint, 25c.; qt., 40c., postpaid; qt., 35c.; 4 qts., $1.25; peck, $2.25; bush., $8.50.

DREER'S IMPROVED OR CHALLENGER LIMA.

Very productive and of superior quality; when green they are nearly as large as the Large Lima, thicker, sweeter and more tender and nutritious, remaining green in the pod for a long time after maturing. Pint, 20c.; qt., 40c.; peck, $2.50.

Pkt., 10c.; pint, 40c.; qt., 75c.; post-paid.

SEEDS FOR MONEY GROWERS

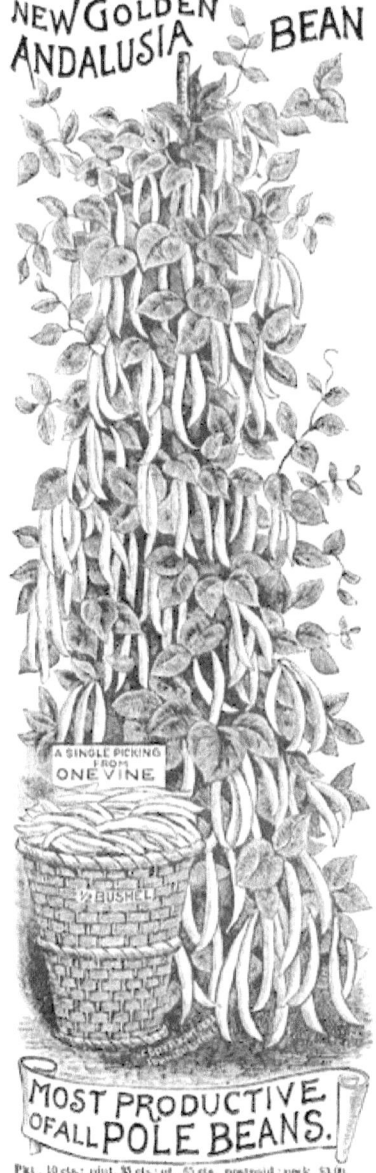

New Golden Andalusia Wax Bean

This new bean, named and introduced by us three years since, has created a decided sensation among bean growers. Nothing we have ever introduced has brought us so many unsolicited letters of the strongest praise from all parts of the United States. Hundreds pronounce it emphatically the *most valuable pole variety ever offered*. It originated at Andalusia, Bucks County, Pa., with a celebrated bean grower. Our illustration, made from Nature, gives some idea of their *wonderful productiveness*, it being nothing unusual to pick one-half bushel to three pecks from a single vine at one picking. The pods are five to six inches long, broad, thick, very fleshy and *entirely stringless, far surpassing all other varieties* in this respect, and retaining these important qualities until almost ripe. The pods when fully grown are from five to six inches long, exceedingly rich, buttery and fine flavored when cooked. The vines cling well to the poles, a very important feature, as on account of their enormous productiveness, the weight of a vine filled with such a mass of large pods is very great. They commence bearing their magnificent pods in great abundance when the vines are quite young, and continue to bear profusely the entire season. The beans when dry are round as a bullet, pure white in color, and also makes a fine shell or winter bean. In great productiveness, fine quality and everbearing character they *stand unequalled by any other pole bean in the world*. Large pkt., 10c.; pint, 35c.; qt., 65c., postpaid; qt., 30c; 4 qts., $1.75; peck, $3.00, by freight or express.

KENTUCKY WONDER.—The largest and most fleshy podded green Pole Bean, rapidly becoming popular in the Middle and Southern States. Vines vigorous, climbing well, and very productive, bearing its pods in large clusters; blossoms white; pods green, very long, often reaching nine or ten inches, nearly round when young, and very crisp, becoming very irregular and spongy as the beans ripen. Dry beans long, oval, dun colored. A very prolific sort and one of the best. Pkt., 10c.; pint, 40c.; qt., 75c., post-paid.

EARLY GOLDEN CLUSTER POLE BEAN.
This new variety leads all other pole varieties in earliness. It is distinct in seed, color and habit of growth. The pods retain their tenderness and plumpness long after the beans have attained a large size, so that only a few days elapse after they cease to be fit for string beans before they are fit to shell. The pods are a beautiful waxy yellow, and are from six to eight inches long, borne profusely in clusters of four to six. Commencing to bear ten days after the Dwarf Golden Wax, it continues to produce an abundance of pods until frost sets in. Pkt., 10c; pint, 35c.; qt., 65c., postpaid; qt., 30c.; 4 qts., $1.40; peck, $2.80, by freight or express.

SALEM IMPROVED LIMA. A selection from the large Lima Bean, of extraordinary size and generally of a deep green color. Pint, 25c; qt., 50c.; peck, $2.75.

Large White Lima (Extra Selected Size). One of the best of the Pole Beans, either green or dry. Pint, 25c.; qt., 50c.; 4 qts., $1.25; peck, $2.25; bush., $8.00.

Carolina or Sewee. Similar to Large Lima, producing beans about half the size, but more productive. Pint, 30c.; qt., 50c.; peck, $2.25.

Dutch Case Knife. One of the earliest and most productive used, shelled, green or dry. Pint, 30c; qt., 50c.

SOUTHERN PROLIFIC. A splendid, vigorous and productive variety. Pods in clusters, succulent and delicious; matures in seventy days from germination, bearing until frost. Pint, 25c; qt., 45c.

Scarlet Runner. Clusters of beautiful scarlet flowers for ornament and table use. Pint, 30c.; qt., 50c.

Early Maine or Essex Prolific. A new, tender, stringless variety. Green pods. Pint, 25c; qt., 50c.

French Asparagus. We imported our original seed of this variety from France, where it is most popular. The pods are tender, of a beautiful green, growing from two to four feet in length, making them also a great curiosity. Pkt., 10c.; pint, 45c.; qt., 75c.

Horticultural or Wren's Egg. An old favorite; equally good as a snap or shelled. Pint, 25c.; qt., 45c.

German Wax Pole. A pole variety of the German or Black Wax, of splendid quality as a snap and very productive. Pint, 25c.; qt., 45c.; peck, $1.75.

Giant Wax. (Red Seed.) Pods from six to nine inches long; thick and fleshy, of a pale waxy yellow color; very productive. Pint, 35c.; qt., 60c.

BEETS.

One ounce will sow sixty feet of drill; five pounds will sow an acre in drills.

Please remember that our prices are for seeds postpaid by mail. If ordered by freight or express at purchaser's expense, 8c. per pound should be deducted.

NEW SURPRISE. The earliest. See Novelties, Page 3. Pkt., 10c.; oz., 20c.; ¼ lb., 50c.; lb., $2.00

BASTIAN'S EXTRA EARLY BLOOD TURNIP. Excellent for both the family and market garden; very early, of quick, large growth, fine turnip form and bright red color. Pkt., 5c.; oz., 10c.; ¼ lb., 20c.; lb., 60c.

ECLIPSE. This variety, originally from Germany, is a great acquisition to our list of turnip beets. It is as early as the Egyptian and much more desirable, owing to its globe shape, great smoothness and regularity, having a firm small top, very sweet, flesh fine and dark blood color. It is very desirable for market gardeners on account of its extreme earliness. Pkt., 5c.; oz., 10c.; ¼ lb., 25c.; lb., 75c.

EDMAND'S EARLY RED TURNIP. A splendid new variety, originated near Boston. While not as early as some varieties, it has many fine qualities to commend it. Strongly to market and family gardeners, being the most uniform of all turnip beets. It is of handsome, round shape, as shown in the above cut, of good marketable size and deep blood color. It does not grow very large or coarse, has a very small top and can be grown very closely together. Pkt., 5c.; oz., 10c.; ¼ lb., 25c.; lb., 75c.

EXTRA EARLY EGYPTIAN BLOOD TURNIP. A standard sort, ten days or two weeks earlier than the old Blood Turnip. Owing to smallness of the top it can be planted very close. It is of fair quality and medium size; fine for forcing. Pkt., 5c.; oz., 10c.; ¼ lb., 25c.; lb., 75c.

Improved Early Blood Turnip. A selected strain and one of the best; blood red, tender and a good, late keeper. Pkt., 5c.; oz., 10c.; ¼ lb., 20c.; lb., 65c.

Extra Early Bassano. Flesh white and rose, very sweet and tender. Pkt., 5c.; oz., 10c.; ¼ lb., 2 lb., 65c.

MITCHELL'S RED TURNIP BEET. A new home variety. It has the earliness and small top of the Egyptian, but said to be of better quality. Very popular with Philadelphia market gardeners. Pkt., 5c.; oz., 10c.; ¼ lb., 25c.; lb., 80c.

Dewing's Extra Early Red Turnip. Of good form and flavor. Flesh and top deep blood red, an excellent early or winter variety. Pkt., 5c.; oz., 10c.; ¼ lb., 20c.; lb., 60c.

ACME SECOND EARLY. A new variety, of handsome, round shape, the skin and flesh is very deep blood red in color and exceedingly sweet and tender in quality. The beets grow regularly of good marketable size. It has a medium short top, the leaves, like the beet, are of a very dark red, shading at times to almost a black color. It is not only valuable for second early, summer and autumn use, but it is a pre-eminently fine sort for planting in July, to be kept in pits for winter and early spring sales. No market gardener who caters for local trade can afford to be without this highly valuable new sort. Pkt., 5c.; oz., 10c.; ¼ lb., 25c.; lb., 80c.

BASTIAN'S HALF-LONG BLOOD. In color, shape and size it is all that can be desired in a beet; a favorite variety for winter use, and largely planted by market gardeners. Pkt., 5c.; oz., 10c.; ¼ lb., 20c.; lb., 70c.

Long Blood Red. A good late variety for fall and winter use. Pkt., 5c.; oz., 10c.; ¼ lb., 15c.; lb., 50c.

LENTZ'S EXTRA EARLY BLOOD TURNIP. We were the first to offer this valuable variety to the public. It originated with Henry Lentz, the well-known Philadelphia market gardener. We recommend it as containing all the valuable essentials of an early beet. It is nearly as early as the Egyptian, but larger and of better quality, of fine, dark red color, tender and sweet at all times, whether old or young. It has a very small top and will produce a crop in six weeks from time of planting the seed. It is very productive and a perfect keeper. Pkt., 5c.; oz., 10c.; ¼ lb., 25c.; lb., 75c.

"BEETS FROM YOUR SEEDS ARE THE FINEST EVER GROWN ON THE ISLAND OF KEY EAST."
ROLAND ADAMS, KEY WEST, FLA.

GARDEN BEETS—Continued.

FORD'S PERFECTED HALF-LONG. New, the best winter beet. See Novelties, Page 3. Pkt., 10c.; oz., 20c.; ¼ lb., 50c.; lb., $1.50.

PHILADELPHIA PERFECTION. This variety is the result of several years' critical selection by a prominent market gardener, of half-long shape, deep blood red color, with a deep, rich, crimson foliage, tap gradual, tender, sweet, juicy. It is of very quick growth, and is not only one of the best for early use, but also for fall and winter, being an excellent keeper. Pkt., 5c.; oz., 10c.; ¼ lb., 25c.; lb., 75c.

Swiss Chard, or Silver. Cultivated for its leaves; the mid-rib is stewed and served as asparagus, other portions of the leaf as a spinach. Pkt., 5c.; oz., 10c.; ¼ lb., 25c.; lb., 75c.

MANGEL AND SUGAR BEETS.

STOCK-FEEDING VARIETIES.

The attention of farmers to the growing of roots for feeding stock has increased rapidly in the past few years, judging from the increased sales of our selected seeds, which now reaches several tons annually. The wonderful results are plainly shown in the health and general condition of the animals, and the increased yield of milk in cows.

They should be sown from April to June, in drills two feet apart, and afterward thinned out to stand one foot apart in the rows. Keep well cultivated, and you will have an abundant crop of roots for winter use.

From five to six pounds of seed required to the acre. In quantities of five pounds and over, by freight or express, 15 cents per pound may be deducted from prices per single pound.

CARTER'S CHAMPION WARDEN ORANGE GLOBE MANGEL. The best Yellow Globe in cultivation; orange yellow root of large size and fine nutritive qualities, growing partly above ground; succeeds well on light land. Of beautiful shape, neat top, fine clear skin, and of choice quality; a sure cropper and excellent keeper. Pkt., 5c.; oz., 10c.; ¼ lb., 15c.; lb., 40c.; 5 lbs., $1.75.

CARTER'S MAMMOTH PRIZE LONG RED MANGEL. A celebrated variety sometimes called Jumbo and Colossal. It is grown extensively for agricultural purposes, producing large roots, partly above ground. A very heavy cropper, frequently producing forty to fifty tons to the acre; growing enormously in size, but of fine texture and quality. Pkt., 5c.; oz., 10c.; ¼ lb., 20c.; lb., 50c., postpaid; 5 lbs. and over, by express, 40c. per lb.

Yellow Ovoid Mangel. Skin of a deep yellow color, and on account of its shape, being between the Long and Globe varieties, will surpass either, bulk for bulk. It is very nutritious, rich in saccharine matter, and productive. Pkt., 5c.; oz., 10c.; ¼ lb., 20c.; lb., 45c.

LANE'S IMPROVED IMPERIAL SUGAR BEET. An improvement on the French Sugar Beet. Recommended as hardier, more productive, yielding thirty-five to forty tons per acre, and containing a greater percentage of sugar. See cut. Pkt., 5c.; oz., 10c.; ¼ lb., 20c.; lb., 60c.; 5 lbs., $1.50.

Vilmorin's Improved White Sugar Beet. An improvement on the old White Sugar, containing a much larger percentage of sugar. Pkt., 5c.; oz., 10c.; lb., 60c.

Silesian, or White Sugar Beet. Large size and grows considerably above the ground; fine for feeding. Cultivated in Europe for its sugar. Pkt., 5c.; oz., 10c.; lb., 60c.; 5 lbs., $1.25.

LANE'S IMPROVED.

THE CHIRK CASTLE MANGEL

Our attention was first called to this prodigious variety a few years since, while visiting Scotland. We were at first inclined to doubt the statements of the Scotch farmers regarding the enormous weights and yields of this variety, but on our return to Scotland, after visiting the continent, six weeks later, we found them harvesting the crops, and to our astonishment these statements were fully verified. We saw hundreds of specimens taken from the field, weighing over sixty lbs. each, while whole crops averaged thirty-eight to forty lbs. per root, producing a yield of over sixty tons to the acre. We immediately secured seed stock and arranged with an English grower to plant it. The length is about the same as Carter's Mammoth Long Red but it is remarkable for its massive shape and broad shoulders, its diameter being more than twice as great; and its weight very much heavier than this celebrated variety. The flesh is red, of very fine texture and quality, containing less water and more sugar than any other mangel, making it more nutritious and milk-producing, enabling the Scotch Dairy farmers to obtain a higher price per gallon for milk from cows fed on this mangel. Their sheep also thrive better when fed on this variety, picking out pieces of it in preference to other kinds when feeding. We consider this variety by far the most valuable and profitable of all the stock-feeding beets yet introduced. Per pkt., 10c.; oz., 15c.; ¼ lb., 35c.; lb., $1.00, postpaid; 5 lbs. and over, $4.00, by express or freight.

The Largest, Heaviest and Most Profitable. Pkt., 10c.; oz., 15c.; ¼ lb., 35c.; lb., $1.00, postpaid; 5 lbs. and over, 80c. per lb., by express.

"CHIRK CASTLE MANGEL I FIND TO BE ALL AND MORE THAN YOU CLAIM FOR THEM, MAKING AS THEY DO THE BEST WINTER FOOD FOR CATTLE AND SHEEP. THEY ARE FAR AHEAD OF ANY VARIETY EVER RAISED OR USED IN THIS SECTION." J. W. SEAL, MT. CARMEL, IND.

GOLDEN GIANT INTERMEDIATE MANGEL. This entirely new and distinct variety is a great improvement over the old Yellow Intermediate, being much larger and more even in shape, and of a beautiful yellow russet color. It grows more than half above ground, as shown in our illustration, with fine neck and large leaves; flesh white, firm, sweet, greatly relished by cattle. In short it is a magnificent root, easily lifted from the ground, producing enormous crops; an excellent keeper, and the best yellow mangel known. Pkt., 5c.; oz., 10c.; ¼ lb., 20c.; ½ lb. (postpaid), 55c., and over by express 35c. per lb.

GOLDEN TANKARD MANGEL. A distinct, new and valuable yellow-fleshed variety, said to contain a large percentage of sugar. It has already taken the lead of other varieties in England, and is much relished by milch cows and sheep. In shape it is broader than the Long Red but not so long, see illustration, exceedingly hardy, and maturing earlier than other large sorts. Pkt., 5c.; oz., 10c.; ¼ lb., 20c. lb. 55c. postpaid, 5 lbs. and over, by freight or express, 35c. per lb.

NEW GOLDEN YELLOW MAMMOTH MANGEL. A cross between Golden Tankard and Long Yellow. In form and size it resembles Carter's Red Mammoth: the flesh, however, is a bright golden yellow, of fine quality and exceedingly rich in saccharine matter; a heavy cropper. Pkt., 5c.; oz., 10c.; ¼ lb., 20c. lb., 55c.

NEW GOLDEN TANKARD MANGEL.

KINVER YELLOW GLOBE MANGEL. Grows somewhat longer than the Golden Globe. Skin and flesh are very smooth and fine. It is enormously productive and of superior quality, much relished by all kinds of stock. Roots of this variety have been grown to weigh forty-five pounds. Pkt., 5c.; oz., 10c.; ¼ lb., 20c. lb., 1c.; 5 lbs., $1.50.

Long Red Mangel. Not as large as Carter's, but similar in quality. Pkt., 5c.; oz., 10c.; lb., 40c.

Golden Globe Mangel and Red Globe Mangel. Pkt., 5c.; oz., 10c.; ¼ lb., 20c.; lb., 40c.

BROCCOLI.

Early Purple Cape. Best for the North, producing compact bluish-purple heads. Pkt., 10c.; oz., 40c.

Early Walcheren. Very large. Pkt., 10c.; oz., 50c.

BRUSSELS SPROUTS.

Perfection. Producing compact sprouts of fine quality. Pkt., 5c.; oz., 15c.; ¼ lb., 50c.; lb., $1.60.

CAULIFLOWER.

One ounce will produce about fifteen hundred plants and sow about forty square feet.

JOHNSON & STOKES' NEW EARLY ALABASTER. Of American origin; the earliest, best and surest heading variety yet introduced. See Photographic Specialties, page 7. Pkt., 25c.; 3 pkts., $1.00; ¼ oz., $1.50; oz., $6.00.

EXTRA SELECTED EXTRA EARLY DWARF ERFURT. One of the earliest varieties; small-leaved, dwarf for forcing, producing very solid, pure white heads of the first quality; about fifteen inches high. Do not confound this variety with the cheaper Early Dwarf Erfurt. Pkt., 25c.; ½ oz., $1.00; oz., $3.00; ¼ lb., $10.00.

GILT EDGE SNOWBALL CAULIFLOWER.

GILT EDGE EARLY SNOWBALL. The strain we have of this variety is without doubt the very best to be had. Our stock was grown from the very finest specimens, noted for their earliness, dwarf habit, large size, uniform shape and compact growth. None of those we set out for seed failed to produce large, beautiful smooth, snow-white heads. For forcing under glass during winter and early spring, or for planting later in the open ground, no stock of Snowball can surpass it. Pkt., 25c.; ½ oz., $1.00; oz., $3.50; ¼ lb., $10.00.

Early London. A good old variety, with white, compact heads. Pkt., 10c.; oz., 50c.; ¼ lb., $1.75.

Extra Early Paris. A popular early, white, sure-heading variety. Pkt., 10c.; oz., 75c.; ¼ lb., $2.25.

Veitch's Autumn Giant. Large fine heads, well proportioned. Pkt., 10c.; oz., 60c.; ¼ lb., $2.00.

Algiers. One of the best, sure-heading late varieties. Pkt., 10c.; oz., 75c.; ¼ lb., $2.50.

Lenormand's Short Stem. A large late variety, with well-formed white heads of extra quality. Pkt., 10c.; oz., 75c.; ¼ lb., $2.50.

New Seeds Free for Trial

As has been our usual custom for some years past, we have again put up this season several thousand packages of new and improved varieties for trial, which have never yet been offered for sale by any seedsman, and shall be glad to add a few packages, free of charge, to customers whose orders exceed $1.00 and indicate an interest in new varieties of vegetables and flowers. All who deal with us will be treated liberally.

IT WILL PAY TO RAISE AN ACRE OR SO OF MANGEL-WURZEL AND SUGAR BEETS FOR THE BREEDING SOWS AND EWES NEXT WINTER.

RELIABLE CABBAGE SEEDS
SELECTED AMERICAN GROWN STOCKS

There is nothing of greater importance to the market or family gardener than reliable cabbage seeds. We need say nothing to those who have purchased our cabbage in former seasons, as to them its high quality is already known. To those who have never tried us, we can only say that our cabbage is the very best procurable and vastly superior to the seed generally sold. Every grain of seed produced is from our fully selected heads, and our stocks are unsurpassed in this country. We annually supply hundreds of the best market gardeners around Philadelphia, New York and other large cities of the Union. This fact alone is an evidence of high quality.

For full information read our "$100 Prize Essays on Cabbage and Onion Culture," price, 30c., or can be obtained free as a premium on all orders amounting to $2.00 and over.

Early and Summer Varieties.

One ounce of seed will produce about two thousand plants and sow a bed of about forty square feet.

JOHNSON & STOKES' WONDERFUL CABBAGE. Wonderfully early, producing good heads in seventy-five to eighty days from sowing. See Specialties, page 4. Pkt., 10c.; oz., 40c.; ¼ lb., $1.25; lb., $4.00.

JOHNSON & STOKES' EARLIEST. The money growers' cabbage. See Photographic Specialties, page 4. Pkt., 10c.; oz., 40c.; ¼ lb., $1.25; lb., $4.00.

EXTRA EARLY EXPRESS CABBAGE.

EXTRA EARLY EXPRESS. A new French cabbage, resembling the well-known Etampes cabbage, but a few days earlier and a little lighter in color. It comes off almost as early as our Johnson & Stokes' Earliest Cabbage, but does not form so large or solid a head. Do not be deceived into buying these French cabbages as the earliest and best, as after three years comparative trials, each variety planted alongside, we find them some days behind our Wonderful and Earliest, which are thoroughbred American varieties, and form both larger and harder heads. Pkt., 10c.; oz., 25c.; ¼ lb., 75c.; lb., $2.50.

LOUDERBACK'S ALL-YEAR ROUND CABBAGE. New and extra fine, equally good for early, intermediate or late. See Novelties, page 6. Pkt., 10c.; oz., 40c.; ¼ lb., $1.25; lb., $4.00.

JOHNSON & STOKES' MARKET GARDENERS' CABBAGE, No. 2. The earliest and most compact of all large cabbages. See Specialties, page 5. Pkt., 15c.; oz., 50c.; ¼ lb., $1.75; lb., $6.50.

HENDERSON'S SUCCESSION CABBAGE. See Specialties, page 12. Pkt., 10c.; oz., 30c.; ¼ lb., 85c.; lb., $3.00.

VERY EARLY ETAMPES.

VERY EARLY ETAMPES.

This variety comes originally from France. Ripening a week later than Johnson & Stokes' Earliest, and coming in a few days ahead of Wakefield, which, previous to the introduction of Johnson & Stokes' Earliest, was considered the earliest of all. It forms a good, hard, pointed head, with a very short stem, growing close to the ground. Pkt., 5c.; oz., 20c.; ¼ lb., 65c.; lb., $2.25.

Early Dwarf Flat Dutch. A standard second early market variety. Pkt., 5c.; oz., 20c.; ¼ lb., 75c.; lb., $2.50.

EARLY WINNINGSTADT (PRUSSIAN PRIZE STOCK).

EARLY WINNINGSTADT, THE PRUSSIAN PRIZE STOCK. Many consider the Early Winningstadt the very best for early market sales, as it invariably grows very hard and will head on soils where many other sorts fail entirely. Reliable stock is hard to get, as seedsmen usually import it from England and France. The seed we offer, however, is American-grown, acclimated and selected from the original Prussian Prize Stock. Those intending to plant this variety will find this strain far superior in earliness, size, solidity and great uniformity of heading to any other ever sold in this country. Pkt., 10c.; oz., 20c.; ¼ lb., 70c.; lb., $2.40.

EARLY BLEICHFIELD GIANT. It is seldom we are able to recommend a new foreign cabbage so highly as this variety. Since its introduction a few years ago it has grown very popular with market gardeners as a second early and summer sort. It is a short stemmed, large heading sort, tender and solid, ripening a few days earlier than Brunswick. Cabbage growers in all sections should not fail to give it a trial. Pkt., 5c.; oz., 25c.; ¼ lb., 70c.; lb., $2.40.

Early Drumhead. A second early, large, solid heading variety. Pkt., 5c.; oz., 20c.; ¼ lb., 70c.; lb., $2.50.

FOTTLER'S IMPROVED EARLY BRUNSWICK. A splendid second early and late sort, short stem, large, solid heads. Pkt., 5c.; oz., 25c.; ¼ lb., 70c.; lb., $2.40.

VANDERGAW MIDSUMMER. This valuable new variety is the result of many years' selection by Mr. Vandergaw, a noted Long Island market gardener. In some respects it resembles "All-Seasons," coming in about a week after Early Summer, making much larger heads than that well-known variety. Heads are very uniform in color and size, very solid, and in quality all that could be desired as a midsummer and winter cabbage. Long Island cabbage growers have been unusually paying Mr. Vandergaw $10 per pound for the seed, and it has never been offered before at a less price. Pkt., 10c.; oz., 30c.; ¼ lb., 75c.; lb., $2.75.

The following well-known varieties of cabbage are each 5c. per pkt.; oz., 15c.; ¼ lb., 45c.; lb., $1.50.

Deep Head Early, Peerless, Extra Early York, Early Sugar Loaf, Imperial Ox-Heart, Early Large York, Early Bacalan, Early Large Schweinfurt.

WE PERSONALLY CONDUCT OUR BUSINESS, JUST AS MUCH FOR PLEASURE AS FOR PROFIT; OUR HEART IS IN IT AS WELL AS OUR PURSE.

Three Good Summer Cabbages

SELECTED EARLY SUMMER. NEW LARGE JERSEY WAKEFIELD. ALL SEASONS.

NEW LARGE OR CHARLESTON JERSEY WAKEFIELD CABBAGE.

We were the first seedsmen to introduce, 5 years since, this now popular market cabbage. It is about 5 days later than Early Jersey Wakefield. The heads are fully one-half larger and quite solid. It is very compact in growth, and can easily be planted in rows 2 feet apart and 20 inches in the rows. One great advantage is, it does not burst open when ripe, like many other early sorts, and consequently can be left standing on the ground a long while without injury, until a favorable opportunity for cutting. No market gardener, desiring a cabbage of this kind, should fail to plant some of this valuable sort. Pkt., 10c.; oz., 35c.; ¼ lb., $1.00; lb., $3.50; 2 lbs., $6.00.

HENDERSON'S EARLY SUMMER CABBAGE (SELECTED).

The illustration above gives the true shape and compact habit of our strain of this valuable sort. It is 10 or 12 days later than the Early Jersey Wakefield, but much larger in size and will stand on the ground much longer without bursting open. In this respect it is much superior to Fottler's Brunswick. While the heads are much larger than the Early Jersey Wakefield, its very compact habit enables it to be planted almost as close. The heads are very hard and solid throughout and of fine uniform shape. Pkt., 10c.; oz., 25c.; ¼ lb., 75c.; lb., $2.75; 2 lbs., $5.00.

ALL-SEASONS CABBAGE.

This strain of Early Drumhead Cabbage we first offered to the public 5 years since under the broad claim of being about as **early as the Early Summer and growing much larger.** Our best market gardeners say they find our claims are fully substantiated in every particular. As its name indicates, it can be planted at all seasons. It forms a fine, large, hard head, of superior quality, not bursting after heading; the heads are of *great thickness*, which make it a capital sort to keep through the winter. Pkt., 10c.; oz., 25c.; ¼ lb., 75c.; lb., $2.50; 2 lbs., $4.50.

SELECTED EARLY JERSEY WAKEFIELD CABBAGE.

EXTRA STOCK.

SELECTED EARLY JERSEY WAKEFIELD CABBAGE.

This variety is a most important one, because it is planted largely for the main early crop, and recognizing the great interests at stake with the growers of this sort, we have been unusually careful in selecting the stock from which our seed was grown. While it is not so early as *Johnson & Stokes' Earliest* and *New Wonderful*, it will be found to be the very best sort to come in immediately after them. We offer the very finest strain of this valuable variety. Many of the leading *market gardeners* around Philadelphia, New York, Boston and elsewhere, pronounce it "the very best they can get." Pkt., 10c.; oz., 25c.; ¼ lb., 75c.; lb., $2.75; 2 lbs., $5.00.

∴ SEEDS ∴ FOR ∴ MONEY ∴ GROWERS ∴

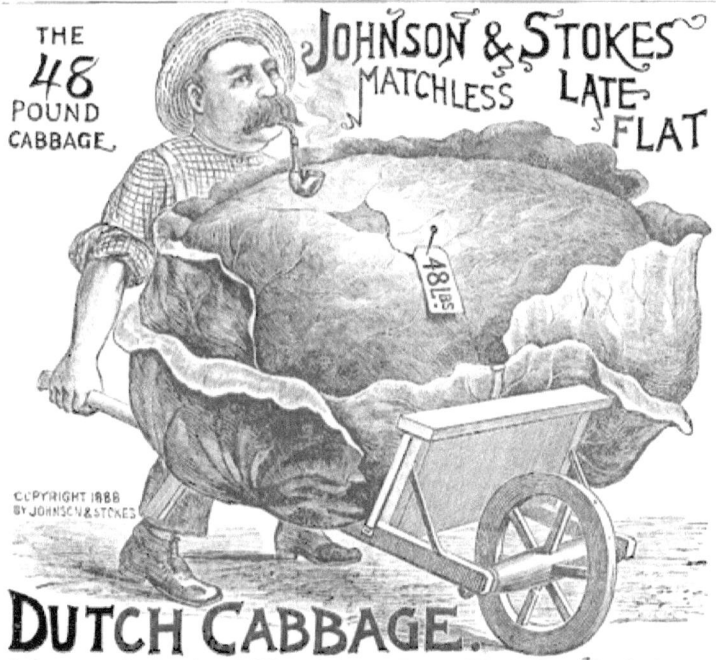

DUTCH CABBAGE.

Johnson & Stokes' Matchless Late Flat Dutch Cabbage.

In this new strain of late cabbage we believe we have combined every good quality essential to perfection. It is the result of several years' continued selection for our seed stocks of the most perfect and largest heads, with low stocks, and especially those that show greater earliness in heading, with few outer leaves and of very uniform color. By such persistent selection, year after year, we have a highly improved strain, pronounced by experienced cabbage growers and market gardeners, who, after four years' trial, now grow it in preference to all others for a main crop, **the finest strain of late cabbage in the world.** It grows larger and weights heavier than any other variety, never fails to make a perfect, solid head, and is most uniform in size and color. We can honestly recommend this superior sort to all growers as standing alone and unequalled by any other late cabbage. Pkt., 10c.; oz., 30c.; ¼ lb., $1.00; lb., $3.00; 2 lbs., $5.50, post-paid.

NEW LATE CABBAGE.
AUTUMN KING.

A new strain of late cabbage which is highly spoken of by all market and family gardeners who have thus far tested it. The heads are of enormous size and very solid. It has few outer leaves, as shown in the accompanying illustration, and owing to this fact it is claimed that "Autumn King" will produce a greater weight of crop from the same space of ground than any other late cabbage. Pkt., 10c.; oz., 40c.; 2 oz., 75c.; ¼ lb., $1.25; lb., $4.00; 2 lbs., $7.00.

AUTUMN KING CABBAGE.

JOHNSON & STOKES

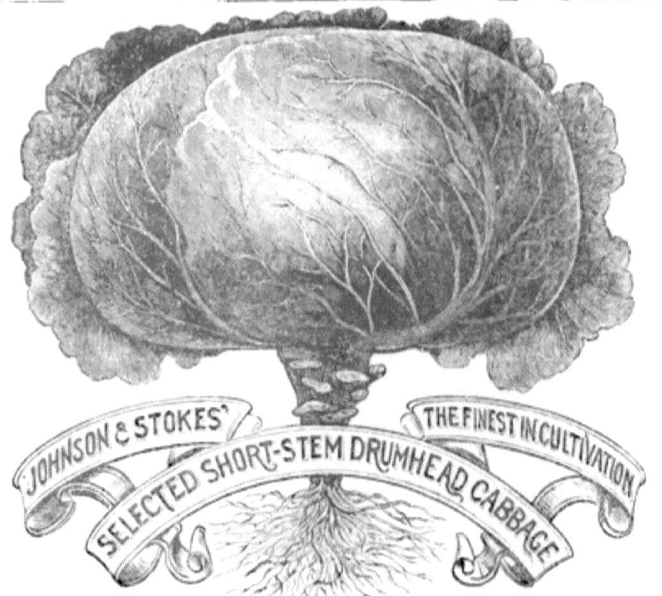

Johnson & Stokes' Short-Stem Drumhead

This improved variety far surpasses the old strain of Large Late Drumhead Cabbage, ripening *earlier*, with very short stock or stem, forming large *solid thick* heads, of fine quality and the best of keepers. Owing to our long continued selection for several years past, this variety is remarkable for *reliability of heading*; every one who plants it can expect at least *ninety-eight* large *solid* heads from every one hundred plants. Our customers in the South, and in all other sections where many varieties till to head, will find the Short-Stem Drumhead a sure thing and can depend on big crops every time. It heads the *best* of the winter Drumheads. Pkt., 10c.; oz., 30c.; 2 oz., 60c.; ¼ lb., $1.00; lb., $3.50; 2 lbs., $5.50, post-paid

GENUINE SUREHEAD CABBAGE

CABBAGE.—Late or Winter Varieties.

GENUINE SUREHEAD. This popular cabbage is rightly named Surehead, and never fails to make a remarkably fine, solid, large head, with few outer leaves, as shown in our illustration. It originated some years since with a practical market gardener, by crossing the Flat Dutch and Drumhead varieties, and has always brought the highest price in our markets. It is a strong, vigorous grower, ripening late for a maincrop and very uniform in size and color. Our supply is grown from the *original seed*, now let ter to be had at any price. Pkt. 10c ; oz., 25c., ¼ lb., 75c., lb., $2.50.

BRIDGEPORT DRUMHEAD. This is the standard shipping cabbage around Chicago, where head growers will raise no other, and have paid as high as $2.00 per pound for the seed in seasons when scarce. It makes a large, even, firm, round head, seldom rots or bursts and is unquestionably one of the finest shipping cabbages grown. *Extra* selected seed. Pkt., 10c; oz., 25c.; ¼ lb., 75c ; lb., $2.50

PREMIUM FLAT DUTCH. This variety is largely grown for late or main crop being the favorite winter market variety. Heads very large, solid and broad, with flat tops, of fine flavor and quality, very short stems. Pkt., 5c., oz., 20c.; 2 oz., 35c.; ¼ lb., 60c.; lb., $2.00; 5 lbs., and over, by express, $1.75 per lb.

LARGE LATE DRUMHEAD. A favorite winter variety; extra large, solid heads; slightly later than the *Flat Dutch*. Pkt., 5c.; oz., 20c.; ¼ lb., 50c.; lb., $1.75, postpaid ; 5 lbs. and over, by express, $1.50 per lb.

"YOUR MATCHLESS LATE FLAT DUTCH CABBAGE WAS THE VERY BEST IN A LOT OF SIX LEADING SORTS." C. C. BALL, RAMEY, PA.

Our Vegetable Collections for 1892.

50c. and $1.00.

The prices of these collections, named below, are about cost of growing the seed in large quantities, and being packed in the fall, when our hands have little else to do, we do not estimate the cost of labor. The seeds alone would cost, at regular catalogue prices, more than twice the price asked here for them. These offers are made solely to extend our trade and induce thousands of new customers to give our seeds a fair trial and prove their great superiority. We cannot sell any other seeds so cheaply, nor can we make any changes in the collections.

COLLECTION No. 1.
FOR 50 CENTS.

WE WILL SEND BY MAIL, ALL POSTAGE PAID, 15 FULL-SIZED PACKETS OF THE CHOICEST VEGETABLE SEEDS, DESCRIBED BELOW.

1. **NEW GIANT PASCAL CELERY.** A selection from our celebrated *Golden Self-Blanching*; large, crisp, solid, unsurpassed in delicious quality and flavor, easily grown and bleached, the best of keepers. See page 37.
2. **NEW GOLDEN BALL ONION.** A very distinct and handsome new onion, finest of all. See page 56.
3. **EARLY SCARLET GLOBE RADISH.** One of the earliest and handsomest red radishes, crisp, mild.
4. **NEW GIANT OF PERA CUCUMBER.** A magnificent variety, the best for the table. See page 41.
5. **NEW EARLY PEERLESS CABBAGE.** Extra early, very large and fine, solid heads of superior quality.
6. **NEW BUDLONG OR BREADSTONE TURNIP.** The very best for table use. See page 74.
7. **IMPROVED DEFIANCE LETTUCE.** Large solid heads of the finest quality.
8. **NEW GIANT OF COLORADO MUSKMELON.** Largest and handsomest, delicious quality. See page 51.
9. **IMPROVED RUST-PROOF GOLDEN WAX BEAN.** One of the hardiest and best. See page 24.
10. **LONG GREEN CROOK-NECK SQUASH.** The best frying squash, superior in flavor to Egg Plant.
11. **NEW CELESTIAL PEPPER.** The most beautiful and useful of peppers.
12. **EDMAND'S EARLY RED TURNIP BEET.** Quite early, fine form, deep blood color, sweet and juicy.
13. **NEW GIANT ITALIAN LEEK.** The largest of all and mildest in flavor.
14. **LIVINGSTON'S FAVORITE TOMATO.** Very early, bright red, large, smooth and solid.
15. **AMERICAN SWEET MARJORAM.** The most popular herb, indispensable in every garden.

We send the above **FIFTEEN PACKETS**, neatly packed, post-paid, by mail, for only 50 CENTS IN STAMPS or cash; FIVE COLLECTIONS, each separate, to different addresses if desired, FOR $2.00.

A COMPLETE VEGETABLE GARDEN FOR $1.00.

OUR SPECIAL INTRODUCTION BOX OF SEEDS. (Collection No. 2) embraces thirty full-sized packets of the choicest Vegetable Seeds, including all the above named, and the fifteen varieties described below. We will also put in each box three packets of choice Flower Seeds as a present for your wife, mother or daughter.

16. **NEW SHOE PEG SWEET CORN.** Deliciously sweet and best of all for the family garden.
17. **NEW RUBICON CARROT.** The best half-long, smooth, beautiful rich orange color.
18. **JOHNSON'S DIXIE WATERMELON.** The hardiest and best ever introduced, succeeds everywhere. $100 cash prizes for the heaviest grown in 1892. See page 18.
19. **LONG BRANCH TOMATO.** A fine new extra early variety, has never been offered for sale and can only be obtained in this collection.
20. **MADRID GIANT ONION.** The largest and handsomest of all red onions. See page 59.
21. **PHILADELPHIA LONG SCARLET RADISH.** The earliest and best long red radish.
22. **BLUE BEAUTY PEA.** New extra early, extremely prolific, and delicious in quality.
23. **VANDERGAW CABBAGE.** A very desirable early or late variety. One of the finest new sorts.
24. **IMPROVED LARGE SUGAR PARSNIP.** Beautiful, smooth and very sweet.
25. **TRUE TENNESSEE SWEET POTATO PUMPKIN.** The best pie pumpkin.
26. **LARGE WHITE GLOBE RADISH.** One of the finest summer radishes.
27. **NEW FERN-LEAVED PARSLEY.** Beautifully curled and one of the best for table and garnishing.
28. **ENKHUIZEN SPINACH.** The only genuine Long Standing. Best for spring sowing.
29. **MARBLEHEAD SQUASH.** Fine for cooking, splendid winter keeper.
30. **LETTUCE.** Ten of the best American varieties, mixed. Giving fine lettuce for the table the entire season.
31. **THREE PACKETS OF CHOICE FLOWER SEEDS.** To beautify your home.

Send a $1.00 bill, Postal Note, P. O. Order, or Stamps, in an ordinary letter, and you will receive the box, containing all the above neatly and securely packed, by return mail, all postage paid, and if not satisfactory, we will return your money. What can be fairer? Show this to your neighbors, and get them to send with you. We will mail three of the above **Special Introduction Boxes** to one address, or different addresses, for only $2.50.

Cheap, but Choice
Flower Seed Collections.

PETUNIA,
STRIPED AND BLOTCHED.

TEN CHOICE ANNUALS (Collection No. 3) FOR 25c.

FOR 25c. OR FIVE COLLECTIONS FOR $1.00.

1.—ASTERS. Choice varieties, mixed. Perhaps you don't know the possibilities of the *Modern Aster*.
2.—BALSAM. Challenge prize. Very choice strain, of very double kinds.
3.—EMPRESS CANDYTUFT. Pure white flowers. A choice novelty.
4.—MIGNONETTE. The sweetest of all.
5.—PETUNIAS. Choice striped and blotched varieties. (See cut.)
6.—POPPIES. The carnation flowered varieties. Dazzling colors.
7.—VERBENAS. Mixed, striped and self-colored kinds.
8.—PANSIES. A choice variety of colors and markings. Everybody loves them.
9.—CALLIOPSIS. A veritable "Wave of Gold." Flower the whole season.
10.—WILD FLOWER GARDEN. A mixture full of delightful surprises, and worth the cost of the entire collection.

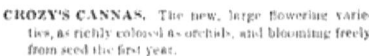
ANOTHER LIBERAL OFFER (Collection No. 4).

TEN FLORAL NOVELTIES FOR 50 CENTS.

CROZY'S CANNAS. The new, large flowering varieties, as richly colored as orchids, and blooming freely from seed the first year.
MARGARET CARNATIONS. This new carnation blooms four months from sowing the seed.
CUP AND SAUCER CAMPANULA. Exquisite rose, blue, lilac and white flowers resembling a cup and saucer in shape. (See cut.)
NEW SHIRLEY POPPY. Exquisitely delicate flowers, ranging from white through all shades of pink and red to fiery crimson. (See cut.)
EMPRESS CANDYTUFT. The most beautiful pure white flower we have. Excellent for bouquets.
ECKFORD'S NEWEST SWEET PEAS. Embracing the finest-named varieties in superb mixture.
TUBEROUS BEGONIAS. The grandest flower for bedding purposes in the whole list. They flower equal to a Geranium, but in a choice of colors rivalling the rose.
FORGET-ME-NOT, VICTORIA. Makes a perfectly round plant with large umbels of exquisite blue flowers.
PANSIES. Imperial German large flowering. Flowers of choice markings and largest size.
WILD FLOWER GARDEN. This is so justly popular that we put it into both collections, knowing the results cannot help being abundantly satisfactory.

NEW CAMPANULA, "CUP AND SAUCER."

NEW "SHIRLEY" POPPY.

We believe the two collections offered above were **never before equalled** at such a moderate price. The 50c. novelty collection is a beauty and wonder. No changes can be made in either, as they are all put up in advance. To those who desire to get up clubs for these collections, we will sell five 25c. collections and three 50c. collections for $2.00, or fifteen 25c. collections and eight 50c. collections for $5.00.

SPECIAL · COLLECTIONS
OF
Summer Flowering Bulbs.
FREE BY MAIL.

WHITE SPIDER LILY. 25c. each.

ROSE OF JERICHO. 20c. each.

SPOTTED CALLA LILY. 15c. each.

Collection No. 5, EIGHT BEAUTIFUL BULBS FOR 50c.

1 **WHITE SPIDER LILY.** A free blooming bulb, bearing pure white, deliciously fragrant flowers. Price, 25c. each.
1 **PURE WHITE CALLA LILY.** The old, beautiful lily we all know and love. Price, 25c. each.
3 **GLADIOLUS.** Assorted colors, all different, one of our most beautiful and satisfactory bulbs. Price, 5c. each.
1 **GIANT LEAVED CANNA.** Growing ten feet high, with immense bronze colored foliage. Makes a magnificent tropical effect in the centre of a bed. Price 15c each.
2 **TUBEROSES.** Deliciously scented, pure white, double flowers. Everybody's favorite. Price, 5c. each.

Collection No. 6—FOR $1.00, we send collection No. 5 and add to it the following nine magnificent flowering bulbs and roots making the finest collection of the kind ever offered for the money.

2. **MONTBRETIAS.** These exquisite Gladiolus-like flowers are not as well known as their beauty deserves. They bloom till long after frost. Price, 10c. each.
1 **TRITOMA, or RED HOT POKER PLANT.** Very effective for planting among shrubbery, lifting its immense fiery scarlet head well above the dark green foliage. Price, 20c. each.
1 **IRIS** (Flower-de-luce). These rival the orchid in exquisite coloring and marking. Are perfectly hardy, and when once planted increase in beauty and size every year. Price, 20c. each.
1 **SPOTTED CALLA LILY.** The flowers of this lily are not as large as the common Calla, but the leaves are beautifully marked with white spots. Price, 15c. each.
2 **TIGRIDIAS.** Producing handsome flowers of large size and gorgeous colors. Price, 10c. each.
1 **ROSE OF JERICHO.** (See cut.) A new resurrection plant from the Holy Land. Is hard wooded and grows in the form of a little bush. As we send it out it looks like a dry, dead stick, but when placed in water it quickly unfolds and sometimes green leaves appear. It is a native of the border of the Dead Sea, where it grows and blooms freely. Price, 20c each.
1 **LARGE FLOWERING CANNA.** Makes a stately plant, growing six to eight feet high, and holding its magnificent stalk of immense crimson flowers well up above the foliage, making a striking plant either for the lawn or flower bed. Price, 20c. each.

❈ RARE · CACTI ❈

Cactus require absolutely no care. They grow for months in the house or garden without watering, and increase in value yearly. No wonder they have become all the rage, for their flowers, which are of **exquisite beauty and fragrance**, and their curious forms, render them exceedingly interesting. In winter they require scarcely any water.

CORN-COB CACTUS.   LIVING ROCK CACTUS.

CORN-COB CACTUS.

The best and finest bloomer of all the Echinocerei; blooms profusely when quite young, and makes valuable plants, as well as large clusters, which often bear forty to fifty flowers at one time. Single plants. 25c. to 75c.

LIVING ROCK.

Anhalonium Fissuratus.

No one would think it is a plant, looks like a piece of curved woodwork on which days of labor have been spent. So tenacious of life is it, that it need not be watered more than once a month. When in bloom it is yet more attractive. Sold elsewhere at $2 to $5 each. Our price is 30c. each.

THE QUEEN CACTUS.

This is certainly the most desirable large-flowering cactus in existence. It is of rapid growth, sure to bloom, and easy to manage; bears flowers often ten inches across, delightfully fragrant, and pure white in color. Grows anywhere. 25c., 50c., and $1.00 each, according to size.

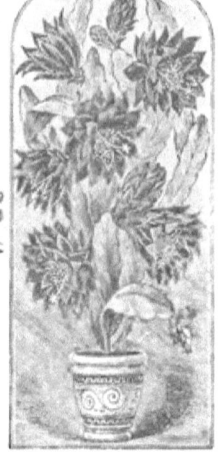

THE KING CACTUS.

A magnificent day bloomer with flowers **five to six inches across**, of the most **brilliant crimson color** imaginable. Blooms first year. One of our best. 25c., 50c., and $1.00 each, according to size.

PHYLLOCACTUS ROSEA.

Flowers pink; 25c. Four distinct sorts for 75c.

SILVER STAR CACTUS.

Is greatly admired for its bright silvery spines radiating in the sun, as well as for the neat yellow flowers which it produces freely when only one inch high. This is a very cheap plant, it should not be overwatered; has bright red seeds. 25c. to 50c. each.

CACTUS COLLECTION (No. 7).
Ten Curious Cactus Plants, as illustrated in above cut, free by mail for $1.00.

THE BUTTON CACTUS.

(*M. Micromeris*.)

A real beauty. Single plant resembles more a fine silk embroidered button than a plant; makes large clusters as it becomes old, as shown in the illustration. Price reduced to 50c. for single plants.

CACTUS SEED. There is a great deal of pleasure in raising cacti from seed, though some of the varieties are slow growth. Below we give directions for sowing the seed. In the seeds we offer there is a mixture of some twenty varieties. Price per pkt., 15c.; 10 pkts for $1.00.

CACTUS SEEDS. Directions of Culture. Sow the seed in flat pans or flower-pot saucers filled with sand and place it in one of larger size, which can be kept full of water. This will keep the sand in the smaller saucer to the required moisture. Cover with a pane of glass and watch for the little plants in from two to four weeks. As soon as these are large enough to handle, transplant to two-inch pots. Price, per pkt., 15c.

All the foregoing collections can be ordered by the numbers. Address,

Johnson & Stokes, Seed Growers, PHILADELPHIA, PA.

NEW DIAMOND WINTER CABBAGE.

In this fine new cabbage, we have a strain entirely distinct from any other, viz: a cross between Short Stem Drumhead and Danish Round Winter. Our customers well know the many valuable characteristics of the former, while as to the latter, it is a universally admitted fact that it is the best, heaviest and most solid heading sort grown in Europe. It has cost the originator, a prominent Long Island market gardener, seven years of constant and unremitting care to select and fix this truly fine type of winter cabbage.

The New Diamond Drumhead combines all those qualities so desirable to an experienced gardener to produce a late cabbage perfect in every respect, viz: size, weight, quality, sure-heading and a long keeper. It grows very compactly, the stem is short and it can be planted closer together than any other late variety, besides this it does not crack open. The heads will average from fifteen to eighteen pounds in weight after they are trimmed for market; they grow very uniform in size and shape, and present a handsome appearance to the eye. In fact, one head is almost an exact duplicate of the other. They are extra hard, solid, round and somewhat flattened on top; possess a fine, small rib and are always of the finest possible quality and a sure-header. Pkt., 10c.; oz., 40c.; ¼ lb., $1.25; lb., $4.00.

ROYAL DRUMHEAD. This variety, from Germany, has become a standard late sort. It grows a beautiful, solid, round, compact head, with bright green foliage and short stem, ripening a few days earlier than our Premium Flat Dutch. Pkt., 10c.; oz., 30c.; ¼ lb., $1.00; lb., $3.00.

Marblehead Mammoth Drumhead. The largest variety grown. Pkt., 5c.; oz., 20c.; ¼ lb., 50c.; lb., $1.75.

Stone Mason. A large solid, tender, free-heading variety. Pkt., 5c.; oz., 20c.; ¼ lb., 60c.; lb., $2.00.

Filderkraut. A German variety, with large, solid, conical heads. In Germany it is much used for making sauerkraut. Pkt., 5c.; oz., 25c.; ¼ lb., 60c.; lb., $2.00.

Green Glazed. A late, large-heading variety, leaves of a glossy pea-green; very popular South, as it resists attacks of bugs and insects. Pkt., 5c.; oz., 20c.; ¼ lb., 60c.; lb., $2.00.

MAMMOTH ROCK RED. This is by far the best, largest and surest-heading red cabbage ever introduced. The plant is large, with numerous spreading leaves. The head is large, round, very solid, and of deep red color. Ninety-eight per cent. of the plants will form extra fine heads. The best of the red cabbages. Pkt., 10c.; oz., 40c.; ¼ lb., $1.25; lb., $4.50.

Red Dutch Erfurt. Very early, of deep blood color; head solid. Pkt., 5c.; oz., 20c.; ¼ lb., 60c.; lb., $2.00.

Large Red Drumhead. Valuable for pickling. Pkt., 5c.; oz., 15c.; ¼ lb., 50c.; lb., $1.50.

LOUISVILLE DRUMHEAD CABBAGE.

LOUISVILLE DRUMHEAD. This is the most popular intermediate and late sort with market gardeners around Louisville and in the Southwest. It comes off medium early, withstands heat to a remarkable extent, heads large, solid and uniform in size and color. We can recommend this sort very highly for the Southern and Middle States. Pkt., 10c.; oz., 25c.; ¼ lb., 75c.; lb., $2.50.

JOHNSON & STOKES' HARD-HEADING SAVOY. (Market Gardeners' Private Stock.) The best of all the Savoys. See Specialties, page 4. Pkt., 10c.; oz., 30c.; ¼ lb., $1.00; lb., $4.00.

PERFECTION DRUMHEAD SAVOY. Grows large, heads nearly round, tender, excellent flavor. Pkt., 5c.; oz., 20c.; ¼ lb., 50c.; lb., $1.75.

Green Curled Savoy. This does not make a solid head, but being very tender is used for boiling. Pkt., 5c.; oz., 15c.; ¼ lb., 50c.; lb., $1.70.

CARROT.

One ounce will sow about one hundred and twenty-five feet of drill and four pounds will sow an acre.

RED PARISIAN FORCING. A new and very distinct variety from France, being the earliest of all carrots, forming roots much quicker than the well-known French Forcing. It is as round as a turnip, has a fine neck; leaves short and erect; quality excellent. Pkt., 5c.; oz., 15c.; ¼ lb., 40c.; lb., $1.25.

NEW RUBICON HALF-LONG. In the Rubicon we have an entirely new and distinct American carrot; very symmetrical in shape and of a dark orange color, selected and perfected by a Connecticut gardener. The stock is so finely bred that the carrots have attained such uniformity that they are almost exact duplicates of each other. It is earlier than the Danvers and about the same length; the leaves are one-third slimer, fewer and finer than this well-known sort; these features make it extremely well adapted to growing under glass. It is a splendid sort, however, for growing outside at any season of the year. It grows without neck, the crown is hollow and it grows well under the ground, which prevents it from becoming sunburnt—a very important feature. Many leading gardeners are now planting the Rubicon to the exclusion of all others. Pkt., 5c.; oz., 15c.; ¼ lb., 40c.; lb., $1.25.

Very Early Short Horn Scarlet, or French Forcing. An early forcing variety; small root and excellent flavor. Pkt., 5c.; oz., 10c.; ¼ lb., 30c.; lb., $1.00.

HALF-LONG NANTES. (Stump Rooted.) A fine intermediate variety, bright scarlet color, smooth, large and of excellent quality. Pkt., 5c.; oz., 10c.; ¼ lb., 30c.; lb., $1.00.

CHANTENAY. This variety resembles the Half-Long Nantes, but has larger shoulders. Fine deep scarlet color. Pkt., 5c.; oz., 10c.; ¼ lb., 25c.; lb., 75c.

Early Scarlet Horn. The favorite summer variety. Pkt., 5c.; oz., 10c.; ¼ lb., 25c.; lb., 90c.

"DIAMOND WINTER CABBAGE CAN'T BE BEAT. IT EXCELS EVERY KNOWN VARIETY."
N. HERRIG, LEAVENWORTH, KANSAS.

JOHNSON & STOKES

NEW OX-HEART, OR GUERANDE CARROT

OX-HEART, or HALF-LONG GUERANDE. (*Shamp-carola.*) This is one of the most valuable of all recent introductions, either for family use or market. It is an intermediate between the half-long and horn varieties, attaining a diameter of three to four inches at the neck, and of most beautiful shape, as shown in above cut, and rich orange color. It is of extra fine quality and very productive. Pkt., 5c.; oz., 10c.; ¼ lb., 30c.; lb., $1.00.

NICHOLS' IMPROVED LONG ORANGE CARROT. We procured this stock from Mr. Robert Nichols, one of the most successful market gardeners of this city. The strain is *earlier* than either the well-known Danvers or Long Orange as usually sold. The color is of a deep orange when no thicker than an ordinary lead pencil, shading to a deep orange red when fully grown. The root is *perfectly* smooth from the shoulder to the extreme tip, and entirely devoid of side roots *in its villous softgrowth.* It grows without any neck whatever, the top is short, and this, together with its *extreme coriness*, admirably fits it for early use.

We pronounce it the ideal carrot, either for early or late use, being of uniformly large size, enormously productive, the best of Keepers, and highly nutritious for stock when grown as a field crop. Pkt., 5c.; oz., 10c.; ¼ lb., 30c.; lb., $1.00; 5 lbs., $4.75, by express.

IMPROVED LONG ORANGE. The well-known and popular old standby for late summer and winter use; grown extensively for feeding stock. Pkt., 5c.; oz., 10c.; ¼ lb., 25c.; lb., 60c.; 5 lbs., and over, 50c. per lb.

Early Half-Long Scarlet. A desirable variety, remarkably smooth and rich color, very fine for table use or forcing. Pkt., 5c.; oz., 10c.; ¼ lb., 25c.; lb., $1.00.

SAINT VALLERY, or NEW INTERMEDIATE RED. This splendid variety originated in France, near the city of St. Vallery, from whence it takes its name. It grows to uniform large size, intermediate in shape between the Half-Long and Long Orange. The roots are straight and smooth, broad at the top, measuring about two and three-fourths inches across with a length of about eleven inches. The color is a rich orange red, its table qualities are faultless. It will be found a most excellent variety for either garden or field culture. Pkt., 5c.; oz., 10c.; ¼ lb., 30c.; lb., $1.00.

IMPROVED DANVERS CARROT. Our pure American stock of this valuable variety is preferred by many gardeners to any other sort. The top is very small, color of a rich shade of orange, shape very handsome and smooth; quality the very best. One highly valuable feature of our strain is that it has its full color when quite young, which enables it to be pulled sooner. It is equally valuable to grow for feeding stock, being well adapted to all soils and will yield the *greatest bulk* with the smallest length of root of any other sort. Under good cultivation we have known it to produce thirty tons to the acre. Pkt., 5c.; oz., 10c.; ¼ lb., 25c.; lb., 80c.; 5 lbs., by express, $3.75.

NEW LONG RED CORELESS. One of the best long carrots we have ever grown; it grows ten to twelve inches long and two inches in diameter; very *smooth*, stump-rooted, good color, of excellent quality, free from any heart or pith. Pkt., 5c.; oz., 10c.; ¼ lb., 30c.; lb., $1.00.

LARGE WHITE VOSGES. A valuable variety, with fine white flesh of excellent quality, large size, and, by reason of its shape is easily dug, very productive and nutritious; excellent for stock. Pkt., 5c.; oz., 10c.; ¼ lb., 20c.; lb. 6c.

Large White Belgian. Grows one-third above ground; large white root, with green top grown exclusively for feeding stock. Pkt., 5c.; oz., 10c.; ¼ lb., 20c.; lb., 60c.

Large Yellow Belgian. A good stock-feeding variety, differing from the above only in color. Pkt., 5c.; oz., 10c.; ¼ lb., 20c.; lb., 60c.

CELERY.

One ounce will produce about twenty-five hundred plants and sow about two hundred feet of row.

JOHNSON & STOKES' GOLDEN SELF-BLANCHING. The best celery in cultivation for the family garden and for early market. See photograph and Specialties, page 5. Pkt., 15c.; oz., 60c.; ¼ lb., $1.10; lb., $4.00.

EARLY ARLINGTON. This new celery comes from the same source as the Arlington Tennis Ball Lettuce, described on another page. It was an improved selection of the well-known Boston Market Celery, made by an Arlington market gardener. It has received *first prize* in both the regular and special premiums offered by the Massachusetts Horticultural Society. Its very early, coming in quite three weeks in advance of the Boston market; and its superiority over this variety is in the fact that it is earlier, of larger size, and more vigorous growth, does not blight or run to seed so badly, and blanches easily and more quickly. Pkt., 10c.; oz., 30c.; ¼ lb., 80c.; lb., $3.00.

DILKS' MANY HEARTED. This fine new celery was originated by Mr. Geo. Dilks, a noted Philadelphia market gardener, from one stalk found growing in a field of Golden Dwarf in 1884. It is very distinct in appearance, being much stouter, thicker and heavier near the root than any other variety. We have seen four stalks in a bunch weigh thirteen and a quarter pounds, and entirely cover the top of an ordinary flour barrel. It surpasses all other celeries in keeping qualities, having for a few years past been sold in our markets as late as May, after Golden Dwarf and all other varieties were done. Pkt., 10c.; oz., 50c.; ¼ lb., $1.25; lb., $3.00.

GOLDEN HEART DWARF. This distinct variety is the most popular old variety among market gardeners. It is entirely solid, an excellent keeper and of fine, nutty flavor. In size and habit of growth it is much the same as Half-Dwarf White kinds, except, when blanched, the heart, which is large and full, is of a waxy golden yellow, rendering it very striking and showy for either market or private use. We have an unusually fine strain, and sell hundreds of pounds each season to our most critical market gardeners. Pkt., 10c.; oz., 25c.; ¼ lb., 60c.; lb., $2.25.

"YOUR CELERY IS AS GOOD AS GOLD. I HAVE THE FINEST IN BALTIMORE CITY MARKETS."
GEO. P. MARBLE, BALTIMORE, MD.

.˙. SEEDS .˙. FOR .˙. MONEY .˙. GROWERS .˙.

KALAMAZOO BROAD RIBBED CELERY.

This magnificent New *Half Dwarf* Celery, which we offered for the first time three years since, originated with a prominent celery grower at Kalamazoo, Mich., and is pronounced by all gardeners who have grown it, "*The most perfect type of Dwarf White Celery known.*"

It is very distinct and handsome, of a beautiful cream-white color throughout, attains a very large size, of quick growth, stiff and close habit, remarkably solid and fine flavored. Ribs are very broad, thickly and closely set, while by reason of its neat growth and showy appearance, it is a specially valuable variety for market. It is also a first-class keeper, remaining fit for use as long as the Golden Dwarf and other good keeping sorts. For the use of hotels, restaurants and other large establishments it is superior to most other kinds, there scarcely being any waste in dressing it for the table. It has such a distinctive appearance in growth as to cause almost everyone seeing it to exclaim; "What celery is that?" Long rows of it being as level and even as though each plant had been shaped in the same mould. It has already takes the lead as a keeping celery for winter use. Pkt., 10c.; oz., 30c.; ¼ lb., $1.00, lb., $3.50.

GIANT PASCAL CELERY.

NEW GIANT PASCAL CELERY.

This variety is a sport thoroughly established by skillful selection from our Golden Self-Blanching Celery, which has become so popular within the last few years; it partakes of the best qualities of that variety but it is somewhat larger and taller. It is of a fine nutty flavor, being entirely free from any bitter taste. It grows about 2 feet high; the stalks are very broad, thick and crisp; the width and thickness of these are distinctive features of this variety. It bleaches with but slight "earthing up," and very quickly, usually in 5 or 6 days. It is a splendid keeper. The heart is golden yellow, very full and attractive in appearance. Market gardeners, try this new celery. You will make no mistake in planting it largely, as it is destined to become one of the most valuable celeries for second early and mid-winter use. We offer *extra selected seed* of our own growing. Pkt., 10c.; oz., 25c.; ¼ lb., 75c.; 1 lb., $2.75.

NEW PERFECTION HEARTWELL.

PERFECTION HEARTWELL CELERY.

A very large, solid growing variety of excellent flavor and a creamy white color. In size it is between the Golden Dwarf and Large White Solid. It makes an excellent market sort, for winter use, as the stalks are clear and attractive in color, with large golden yellow heart, and of a size to influence purchasers. Very popular in the New York markets where it is considered by many the finest of all winter varieties. Pkt., 10c.; oz., 30c.; ¼ lb., 85c.; lb., $3.00.

WHITE PLUME CELERY (Extra Selected).

Each year adds to the popularity and value of this variety. Like our *Golden Self-Blanching*, it requires very little earthing up to blanch it, and although its keeping qualities are not equal to our *Golden Self-Blanching*, yet as a celery for the fall and early winter use it is unsurpassed. Our strain of this variety is closely selected each year and will be found entirely free from green celery, so prevalent in much of this seed sold. Market gardeners who purchased from us the past five years are unanimous in pronouncing our White Plume the best and purest they can get. Pkt., 10c.; oz., 30c.; ¼ lb., $1.00; lb., $3.50; 2 lbs., $6.00.

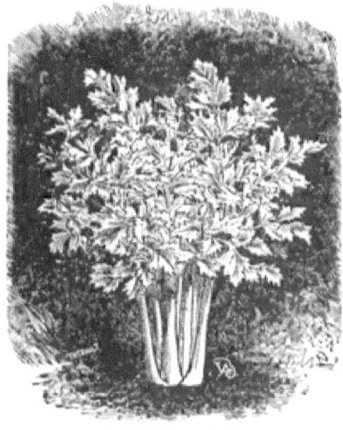

WHITE PLUME CELERY.

JOHNSON & STOKES

CELERY—Continued.

CHICAGO GIANT GOLDEN HEART. This new sort is a selection made by a Chicago gardener from Dwarf Golden Heart. It is grown extensively in Chicago, growing much taller than its parent, with very broad stalks, very solid, and a fine winter keeper. We recommend it highly. Pkt., 10c.; oz., 30c.; ¼ lb., 60c.; lb., $2.00.

GIANT WHITE SOLID. The best of the large growing sorts and a favorite variety, solid, crisp and tender. Pkt., 5c.; oz., 15c.; ¼ lb., 60c.; lb., $2.00.

CRAWFORD'S HALF-DWARF, also known as Henderson's Half Dwarf. This variety is a great favorite. When blanched, it is of a yellowish white making it very ornamental; entirely solid, possessing the nutty flavor peculiar to the dwarf kinds, while it has much more vigor of growth, surpassing most of the large-growing sorts in weight. Pkt., 5c.; oz., 20c.; ¼ lb., 60c.; lb., $2.00.

Imperial Dwarf Large Ribbed. An excellent variety, white, very solid, fine, sweet flavor and a good keeper. Pkt., 5c.; oz., 20c.; ¼ lb., 60c.; lb., $2.00.

Sandringham Dwarf White. White, solid, crisp, and of fine flavor. Pkt., 5c.; oz., 20c.; ¼ lb., 60c.; lb., $2.00.

Boston Market Dwarf. A bushy, white, solid, fine flavored market celery. Pkt., 5c.; oz., 25c.; ¼ lb., 75c.; lb., $2.50.

NEW FERN-LEAVED. A splendid, unusually large and solid new variety. The leaves resemble those of the female or of parsley, rendering it the most ornamental variety in cultivation. Pkt., 10c.; oz., 25c.; ¼ lb., 75c.

NEW ROSE. In England, the Pink or Red Celeries are much more largely used than the White varieties, and we have often wondered why they were not more grown in this country. They possess many advantages over the White, being hardier, more solid and better keepers. The New Rose is the best of all the red varieties, combining all these desirable qualities, and is the most ornamental for the table, with its beautiful pink-shaded heart and pink stems. Pkt., 10c.; oz., 30c.; ¼ lb., 75c.; lb., $2.75.

Incomparable Dwarf Crimson. A fine red variety, large, solid, crisp, of superior quality and rich color. Pkt., 5c.; oz., 20c.; ¼ lb., 60c.; lb., $2.00.

Soup, or Flavoring Celery (Old Seed). Used for flavoring soups, stews and preparations. Oz., 10c.; lb., 50c.

A New Celery—Free for Trial.

THE MARKET FAVORITE. This handsome new celery has never been offered for sale in America, but being desirous of having it tested in all sections this season, we will include a liberal trial package to all orders of $1.00 and over from this catalogue.

CELERIAC—(Turnip-Rooted Celery).

LARGE SMOOTH PRAGUE. The largest, smoothest and best of the celeriacs. Pkt., 5c.; oz., 20c.; ¼ lb., 75c.; lb., $2.75.

Apple-Shaped. A new knob, with small foliage, the roots being smoother and rounder than the old sort. Pkt., 5c.; oz., 20c.; ¼ lb., 60c.; lb., $2.00.

CHERVIL.

Curled. Pkt., 5c.; oz., 15c.; ¼ lb., 60c.; lb., $1.00.

CHICORY.

Large Rooted. Pkt., 5c.; oz., 15c.; ¼ lb., 30c.; lb., 90c.

COLLARDS (Colewort.)

True Georgia, or Southern. Pkt., 5c.; oz., 10c.; ¼ lb., 30c.; lb., 90c.

CORN—Sweet or Sugar.

One quart will plant about two hundred hills and one peck is required to plant an acre in hills.

> *N.B.*—Please remember our prices on Sweet Corn by the pint and quart include prepayment of postage by us. Customers ordering Sweet Corn to be sent by freight or express can deduct 8c. per pint and 15c. per quart from these prices.

LARGE PACKETS OF ANY VARIETY, 10c. EACH, POST-PAID BY MAIL.

EARS OF EARLY VARIETIES, 10c. EACH; LATE VARIETIES, 15c. EACH, POSTAGE PAID.

SWEET CORN—Early and Intermediate Varieties.

If ordered half bushel at peck and bushel rates.

BONANZA.   MINNESOTA.

New Early Bonanza.

This valuable variety originated a few years since with an enterprising market gardener of this city, who astonished his brother gardeners by having in market, several weeks ahead of any of them, large, fine ears of sweet corn in great abundance, and for which he obtained almost fabulous prices. It having become quite celebrated for its fine quality, and was much sought after. It is undoubtedly as early as Minnesota, Crosby's and other extra early varieties, while the ears are much larger. It is exceedingly prolific bearing two or three good ears to the stalk. Pint, 25c.; qt. 40c.; peck, $1.25; bush., $4.00.

EARLY MINNESOTA. One of the earliest, of dwarf habit, ears small, productive and good. Pint, 20c.; qt., 35c.; peck, $1.00; bush., $3.50.

THE CORY. After carefully testing this new variety, we were the first to offer it five years since; grown side by side with Marblehead and other early varieties, it took them all by jolly a week. It will produce good ears for boiling in seventy-six days from planting. It has a larger kernel than the Marblehead and is quite distinct, being whiter in color. Market gardeners and others who have grown the Cory Corn, have completely controlled the early market. Our stock comes directly from Mr. Jos. Cory, the originator. Pint, 20c.; qt., 40c.; peck, $1.00; bush., $3.75.

STABLER'S PEDIGREE EXTRA EARLY. A very popular variety with Philadelphia gardeners, noted for its earliness and great sweetness. Pint, 25c.; qt., 40c.; peck, $1.00; bush., $4.00.

EARLY GOLDEN or ORANGE. We introduced this new and distinct variety after a two years' trial. It is of delicious quality. The seed when dry is of a beautiful golden color, hence the name given it. Pint, 25c.; qt., 40c.; peck, $1.00.

MARBLEHEAD EARLY. This variety, before the introduction of the Cory, was considered the earliest of all. The stalk is of dwarf growth and ears set very low down; it is apt for market size and very sweet. Pint, 20c.; qt., 35c.; peck, 85c.; bush., $3.00.

THE COMMAND WAS "BY THE SWEAT OF *THY* BROW SHALT THOU EAT BREAD"—NOT SOME OTHER FELLOW'S BROW.

∴ SEEDS ∴ FOR ∴ MONEY ∴ GROWERS ∴ 39

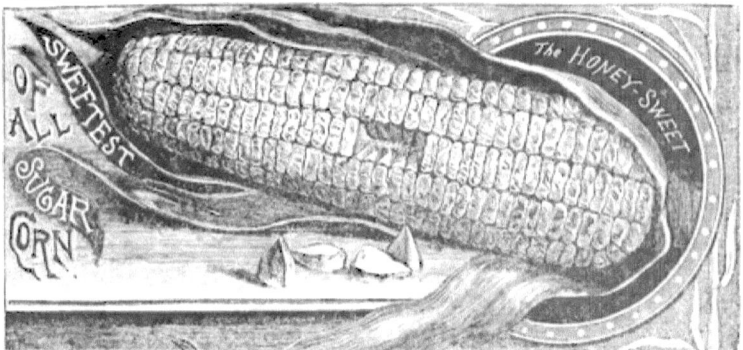

The Honey. Engraved from Nature. Pkt., 10c.; pint, 25c.; qt., 45c., post-paid; peck, $1.25; bush., $4.50.

THE HONEY SWEET CORN.

Nothing we have ever introduced has elicited from both market and family gardeners such enthusiastic praise in all parts of the country. It originated with a German market gardener near Allentown, Pa., who had the reputation of bringing the finest and sweetest corn to that market, for which he realized fabulous prices. In growth and appearance it is unlike any other variety, the husks and silk being of a deep red color during growth, while the corn itself is of a beautiful cream white, much shrivelled when dry, with deep grain and small cob. It is also a most productive variety, bearing three to four good, large ears on a stalk, growing vigorously, and coming in as early as Moore's Concord. No market or private garden is complete without it. Pkt., 10c.; pint, 25c.; qt., 45c., post-paid; peck, $1.25, bush., $4.50, by express or freight.

BURLINGTON HYBRID. A cross between Adams' Extra Early and Sweet Corn, as early as the Adams', but much larger and sweeter. See Photographic Specialties, page 9. Pkt., 10c.; pint, 25c.; qt., 45c., post-paid; peck, $1.25; bush., $4.50.

EARLY DAWN. A new Extra Early Sugar Corn with ears as large as Evergreen. See Photographic Specialties, page 9. Pkt., 15c.; pint, 30c.; qt., 50c.; post-paid; peck, $1.75; bush., $6.00.

Adams' Extra Early. An old variety well known as one of the hardiest and earliest varieties for table use, but not a sweet corn; white grain and short ear. Pint, 20c.; qt., 35c.; peck, 85c.; bush., $3.00.

CROSBY'S EXTRA EARLY. An early market variety; very productive, ears rather short and rich sugary flavor. Pint, 20c.; qt., 35c.; peck, 90c.; bush., $3.25.

EARLY MAMMOTH, OR ASYLUM. Ripens about two weeks earlier than Late Mammoth; ears somewhat smaller, but of good market size. Pint, 20c.; qt., 35c.; peck, $1.00; bush., $4.50.

ROSLYN HYBRID. A medium early variety, with large, fine ears, and in quality equal to Stowell's Evergreen. Much prized by canners and fine for market. Pint, 20c.; qt., 35c.; peck, $1.00; bush., $3.75.

THE GUARANTEE. This new variety has had quite a reputation for a few years in one of the largest market houses in Philadelphia, where it has been brought to market in its season by a Chester County, Pa., market man, and had become known to its patrons as "The Guarantee," he having always, in disposing of it, guaranteed it to be the sweetest in the whole market. We have seen his supply of this corn sold out before 8 o'clock in the morning, long before the market was half over, notwithstanding the fact that his prices was always 10c. per dozen above his competitors. He has always kept the seed in his own hands until recently, when, after great persuasion and at high cost, we obtained from him a few quarts two years since, from which our present stock was grown. It grows a fair-sized, handsome, white ear, grain very much shrivelled when dry, coming in second early or intermediate and producing three to four ears on each stalk. Pint, 2½c.; qt., 45c.; peck, $1.50.

Early Large Eight-Rowed. A fine early sort; the ears are of large size and have but eight rows; delicious quality. Pint, 20c.; qt., 35c.; peck, 90c.; bush., $3.25.

PERRY'S HYBRID. A new extra early variety, with large, fine ears, about twice the size of Minnesota; twelve-rowed and of fine quality. Pint, 20c.; qt., 35c.; peck, 90c.; bush., $3.40.

HICKOX IMPROVED. An excellent second early, very sweet and productive, excellent for canning. Pint, 20c.; qt., 35c.; peck, $1.00; bush., $3.50.

OLD COLONY. A very sweet and wonderful productive variety, averaging three ears on every stalk. The ears are of large size and well filled out. It ripens extra early. Its distinctive value lies, however, in its fine sugary flavor. Pint, 20c.; qt., 35c.; peck, $1.00; bush., $3.50.

SHAKERS' EARLY. A new variety of excellent quality, ripening with the Early Minnesota, but with larger ears; produces two or three large ears with each stalk. Pint, 20c.; qt., 35c.; peck, $1.00; bush., $3.50.

SQUANTUM, or POTTER'S EXCELSIOR. An excellent variety of the finest quality for table use and market; ripens early with fine large ears and deep grain. Pint, 20c.; qt., 35c.; peck, $1.00; bush., $3.50.

Amber Cream. This handsome, medium early sort is a strong, vigorous grower; stalks six to seven feet high, the ears are large, white, handsome and very sweet. When dry the seed is of amber color, varying from a light to a dark shade. Pint, 20c.; qt., 35c.; peck, $1.00; bush., $3.50.

Moore's Early Concord. Very early, with large corn, twelve to eighteen rows, excellent in quality for table or market. Pint, 20c.; qt., 35c.; peck, $1.00; bush., $3.50.

Triumph. An early large-eared variety, very productive and rich in flavor. Pint, 20c.; qt., 35c.; peck, $1.00.

SWEET CORN—Late Varieties.

Large pkt., 10c.; ears, 15c., post-paid.

STOWELL'S EVERGREEN. The best and one of the sweetest; ears large, remaining green longer than any other variety. Pint, 20c.; qt., 35c.; peck, 85c.; bush., $3.00. Special prices for larger quantities.

NEW RED COB EVERGREEN. A sport from Stowell's Evergreen with reddish cob slightly earlier. Pint, 2½c.; qt., 40c.; peck, $1.25; bush., $4.25.

LATE MAMMOTH. The largest of all varieties; ears very large, productive, flavor rich and sweet; a fine market variety. Pint, 20c.; qt., 35c.; peck, 85c.; bush., $3.00.

EGYPTIAN, or WASHINGTON MARKET. A large variety somewhat resembling the Evergreen; flavor peculiarly rich and sweet, and superior quality; fine for market. Pint, 2½c.; qt., 35c.; peck, $1.00; bush., $3.50.

Black Mexican. A variety with black ears, one of the sweetest. Pint, 20c.; qt., 40 c.; peck, $1.00.

Fodder Sweet Corn. For soiling and green fodder. Bush., $1.50; 5 bush. and over, $1.40 per bush.

"THE HONEY SWEET CORN IS SWEETEST AND BEST, WITH FOUR TO SIX EARS ON A STALK."
WM. G. SICKES, STUYVESANT, N. Y.

JOHNSON & STOKES

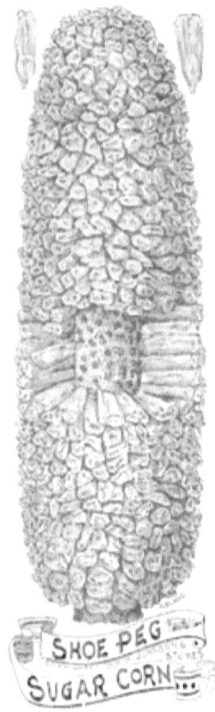

SHOE PEG SUGAR CORN

POP CORN FOR THE BOYS.

MAPLEDALE PROLIFIC

QUEEN'S GOLDEN POP CORN.

SHOE PEG SWEET. This very excellent new and distinct variety, offered two years since for the first time, originated at Bordentown, N. J., in which market it is considered the sweetest and choicest sort grown, selling at double the prices of all other varieties. It is sometimes confounded with the Ne Plus Ultra, owing to the resemblance of the seed to that variety. It is, however, very distinct in growth from any other and has the deepest grain and smallest cob of any known variety. The accompanying cut is an exact representation of an ear from nature. The stalks are of medium height, without suckers, joints short, and sometimes yield as many as five ears, well filled out. The kernel is small, very long, white and exceedingly tender, sweet and of a rich, juicy flavor that is not equalled by any other sort. In maturing it is medium late. In our extended experience we have grown every known variety of sugar corn, but have never found a variety possessing so many desirable qualities as Shoe Peg. Pkt., 10c.; pint, 25c.; qt., 45c.; post-paid; peck, $1.25; bush., $3.75 by freight or express.

Ne Plus Ultra, Little Gem, or Quaker Sweet. A variety first sent out by us a few years since. The ears are medium size, grain deep and rows very irregular; produces three to four good ears to a stalk. It is a valuable and distinct acquisition. It's delicious flavor is unsurpassed. Pkt., 20c.; qt., 45c.; peck, $1.00; bush., $3.75.

CRESS, or PEPPER GRASS.

One ounce will sow about fifteen square feet.

NEW UPLAND CRESS. A perennial grown same as spinach but closely resembles watercress in flavor. Pkt., 10c.; 3 pkts., 25c.; oz., 75c.

Extra Curled. Fine Flavor, and can be cut several times. Pkt., ½ oz., 10c.; ¼ lb., 20c.; lb., 60c.

TRUE WATER-CRESS. A well-known aquatic plant, with oval leaves, making a delicious and appetizing salad. Pkt., 10c.; oz., 75c.; ¼ lb., $1.25; lb., $4.00.

QUEEN'S GOLDEN. This new sort is by far the largest eared and best of all for popping, owing to its large size, extreme tenderness and pure white color when popped. It grows about six feet in height and bears three to four good ears to a stalk. Ear, 10c.; 3 ears, 25c.; pkt. shelled, 10c.; pint, 25c.; qt., 45c. post-paid; lb., 15c.; 2 lbs., 25c.; 10 lbs., $1.00; 25 lbs., $2.25, by express.

MAPLEDALE PROLIFIC POP CORN. The most prolific tree pop corn, averaging eight to twelve good ears to the stalk; as many as nineteen ears having been taken from a single stalk. It grows five and a half to six feet high, with ears of uniformly large size; grain pearly white; pops to a large size, and very tender. Ear, 15c.; large pkt., shelled, 10c.; pint, 25c.; qt., 45c., post-paid; lb., 15c.; 10 lbs., $1.00; 25 lbs., and over, 8c. per lb., by express.

RICE POP CORN. A splendid variety for popping purposes; grains sharply pointed. Ear, 10c.; pkt., 10c.; pint, 25c.; qt., 45c., post-paid; lb., 15c.; 10 lbs., $1.00; 25 lbs., $2.00; 50 lbs. and over, 8c. per lb., by express.

SILVER LACE POP CORN. Pearl Pop Corn. (Small Grain.) **Eight-Rowed Pop Corn.** (Large Grain.) Each, pkt., 10c.; pint, 25c.; qt., 45c.; postpaid; by freight or express, lb., 15c.; 3 lbs., 25c.; 25 lbs., $2.00; 100 lbs. and over, 6c. per lb.

Corn for Field Culture. Will be found under Farm Seeds.

MARKET GARDENERS AND INSTITUTIONS Wanting to purchase seeds in unusually large quantities will please write for special prices. Although we have made prices very low in this Catalogue, yet, where several pounds or bushels are wanted, we can frequently supply at a lower price than by the single pound or bushel. Address

JOHNSON & STOKES, SEED GROWERS,
WAREHOUSES: 217 & 219 MARKET STREET, 206 & 208 CHURCH STREET. PHILADELPHIA, PA.

☞ If at any time you forget our Street and Number, any letter addressed simply JOHNSON & STOKES, PHILADELPHIA, will reach us, though mailed in any part of the world.

PLEASE TAKE THIS CATALOGUE WITH YOU WHEN YOU GO BY A NEIGHBOR'S NEXT TIME; SHOW IT TO HIM, AND ASK HIM TO CLUB WITH YOU IN SENDING YOUR ORDER.

CORN SALAD—FETTICUS, or LAMBS' LETTUCE.

One ounce will sow about eighteen square feet, and six pounds will sow one acre.

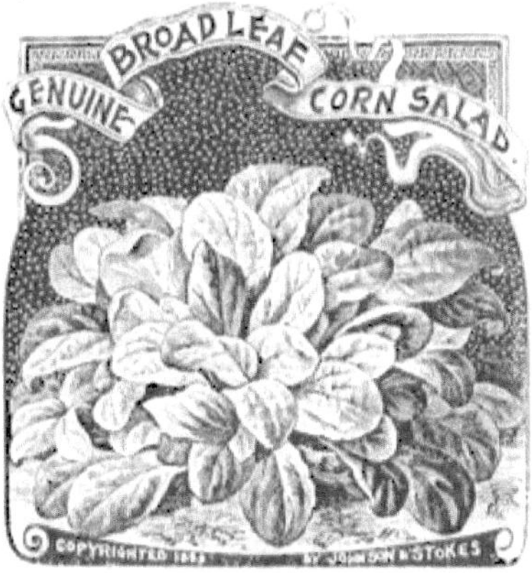

BROAD LEAVED (LARGE SEEDED). The best variety for family use and market purposes and deserving of more wide-spread cultivation.

It makes a delicious small salad used during the winter and spring months as a substitute for lettuce, and is also cooked and used like spinach. Sow in spring in drills one foot apart. Keep clean from weeds. It will mature in six weeks when sown in the spring. For early spring use sow in September, thickly in drills ¼ inch deep. Tread the ground if dry weather. Protect with litter when cold weather comes and winter over like spinach. Pkt., 5c.; oz., 10c.; ¼ lb., 20c.; lb., 60c.

Northern Grown from Carefully Selected Seed Stocks.

One ounce will plant about fifty hills; two pounds will plant one acre.

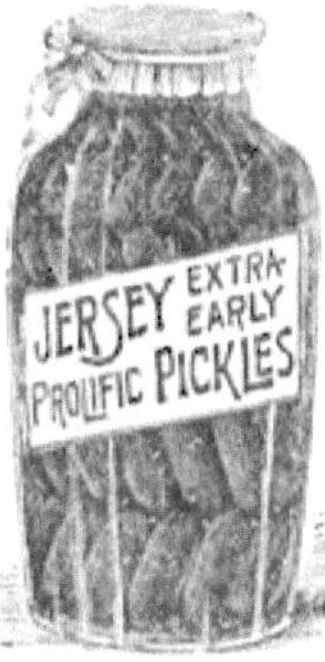

Early Russian. Very early, hardy and productive; produced in pairs. Pkt., 5c.; oz., 10c.; ¼ lb., 25c.; lb., 75c.

Early Frame, or Early Short Green. Of medium size, straight and excellent for table use or pickling. Pkt., 5c.; oz., 10c.; ¼ lb., 25c.; lb., 75c.

JERSEY EXTRA EARLY PROLIFIC PICKLE. This splendid new variety was originated and selected by a prominent New Jersey pickle grower in the celebrated pickle section on the Delaware River, about twenty-five miles above Philadelphia, where more pickles are grown than in any other section of the United States. It is ten days earlier than the old Long Green or Jersey Pickle and more productive. It is pronounced by growers of thirty years' experience "a perfect pickle in all respects." Try it. Pkt., 5c.; oz., 15c.; ¼ lb., 35c.; lb., $1.25.

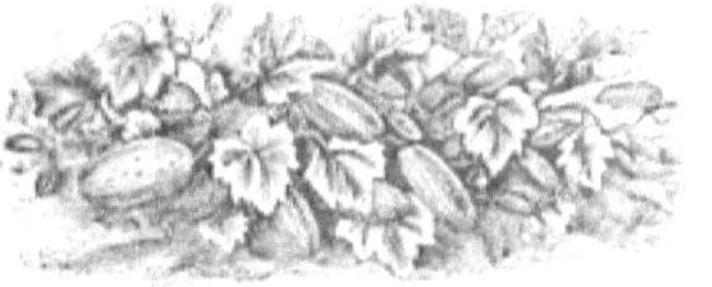

THORBURN'S NEW EVERBEARING CUCUMBER.

THORBURN'S EVERBEARING. This variety is entirely new and unique, and will prove valuable both for the table and for pickling. It is of small size, *very early, enormously productive*, and extremely valuable as a green pickler. The peculiar merit of this new cucumber is, that the vines continue to flower and produce fruit until killed by frost, *whether the ripe cucumbers are picked off or not*—in which respect it differs from all other sorts in cultivation. Cucumbers in every stage of growth will be found on the same vine. Pkt., 10c.; oz., 20c.; ¼ lb., 45c.; lb., $1.50.

NEW PARIS PICKLING CUCUMBER. A very desirable and distinct new French sort, which promises to be a great acquisition. The fruit is very long, slender, cylindrical, densely covered with fine prickles and deep, rich green in color. The flesh is very crisp and tender, making it one of the best for slicing as well as for pickles. The vine produces its fruit in clusters and is enormously productive. On our trial grounds the past two seasons it surpassed all others in **pickling qualities**, which constitute brittleness or crispness and showing no sign of seeds when in a proper stage for pickling. Pkt., 10c.; oz., 20c.; ¼ lb., 45c.; lb., $1.50.

PEERLESS, OR IMPROVED EARLY WHITE SPINE. Very early and productive, medium to large size, deep green, crisp, fine flavor. Pkt., 5c.; oz., 10c.; ¼ lb., 25c.; lb., 75c.

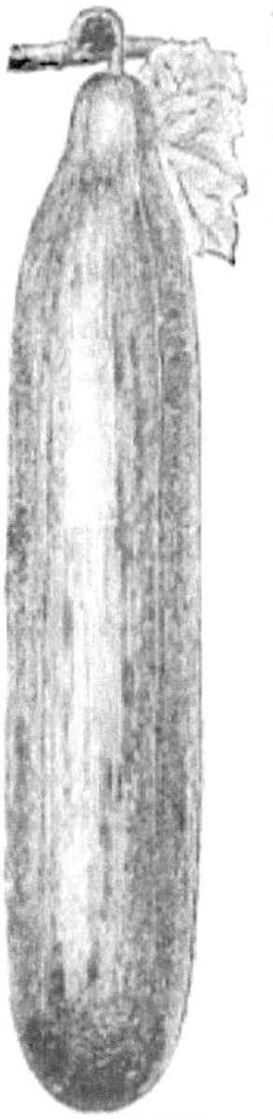

GIANT OF PERA.

NEW GIANT OF PERA. This magnificent variety was first brought here from Turkey by Dr. Harris, of Philadelphia. They are of the most delicious flavor, no other cucumber we have ever eaten surpassing them. Another remarkable quality is that they are very crisp and tender at all stages, and can be eaten at any time during growth. They grow to an enormous size, frequently to one and a half feet in length and ten to eleven inches in circumference; very smooth and straight, with a beautiful green skin. The vines grow vigorously, fruit sets near the hill and grows closely together, making them exceedingly prolific. The seed cavity is very small and the seeds are slow to form and few in number. Pkt., 5c.; oz., 15c.; ¼ lb., 35c.; lb., $1.25.

White Japan. Very desirable for the table or pickles, being pure white, productive and of superior quality. Pkt., 5c.; oz., 10c.; ¼ lb., 25c.; lb., 90c.

Tailby's Hybrid. A hybrid of the White Spine, with a large English variety, retaining the prolificness of the former, united with *large size, hardiness and desirable market qualities*. Pkt., 5c.; oz., 10c.; ¼ lb., 30c.; lb., $1.00.

Long Green Turkey. A leading variety for pickling; of excellent quality, dark green, firm, crisp. Pkt., 5c.; oz., 10c.; ¼ lb., 25c.; lb., 85c.

NICHOLS' MEDIUM GREEN. This new variety was originated near Columbus, O., by an extensive grower for market. In length it is medium between the White Spine and Long Green; very thick through and full at both ends, presenting a beautiful type; skin of a light green color and very smooth; the vines are very hardy and productive; they are excellent for slicing or pickling. Pkt., 5c.; oz., 10c.; ¼ lb., 25c.; lb., 80c.

"AFTER MANY YEARS' EXPERIENCE I FIND YOUR SEEDS THE PUREST AND BEST. RELIABLE AS THE SUN."

MARTIN YAKLEY, PITTSFIELD, ILLS.

EVERGREEN EARLY WHITE SPINE CUCUMBER.

We first introduced this new and improved strain five years ago, and have received hundreds of letters from customers in all sections, who purchased the seed, all of whom agree in pronouncing it the handsomest and most productive of any they have ever grown. To those who have never seen or grown this valuable variety, we would state that it differs from the ordinary White Spine, in the fact of always *remaining of a deep green color* in all stages of growth. It grows to good length, of handsome, smooth shape, *very early and prolific.* It is a very hardy sort and will not turn yellow after being picked from the vine, but will permanently retain its deep green color. The flavor is delicious, the flesh being unusually *tender and crisp,* whether grown for the family garden or as a shipping variety, it is superior to any we know of, and its fine appearance always insures "top notch" market price. Pkt., 10c.; oz., 20c.; ¼ lb., 30c.; lb., $1.00.

Green Prolific, or Boston Pickling. A short pickling variety of fine form and flavor, enormously productive, crisp and tender. Pkt., 5c.; oz., 10c.; ¼ lb., 25c.; lb., 80c.

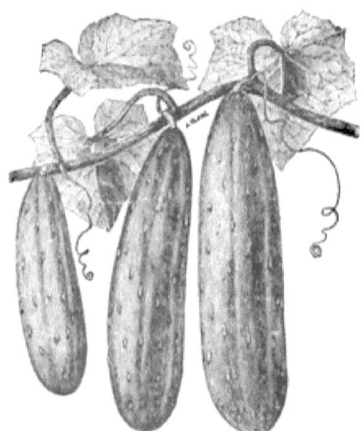

IMPROVED LONG GREEN, OR JERSEY PICKLE CUCUMBER.

IMPROVED EXTRA LONG GREEN. (Jersey Pickle.) A standard pickling variety; dark green, tender, crisp, productive, of fine flavor and medium size. Our strain is unsurpassed. We supply each season hundreds of the most critical Jersey market gardeners and pickle growers, with the most satisfactory results. Pkt., 5c.; oz., 10c.; ¼ lb., 20c.; lb., 70c.

WESTERFIELD'S CHICAGO PICKLE. In recent years Chicago has become the centre of a very large pickling industry. This variety, originated by Mr. Westerfield, a gentleman largely interested in the business, is preferred for pickling by almost every large pickling factory in that city, and for commercial pickles it is one of the best. We offer the best selected seed of this variety; none better at any price. Pkt., 5c.; oz., 10c.; ¼ lb., 25c.; lb., 80c.

Early Cluster. Quite early, and very productive, medium in size, and of a pale green color, and turns to a brownish yellow when ripe. Pkt., 5c.; oz., 10c.; ¼ lb., 25c.; lb., 70c.

WEST INDIA GHERKIN, or BURR. Also known as the *Jerusalem Pickle.* A very small, oval, prickly variety, quite distinct from all others. It is grown exclusively for pickling; is the smallest and best of all for small pickles, and should always be picked when young and tender. Pkt., 5c.; oz., 15c.; ¼ lb., 40c.; lb., $1.25.

SERPENT OR SNAKE CUCUMBER. Pkt., 10c.

SOOLY QUA, SERPENT, or SNAKE CUCUMBER. A great curiosity, growing six feet long, and coiled like a snake, as shown in above illustration, with the head protruding. The Chinese consider this variety a great delicacy, either raw or boiled. Pkt., 10c.; 3 pkts., 25c.; oz., 50c.

ENGLISH FRAME CUCUMBERS.

Carter's Champion, Blue Gown, Telegraph, Giant of Arnstadt, and other good sorts. Each, per pkt., 25c.

"Myself and neighbors had no luck with seeds until we began purchasing yours."—J. M. BICKEL, Traer, Iowa.

A FEW PIECES OF HORSE RADISH PUT AMONG PICKLES WILL IMPROVE THE FLAVOR AND KEEP THEM FROM MOULDING.

∴ SEEDS ∴ FOR ∴ MONEY ∴ GROWERS ∴   43

Pkt., 15c.; oz., 50c.; ¼ lb., $1.50; lb., $5.50.

New Jersey Improved Large Purple Smooth Stem Egg-Plant.

This superior strain of Egg-plant was brought to perfection by one of the most successful Egg-plant growers of New Jersey, which State supplies the North with the largest and finest Egg-Plants grown. It is a **decided improvement** on the New York Large purple in quality, size and great beauty. The plants are large and vigorous, leaves of a light green shade, fruit early, very large, oval and of a fine deep purple—never red or yellow; flesh white, tender and of a superior quality. A sure cropper. Our customers will find this variety the **very best in cultivation** and our extra selected seed grown by the originator of superb quality. Pkt., 15c ; oz ., 50c.; ¼ lb., $1.50; lb., $5.50.

EGG-PLANT.

One ounce will produce about one thousand plants.

Extra Early Dwarf Round Purple. A distinct variety, ripens a month earlier than the New York Large Purple; is of the same round shape, but smaller in size. It is extremely hardy, well adapted to the North, where it has heretofore been impossible to grow this vegetable to perfection. Pkt., 10c.; oz., 75c.; ¼ lb., $1.00; lb., $3.00.

New York Large Purple. A leading and popular market variety grown extensively in sections where the New Jersey Improved has not been introduced; large, round, dark fruits; excellent and productive. Pkt., 10c.; oz., 45c.; ¼ lb., $1.25; lb., $4.50.

Black Pekin. A very handsome variety with large, round, black fruits; very smooth and glossy, of fine delicate flavor, but not a sure bearer, especially in the North. Pkt. 10c.; 3 pkts . 25c.; oz., 45c.; ¼ lb., $1.25.

TOMATO EGG-PLANT. This curious plant was first discovered a few years ago by Mr. William C. Lesler, a New Jersey trucker, growing in a field of egg-plants. The vine has every appearance of the egg-plant, even to the prickly stem and leaf, but fruits from forty to sixty bright red, solid tomatoes. It is unquestionably the greatest curiosity in the vegetable kingdom that has ever come to our notice; exceedingly ornamental and worthy of a place in either the flower or vegetable garden. Pkt., 15c.; 2 pkts., 25c.; 5 pkts., 50c.

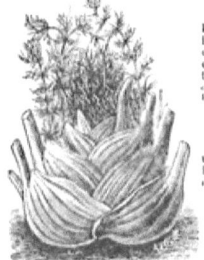

FLORENCE FENNEL.

DANDELION.

Improved Large Leaved. A very early and healthful spring salad. Sow early in the spring in drills eighteen inches apart, and thin out to six inches in the drills. Pkt., 10c.; oz., 50c.; ¼ lb., $1.75.

FENNEL.

Florence Celery-rooted. A novelty from Italy, where, owing to its delightful sweet flavor, it is much preferred to celery. It thrives remarkably well in our climate and is of the easiest culture. Seed can be sown early in spring and cultivated same as parsley, except that the thickened part of the root should be covered with soil a short time before completing its growth. Pkt., 10c.; 3 pkts., 25c.; oz., 75c.

"I am an old market gardener and from experience I place more confidence in your seeds than any others I have ever planted." W. M. Cross, Ono, Wis.

THE BEST IS NONE TOO GOOD, BE IT SEEDS, COAT OR CHARACTER.

ENDIVE.

One ounce will sow fifteen feet of drill and will produce about three thousand plants.

NEW MAMMOTH GREEN CURLED. This very beautiful and valuable variety grows to full twenty inches in diameter. The leaves are very crisp, much cut and curled, tufty and full in every stage of growth. The mid-ribs are pure white, thick, fleshy and tender. It is equally suitable for spring, summer or autumn planting. The quality is exceedingly good, blanches very readily and its handsome appearance causes it to outsell all other varieties. This variety was named and introduced by us three years ago. All who have grown it say that no other variety should be planted. Pkt., 10c; oz., 25c; ¼ lb., 75c; lb., $2.50.

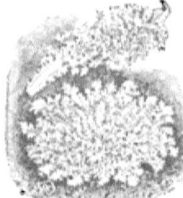

NEW LONG-STANDING WINTER. A most valuable new and distinct variety, growing about as large as the Mammoth Green Curled, but more upright in growth and self-blanching to a remarkable extent, assuming a beautiful cream white in the centre and blending off to a beautiful pale green. It is extremely hardy and will stand longer and keep better than any other known sort. We hope all who grow Endive will give it a trial. Pkt., 10c; oz., 40c; ¼ lb., $1.25.

Green Curled. The well-known old sort, with dark green curled leaves, tender and crisp. Pkt., 5c; oz., 15c; ¼ lb., 50c; lb., $1.75.

Early White Curled. Leaves pale green, large size, crisp and tender. Pkt., 5c; oz., 15c; ¼ lb., 50c; lb., $1.75.

GOURDS.

LUFFA GOURD.

LUFFA, or DISHCLOTH. This remarkable and handsome climber is a native of the East Indies, and in its nature has furnished us with a vegetable dishcloth, the inside being enveloped in a sponge-like cloth, which is tough, elastic and durable. The fruit grows about two feet in length and the vine grows rapidly to a height of twenty to twenty-five feet in a season, producing clusters of large yellow blossoms; many ladies prefer this dishcloth to anything that can be made. It is also called Ladies' Bonnet Gourd, from the fact that it is now frequently made into summer bonnets. For the bath and for all uses of the kind in general, the "Dish Rag Gourd" is taking the place of the sponge. It is, in fact, a sponge, a soft brush and a bath glove combined; the fibre wears away almost imperceptibly, and as long as any part is left they are as good as new. Even with daily use they will last for years. The dried interiors of these gourds have already become an article of commerce; they are sold by druggists in Philadelphia and New York, while in England their sale and use are quite general. Pkt., 10c; 3 pkts., 25c; 7 pkts., 50c; 15 pkts., $1.00.

DIPPER. Named for its resemblance to a dipper. The capacity varies from a pint to a quart, with handles six to twelve inches long. They are convenient for dipping hot liquids, etc. Pkt., 10c; oz., 25c.

SUGAR TROUGH. Very useful for baskets, dishes, buckets, etc. They have hard, thick shells, lasting for years, and capable of holding from two to ten gallons each. Pkt., 10c; oz., 25c.

FINE MIXED. A collection of the most ornamental, including all the above. Pkt., 5c; 2 pkts., 25c; 5 pkts., 50c.

JAPANESE NEST-EGG GOURD. Pkt., 10c; 3 pkts., 25c.

JAPANESE NEST EGG. These exactly resemble in color, shape and size, the eggs of hens, making a capital nest egg, which are superior to glass eggs, as they do not crack or break and are uninjured by cold or wet. As the plant is a rapid growing climber, it is very useful for covering screens, etc. Pkt., 10c; 3 pkts., 25c; oz., 50c.

GARLIC.

GARLIC BULBS.

This is extensively used in many places for flavoring soups, stews, etc. The sets, or small bulbs from which it is propagated, should be planted early in spring in rich soil in rows one foot apart and from three to five inches apart in the rows. Cultivate like onions. In August the tops die off and the crop is ready to gather, and may be kept for future use in the same manner as onions. Sets per ¼ lb., 20c; lb., 50c, post-paid. 10 lbs. and over, 20c per lb., not prepaid.

HORSE RADISH.

Horse Radish is grown from young roots or sets which should be planted out in the spring. They will form a large sized radish fit for use in one season's growth. Roots, per dozen, 25c; per 100, $1.00, by mail, post-paid. Write for special prices by the thousand.

KALE.—Borecole.

One ounce will produce about two thousand plants.

NEW IMPERIAL, or LONG STANDING. A beautiful curled and crimpled sort, selected by a Philadelphia market gardener. Of strong, vigorous habit, perfectly hardy, attractive appearance and a bright green color. It is superior to all other sorts, and will stand longer without shooting to seed than any other variety. Height, about two feet. Pkt., 5c; oz., 10c; ¼ lb., 25c; lb., 75c.

GREEN CURLED SCOTCH. Philadelphia Stock. A favorite with Northern market gardeners; growing about two feet in height and hardier than the Extra Dwarf Green Curled Scotch, being improved by frost; leaves green and beautifully curled and wrinkled. Pkt., 5c; oz., 10c; ¼ lb., 20c; lb., 60c.

SIBERIAN CURLED KALE. This variety grows a little larger and coarser than the preceding; the leaves are not so deeply curled and are of a bluish-green color. In point of hardiness it exceeds all other sorts, being fully capable of withstanding ten degrees below zero without injury. Pkt., 5c; oz., 10c; ¼ lb., 20c; lb., 60c.

CURLED MOSBACH. A particularly fine strain, in bright between the Extra Dwarf Scotch and Green Curled Scotch; leaves bent upwards, light yellow green, double curled, white narrow ribs and veins—very showy, resembling a fine curled parsley. Splendid for garnishing. Pkt., 5c; oz., 20c; ¼ lb., 60c; lb., $1.75.

AN OUNCE OF GUM CAMPHOR IN THE BOTTOM OF THE SEED BOX WILL KEEP OUT INSECTS.

SEEDS FOR MONEY GROWERS

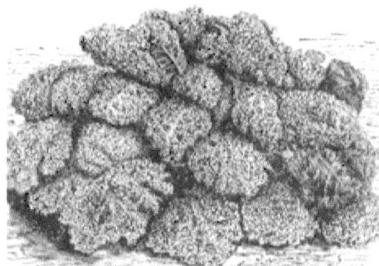

EXTRA DWARF GREEN CURLED SCOTCH KALE.

EXTRA DWARF GREEN CURLED SCOTCH KALE. This is one of the best Kales for spring sowing in the North and is the principal sort grown throughout the Southern States for Northern markets. It is hardy and will remain over winter in any place where the temperature does not go below zero. The habit is very dwarf and spreading, and will rarely exceed eighteen inches in height. The leaves are of a bright green color, beautifully curled and produced in great abundance. Pkt., 5c.; oz., 10c.; ¼ lb., 20c.; lb., $1.00.

MOSS CURLED, or HALF DWARF FRINGED. This new and beautiful variety is very popular with the gardeners around Paris. It is between the dwarf and tall varieties, with yellowish-green, finely fringed leaves. It is one of the handsomest and most ornamental varieties we have ever seen; is extremely early and hardy, and from its upright habit can be grown closer together than other varieties. Pkt., 5c.; oz., 10c.; ¼ lb., 20c.; lb., $1.00.

SEA KALE. Grown for its blanched shoots; cooked like Asparagus. Sow the seed early in the spring, in rows two feet apart; thin out to stand six inches in the rows, before winter, cover with litter or leaves, and the next spring transplant in hills, three feet apart each way. Pkt., 10c.; oz., 25c.; lb., $2.50.

KOHL-RABI—Turnip-Rooted Cabbage.

This is a favorite vegetable in Europe, where it is extensively grown for feeding cattle, as well as for table use.
One ounce will sow one hundred and fifty feet of drill.

EARLY WHITE VIENNA. Flesh tender and white, excellent for table use and market. Pkt., 5c.; oz., 20c.; ¼ lb., 60c.; lb., $2.00.

Early Purple Vienna. A little later than the White; color, bluish-purple. Pkt., 5c.; oz., 20c.; ¼ lb., 60c.; lb., $2.00.

LEEK.

One ounce will sow one hundred feet of drill, and produce about one thousand plants.

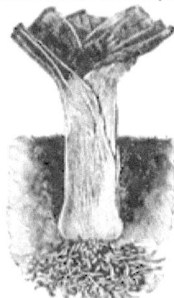

NEW GIANT ITALIAN.

NEW GIANT ITALIAN. We introduced this new Leek from Italy and guarantee it to be the largest and finest leek in cultivation. It is fully twice the size of the ordinary London Leek, and much handsomer in appearance. Like the Italian onions, it is very mild and agreeable in flavor; extremely hardy and a fine keeper. All those who have grown it the past two years, were astonished at its large size and fine white appearance. We knew of no leek as well adapted to market gardeners' purposes as this valuable new sort. Pkt., 10c.; oz., 30c.; ¼ lb., 60c.; lb., $2.00.

LARGE AMERICAN FLAG. Previous to our introduction of the Giant Italian this was the favorite variety with our gardeners. Very fine and large. Pkt., 5c.; oz., 15c.; ¼ lb., 40c.; lb., $1.25.

CARENTAN, or SCOTCH CHAMPION. An extra large variety from Scotland, grows rapidly, and very hardy. Pkt., 5c.; oz., 15c.; ¼ lb., 50c.; lb., $1.50.

London Flag. Large, with broad leaves growing on two sides. Pkt., 5c.; oz., 10c.; ¼ lb., 40c.; lb., $1.25.

Large Musselburgh. Grows to a very large size; of excellent quality. Pkt., 10c.; oz., 20c.; ¼ lb., 60c.; lb., $2.00.

LETTUCE.

One ounce will sow about one hundred square feet and produce three thousand plants.

NEW SENSATION LETTUCE. The best variety ever introduced for all seasons and purposes. See Novelties, page 17. Pkt., 20c.; oz., 50c.; ¼ lb., $1.50.

CHAMPION SPRING AND SUMMER LETTUCE. A valuable new and distinct sort. See Photograph in Specialties, page 2. Pkt., 15c.; oz., 40c.; ¼ lb., $1.25; lb., $4.00.

NEW GOLDEN QUEEN. A splendid new forcing lettuce, of a pleasing golden-yellow color, of very dwarf, compact growth, with few loose outer leaves, enabling it to be planted very close. The quality is very similar to the Boston Market or Tennis Ball, but distinct in appearance. Pkt., 10c.; oz., 30c.; ¼ lb., 75c.; lb., $2.75.

WHITE-SEEDED TENNIS BALL, or BOSTON MARKET. A standard and popular early variety, forming a small, close, hard head; very hardy, crisp and tender. Excellent for forcing. Pkt., 5c.; oz., 15c.; ¼ lb., 40c.; lb., $1.35.

ARLINGTON TENNIS BALL LETTUCE. This strain of seed which we offered last spring for the first time, is saved by one of the most successful market gardeners in Arlington, Massachusetts, where the Tennis Ball, or Boston Market Lettuce originated. His lettuce have carried off first premiums at the Massachusetts Horticultural Shows for several years in succession. The seed is saved from plants started under glass, by which means the valuable forcing qualities are better retained than from plants started outside, and from selected heads only. It is in every respect the same as the originator uses for stock and which his brother gardeners have heretofore been glad to get, paying at the rate of $4.00 per ounce for it. It cannot fail to produce admirable results and please the most critical grower. We highly recommend this special strain, knowing that nothing finer in the way of a forcing lettuce can be obtained. The price we have to ask for this is a slightly enhanced one when compared with ordinary stock; but when the extraordinary pains taken to forcing and setting out the plants, selecting and saving are considered, any one who knows the importance of sowing the best seed will not hesitate in paying the slight difference in price. Pkt., 15c.; oz., 45c.; ¼ lb., $1.25; lb., $4.50.

BLACK-SEEDED TENNIS BALL. A favorite forcing variety, forming a close hard head. It makes but few outer leaves, and for this reason can be planted quite closely under glass—from six to seven inches apart. Pkt., 5c.; oz., 15c.; ¼ lb., 40c.; lb., $1.35.

PHILADELPHIA EARLY WHITE CABBAGE. Produces fine, greenish-white, well-formed heads of extra quality, and remarkably tender and crisp. It is of very quick growth and is largely grown both for forcing and summer use. Pkt., 5c.; oz., 15c.; ¼ lb., 40c.; lb., $1.40.

SILVER BALL. A handsome variety, head of silvery-white color, very solid and firm, of exquisite flavor and attractive appearance. A splendid variety for winter forcing, also for early spring and summer use, coming early and standing a long time before running to seed. It is one of the best all the year round lettuces we know of. We offer an extra selected strain, procured by market and private gardeners who have had it, superior to any they can get. Pkt., 10c.; oz., 25c.; ¼ lb., 65c.; lb., $2.25.

WORK OR REST BUT, WHATE'ER BEFALL, THE FARMER HE MUST FEED THEM ALL.

Reichner's Early White Butter or Ridge Lettuce.

This very excellent new variety is the result of several years' selection from the Philadelphia Early White Cabbage made by the Reichners, who are among the best market gardeners around Philadelphia. It is one of the best forcing lettuces, and very valuable for summer on account of its slowness to shoot to seed. It is also the best variety for sowing in the fall, for planting on ridges, being entirely hardy in the South, and requiring only a slight protection in the North; produces fine, large, white, solid heads of superb quality, and is remarkably early. Philadelphia market gardeners value this lettuce so highly that they will pay almost any price to obtain the seed. No market or private grower can afford to be without this valuable variety. Pkt., 10c.; oz., 25c.; ¼ lb., 70c.; lb., $2.50.

New White Russian Summer Lettuce.

This is pre-eminently one of the best sorts to withstand the extreme heat of our long, hot summer months, as it forms beautiful large, solid heads, without showing the slightest disposition whatever to run to seed. The heads generally have to be cut before any seed-stalk will appear. It is not a forcing variety, but one of the best for open ground crops, both North and South. Of very rapid growth, with few outer leaves; in color it is a light apple-green, yellowish-white inside, and forms a **very large, solid head**, of the finest quality for market and shipping. All who have planted it are enthusiastic in its praise. This lettuce is so distinct that a casual observer could readily discover a single head of it in an acre of any other sort. Pkt., 10c.; oz., 35c.; ¼ lb., $1.00; lb., $3.50.

Denver Market Lettuce.

We were so well pleased with this new lettuce on our trial grounds this season that we have decided to offer it to our customers and append the introducer's description as follows:

"We obtained a few seeds of this new lettuce some years ago from a market gardener in Denver, Colorado. It is an early variety of head lettuce, either for forcing or open ground. It forms large, solid heads, of a good, light green color and is very slow to run to seed. The leaves are beautifully curled and crimped (like the Savoy Cabbages), and are very tender, crisp and of excellent flavor. The crimped leaves distinguish it from any other kind of lettuce now grown. The shape of the head resembles somewhat the Hanson, but is more oblong." Pkt., 10c.; oz., 25c.; ¼ lb., 70c.; lb., $2.50.

LETTUCE IS NOT ONLY COOLING TO THE SYSTEM, BUT PRODUCES SLEEP, ESPECIALLY IF THE STALK IS EATEN.

SEEDS FOR MONEY GROWERS 47

GRAND RAPIDS. This variety originated at Grand Rapids, Mich., where it is largely grown for shipment to distant points and where it is considered by many the best house headed lettuce for forcing under glass. Leaves medium size, of light yellowish-green color, much crimped and frilled, thin, but of very upright growth, forms a fair sized but loose head; crisp, tender and of good quality. Owing to its upright habit it may be planted very closely. It is of extremely rapid growth; very little liable to rot, will stand without spoiling a week to ten days after it is fit to cut, and retains its freshness a long time after cutting. Pkt., 5c.; oz., 20c.; ¼ lb., 60c.; lb., $2.00.

BLOND BLOCKHEAD, or SUNSET. This new variety comes from France. We find it distinct from any other variety in its attractive shape, large solid heads, and beautiful golden-yellow color, hitherto unknown in this class of lettuce. It withstands heat to a remarkable extent, keeps a long time in good fresh condition after being cut, and ships splendidly. Pkt., 5c.; oz., 20c.; ¼ lb., 65c.; lb., $2.75.

PHILADELPHIA DUTCH BUTTER SPECKLED. Producing large heads of excellent quality; one of the best for the market gardener; stands heat well and slow to run to seed. Pkt., 5c.; oz., 15c.; ¼ lb., 40c.; lb., $1.35.

VICTOR DUTCH BUTTER. (Market gardeners' private stock). Notwithstanding this fine variety was only first offered two years since, it has had a famous local reputation around Philadelphia, where market gardeners have heretofore paid very high prices for the seed. It is a selected and greatly improved strain of the Dutch Speckled Butter, and is most highly prized for early spring and autumn sowing, producing crisp, white, solid heads, almost equal to a cabbage; the outer leaves are speckled with a brownish tinge. It is an elegant forcing variety, or for growing in cold frames, and stands the heat and cold to a remarkable degree; we regard it as one of the very best and most profitable varieties to grow. Pkt., 10c.; oz., 35c.; ¼ lb., 90c.; lb., $3.50.

CALIFORNIA ALL HEART. The valley of Santa Clara, California, just south of San Francisco, has of late years been noted for growing the finest lettuce in the world. This new variety was sent from there, with the request that we give it a trial. The originator, a prominent lettuce grower, in sending us the seed, wrote: "No praise is too high for its merits, as its superior does not exist." We are happy to say that, after a fair trial by ourselves and numerous customers, we can fully endorse his strong claims for it, and believe it to be the best of all for the family garden. Its handsome shape and appearance are well shown in the above cut. Its shape is very distinct, heading up like a pointed cabbage and almost as solid, of a beautiful light green shade, almost white and particularly rich and buttery in flavor; very tender and sweet at all times, never bitter. Pkt., 10c.; oz., 25c.; ¼ lb., 75c.; lb., $2.50.

Early Curled Silesia. A fine early curled variety, which does not head; leaves large and tender, of fine flavor. Pkt., 5c.; oz., 10c.; ¼ lb., 30c.; lb., $1.00.

Early Curled Simpson. This does not head, but forms a close, compact mass of leaves; early and excellent for forcing. Pkt., 5c.; oz., 10c.; ¼ lb., 30c.; lb., $1.00.

HUBBARD'S MARKET. A white-seeded variety, very similar to the Black-seeded Tennis Ball. It is not quite so early to mature, but forms a little larger and more open head. Very popular in Boston and other Eastern markets. Pkt., 5c.; oz., 15c.; ¼ lb., 40c.; lb., $1.00.

CALIFORNIA CREAM BUTTER. This variety forms large, solid, round, compact heads, light green outside and creamy yellow within. It is medium early and strongly recommended as a summer variety, being very slow to shoot to seed. Pkt., 5c.; oz., 15c.; ¼ lb., 40c.; lb., $1.50.

DEACON. A fine new variety, originated near Rochester, N. Y., with round, compact heads, four to five inches in diameter; leaves very thick, dark green, tender and of unusual fine quality. Pkt., 5c.; oz., 15c.; ¼ lb., 40c.; lb., $1.50.

IMPROVED HANSON. An improved strain of this superior curled heading variety, of large size, often weighing three pounds; sweet, tender and crisp, of a beautiful greens without and white within. Resisting heat and drought well. Pkt., 5c.; oz., 15c.; ¼ lb., 40c.; lb., $1.35.

BLACK SEEDED SIMPSON. This is by far the best curled lettuce for forcing. In Chicago and other Western cities, it is the most popular and best selling lettuce that can be grown. It differs from the Early Curled Simpson in being much lighter in color, the leaves being nearly white and attaining nearly double the size of that variety. It also stands the summer heat splendidly when grown outside. Our engraving, made from a photograph, will give some idea of its distinctive and handsome appearance. The quality is exceptionally fine; all gardeners who have never grown it will do well to give it a trial. Pkt., 5c.; oz., 20c.; ¼ lb., 60c.; lb., $2.00.

BUTTERCUP. A new variety from Germany, good for winter and summer use or early forcing; forming large, solid heads of bright green colored foliage, crisp, tender and delicate flavor. Pkt., 5c.; oz., 15c.; ¼ lb., 75c.; lb., $1.50.

BIG BOSTON. This new variety resembles the well-known Boston Market Lettuce, but produces heads about double the size, but matures a week later. A valuable sort for open ground or forcing. Pkt., 5c.; oz., 20c.; ¼ lb., 70c.; lb., $2.00.

A FREE PREMIUM.
Johnson & Stokes' Hot House Lettuce.

This is a new lettuce, with which we have been working for a few years past. We believe it to possess very valuable and distinct qualities, for forcing, in the greenhouse or in frames. The supply of seed is so small this season, that we cannot offer it for sale, but will include a liberal trial package free to all who order Lettuce to the amount of $2.00 and over, from this catalogue, and when requested.

"THE BEST OF ALL LETTUCES IS CALIFORNIA ALL HEART, RIGHTLY SAID. ITS SUPERIOR DOES NOT EXIST."
D. LEMER, ADRIAN, OHIO.

∴ JOHNSON ∴ & ∴ STOKES ∴

LONGSTANDER BRONZE HEAD. We first offered this new lettuce for sale three years since. After a thorough and exhaustive trial on our Trial Grounds and from our own experience and the reports of many growers, we feel fully justified in claiming it to be the *largest, handsomest, most tender and compact in head, and longest standing of any brown cabbage lettuce*. Its strong points and beautiful golden bronze color are well expressed by John Wetzel, a well-known market gardener of Reed City, Mich., who writes: "There are not words in the English language to sufficiently praise your new lettuce. Longstander Bronze Head. It goes to seed so very small and continues growing through the whole summer, attaining a size larger than a half bushel. I could not get any of it to go to seed for me; it stood from April until October and never started to seed. It is exceedingly tender and of the best flavor; it looks very grey-oily-like, as though a fine yellow oil had been poured over it, saturating every part of the head and leaf." Pkt., 10c.; oz., 35c.; ¼ lb., sic.; lb., $1.00.

LARGE WHITE PASSION. A very handsome cabbage lettuce, forming very large, hard heads of delicious flavor, and is slow to running to seed. Although quite new, this variety is already very popular with our Southern market gardeners for shipment North. The seed being sown in the fall and transplanted during the winter, it grows to fine, large size, and stands long shipments better than any variety we know of. Pkt., 10c.; oz., 20c.; ¼ lb., 60c.; lb., $1.75.

Philadelphia Early Prize Head, or Brown Cabbage. An excellent family lettuce, it forms a mammoth head, and remains tender and crisp throughout the season. It is prompt to head and slow to run to seed; very hardy, and of superb flavor. Pkt., 5c.; oz., 15c.; ¼ lb., 35c.; lb., $1.25.

STANDWELL. This lettuce will, as its name implies, stand a long time before running to seed. The heads are very large and *solid*. The heart and leaves are of a *buttery yellow-green*. Pkt., 10c.; oz., 25c.; ¼ lb., 70c.; lb., $2.40.

Black-Seeded Satisfaction. A splendid variety, with large, fine, compact heads of rare quality; very solid, stands heat well, and remains in fine eating condition for a long time. Pkt., 5c.; oz., 15c.; ¼ lb., 35c.; lb., $1.25.

NEW PERPETUAL, or IMPROVED SIMPSON. This variety is entirely distinct, not heading, but forming huge compact bushes. The leaf is a *yellowish-green and very tender*. For private use it is especially adapted, as only one sowing is necessary for the whole season. It remains up to the time of seeding of just the same quality for eating as at any time before. Pkt., 5c.; oz., 15c.; ¼ lb., 40c.; lb., $1.35.

NEW CHARTIER. This fine sort will take front rank when thoroughly introduced. A few Pittsburg gardeners have kept it carefully among themselves, until we secured seed stock. It is one of the most striking and distinct varieties in cultivation, and attracts much attention owing to its pinkish color, fine head and beautiful curled leaves. Its quality is faultless. Pkt., 5c.; oz., 15c.; ¼ lb., 40c.; lb., $1.40.

NEW OAK-LEAVED. A distinct and beautiful new variety. The heads are compact, crisp and tender, and entirely free from that bitter taste peculiar to many sorts. Pkt., 5c.; oz., 15c.; ¼ lb., 40c.; lb., $1.40.

IMPROVED DEFIANCE SUMMER. Among the few lettuces of merit recently introduced, we place this sort among the front rank of summer varieties. It produces a splendid large, solid head, of the cabbage type, remaining a long time in prime condition without going to seed. It is of a light green color, fine quality, crisp, tender and nearly every plant will make a fine, solid head in the hottest weather, when many other varieties will refuse even to grow. Pkt., 5c.; oz., 15c.; ¼ lb., 40c.; lb., $1.40.

TOMHANNOCK. A splendid new cutting lettuce of fine quality, which it retains for an unusual length of time during growth; the leaves grow upright, the edges of the leaves growing outward and are handsomely wrinkled. The inside leaves are of a very pale green, and remarkably crisp and tender. Pkt., 5c.; oz., 15c.; ¼ lb., 40c.; lb., $1.40.

SALAMANDER. An excellent summer variety, withstanding drought and heat to a remarkable extent; forms good-sized, compact heads; light green outside, white within; fine for market. Pkt., 5c.; oz., 15c.; ¼ lb., 35c.; lb., $1.60.

IMPROVED YELLOW-SEEDED BUTTER. This is one of the best for late spring or summer planting, producing fine large heads, very crisp and tender. It is of quicker growth and will stand the hot summer sun better than Salamander. Pkt., 5c.; oz., 15c.; ¼ lb., 45c.; lb., $1.60.

NEW YORK. A very large green lettuce with solid heads, often weighing three to four pounds each. Not suited for forcing, but excellent for summer use, being slow to shoot to seed. Pkt., 5c.; oz., 15c.; ¼ lb., 40c.; lb., $1.40.

AMERICAN VARIETIES MIXED. Fifteen kinds mixed in one packet. Early, medium and late sorts, giving lettuce for table during the entire season. Pkt., 10c.; oz., 20c.

COS LETTUCES.

NEW TRIANON COS, or CELERY LETTUCE. This new variety from France is by far the best Cos Lettuce we have ever grown and, after a critical test of two seasons, we can recommend it as the very finest of its class. The Cos Lettuces are now the favorites in Europe, and they are fast becoming more popular here. The long, narrow leaves, which form large solid heads, almost like a Wakefield cabbage, bleach and quickly become snowy white. They excel all other lettuces in quality, having a taste and crispness unequalled. The leaves of this variety when bleached are stiff like celery stalks and can be eaten in the same manner. In many countries of Europe where known this lettuce is preferred to celery. Those of our customers who have never grown the Cos lettuces, will be amply repaid by giving this new sort a trial. Pkt., 10c.; oz., 25c.; ¼ lb., 50c.

Giant Mexican Cos. A variety from Mexico, where it is eaten as a fruit; growing to enormous size. Pkt., 5c.; oz., 15c.; ¼ lb., 50c.; lb., $1.60.

Paris White Cos. Pkt., 5c.; oz., 15c.; lb., $1.40.

MARTYNIA.

Martynia Proboscidea. For pickling. Pkt., 5c.; oz., 25c.; ¼ lb., $1.00; lb., $2.75.

MUSTARD.

One ounce will sow about seventy-five feet of drill.

NEW CHINESE. A giant curled variety; leaves twice the size of the ordinary White Mustard, frequently fourteen to fifteen inches long, with blade of yellowish green color, netted and crumpled like that of a Savoy cabbage; stems more succulent than any other mustard; flavor pleasantly sweet and pungent. In six weeks from the time of sowing the leaves may commence to be gathered, and the plants will continue to yield until frost sets in. The leaves are eaten boiled like spinach. They are very little diminished in substance by cooking, and have a very agreeable flavor. In some countries it forms one of the most highly esteemed of all green vegetables. Pkt., 5c.; oz., 10c.; ¼ lb., 30c.; lb., $1.00.

White London. Best for salads. Oz., 5c.; lb., 45c.

Black, or Brown. More pungent than the white; for salad and culinary use. Oz., 5c.; ¼ lb., 20c.; lb., 45c.

NASTURTIUM—Indian Grass.

Tall Yellow. The best for pickling or salads. Pkt., 5c.; oz., 15c.; ¼ lb., 40c.; lb., $1.25.

Dwarf Mixed. Pkt., 5c.; oz., 15c.; ¼ lb., 40c.; lb., $1.25.

"WHITE RUSSIAN SUMMER AND LONGSTANDER BRONZE HEAD DESERVE MORE PRAISE THAN YOU BESTOW UPON THEM. ALL YOUR SEEDS THE BEST." GRISCOM BROS., WEATHERFORD, TEXAS.

SEEDS ∴ FOR ∴ MONEY ∴ GROWERS ∴

Johnson & Stokes Superior Melon Seeds

We grow our Melon Seed almost exclusively on our own farms and those of our private growers in Southern New Jersey, a locality famous for producing the finest melons in the world. We are to-day the largest growers of melon seeds in the United States, our annual production amounting to many tons. During past years we have annually supplied them, not only in the United States, but to customers in nearly every country in Europe, Africa, South America, Mexico and West Indies. We also supply, every season, over our counter, hundreds of New Jersey truck gardeners with our superior strains. We attribute the popularity of our melon, as well as of other seeds, to our careful and personal selection of the very finest specimens for our seed stocks, thus improving and breeding up our stocks to the highest state of perfection. As will be noted in the following descriptions, several of the best and most popular melons now known were first named and introduced by us. We desire to call special attention to *two new varieties* of muskmelons, viz: **JERSEY BELLE and SUPERB** and also the **JOHNSON'S DIXIE WATERMELON**, which we have illustrated in colors on back of this book; all of these will be found fully described and illustrated under *Novelties and Specialties for 1892*.

MUSKMELON.—Cantaloupe.

One ounce will plant about seventy hills; three pounds will plant one acre.

NETTED BEAUTY. This new variety was first named and introduced by us last spring. It met with large sale and many leading melon growers have written us that they consider it the very best Extra Early sort they have ever grown, and that notwithstanding the low prices last summer, they realized handsomely on their crops of Netted Beauties, owing to their great earliness and distinct handsome appearance. The above engraving, made by our artist from a photograph, is an exact representation of the melon, which, as before stated, is very early, coming in a few days after our **EXTRA EARLY PRIZE** and **JERSEY BELLE** (see Novelties), which are the earliest melons known, being completely covered with a dense netting, and entirely free from any tendency to rib like other sorts. It is also very productive, which is shown in the fact that our whole crop averaged the past two seasons over ten melons to the vine, on good ground. The flesh is pale green, very thick, sweet and high flavored. Pkt., 10c.; oz., 20c.; ¼ lb., 85c.; lb, $3.00.

NETTED PINEAPPLE. A splendid market variety, of good shape, medium size, flesh green and thick, firm, juicy and sweet; very early, and popular in our markets. Pkt., 5c.; oz., 10c.; ¼ lb., 25c.; lb., 75c., 5 lbs. and over, by express, 60c. per lb.

JERSEY BELLE. The earliest of all muskmelons, now offered for the first time. See photograph and description under Novelties, page 11. Pkt., 15c.; 2 pkts., 25c.; 4 pkts., 50c.; 10 pkts., $1.00.

NEW SUPERB. The handsomest and best late green-fleshed melon. See Photographic Specialties, page 17. Pkt., 10c.; oz., 40c.; ¼ lb., $1.00; lb., $3.75

EARLY JENNY LIND. A standard popular sort, rather small, early and flattened on the ends. Flesh green and generally good in flavor. Pkt., 5c.; oz., 10c.; ¼ lb., 20c.; lb., 60c.

Surprise. A good bearer, of excellent flavor and quality. Pkt., 5c.; oz., 10c.; ¼ lb., 25c., lb., 75c.

Improved Orange Christiana. Very early, orange-fleshed, good quality. Pkt., 5c.; oz., 10c.; ¼ lb., 25c.; lb., 80c.

PROLIFIC NETTED NUTMEG. A favorite and profitable early market variety; medium sized, deeply netted, nearly round, flesh thick, sweet and of delicious flavor. Pkt., 5c.; oz., 10c.; ¼ lb., 25c.; lb., 75c.

WARD'S NECTAR. An exceedingly sweet and delicious green-fleshed variety, considered by many growers the very best in flavor and quality of all the green-fleshed sorts. Grows to good size; well netted and of handsome shape. Those seeking a muskmelon for quality will find all they are looking for in the Ward's Nectar. Try it. Pkt., 5c.; oz., 10c.; ¼ lb., 30c.; lb., 85c.

"NETTED BEAUTY IS THE VERY BEST I EVER ATE OR GREW. I DO NOT THINK THERE IS A BETTER VARIETY IN EXISTENCE."
T. R. HUBBARD, HILLS POINT, MD.

JOHNSON & STOKES

EXTRA EARLY PRIZE. A carefully selected and improved strain, made a few years since by a trucker and melon grower, of Swedesboro, N. J. It is prized for its great earliness and rapidity with which it sells in market. It is very popular and already largely grown for, and is the first Northern grown muskmelon offered on the New York and Philadelphia markets. Very thickly netted when grown on good ground, small size and shape, as shown in above cut; of excellent flavor and quality. Pkt., 5c.; oz., 10c.; ¼ lb., 30c.; lb., $1.00; 5 lbs. and over, by express, 80c. per lb.

ACME, or BALTIMORE. This melon is the most popular of all in Baltimore markets and throughout Maryland, where it is known as Baltimore Citron. It has of late years also become prominent in Philadelphia and New York markets as Acme Cantaloupe, and in its season is now much sought after by the best hotels and restaurants, owing to its handsome appearance and excellent quality. It is quite early, very large and showy, pointed at the ends, as shown in cut; strongly netted, thick, rich, green flesh. It is unquestionably one of the best and most profitable varieties for shipping to distant markets. Pkt., 5c., oz., 10c.; ¼ lb., 25c.; lb., 75c.; 5 lbs. and over, by freight or express, 65c. per lb.

NEW EARLY HACKENSACK. This valuable variety is ready for market fully ten days ahead of the well-known Hackensack, its progenitor, which it much resembles in size, shape and quality. The melons are almost equal in size to the old Hackensack, weighing from five to ten pounds each. It is also very productive, averaging from five to six melons on the vine, all of which are very deeply netted. Its carrying and shipping qualities are equal to those of any known variety, and is fast becoming popular in the South, where it is grown for shipment to New York markets. Pkt., 5c.; oz., 10c.; ¼ lb., 25c.; lb., 9 oz.; 5 lbs. and over, 75c. per lb.

CHICAGO MARKET. A superior market variety, developed by Mr. A. Colvin, a well-known Chicago gardener. It is the most popular green-fleshed Nutmeg in Chicago and other Western markets, and is steadily growing in favor in the East. It comes quite early for such a good-sized melon. Very uniform in size, deep green flesh of excellent quality. Pkt., 5c.; oz., 10c.; ¼ lb., 25c.; lb., 90c.; 5 lbs. and over, 75c. per lb.

GOLDEN GEM (Netted Gem, or Golden Jenny). This valuable cantaloupe, first introduced by us, is admitted by prominent melon growers to be one of the very best now grown. The illustration above, engraved from a photograph, shows their shape, which is nearly round. They grow very uniform in shape and size, weighing about two pounds each, skin green and thickly netted. They are very thick meated, flesh of a light green color, the inside surface, when cut open, being of a beautiful golden color. In quality and flavor they are *superior*, being uniformly rich, *sugary and luscious*. They are *extra early* in ripening, coming in a few days after our Extra Early Prize, the vines keeping green longer and producing better than any variety we have ever known. They sell in Philadelphia and other markets, where known, right alongside of other varieties, at double price. Pkt., 5c., oz., 10c.; ¼ lb., 30c.; lb., 85c.; 5 lbs. and over, by express, 70c. per lb.

CHAMPION MARKET, or STARR'S FAVORITE. This new muskmelon is quite distinct from all other varieties. The melons are almost a perfect globe in shape and densely netted. They are very uniform in size, averaging about six pounds each. The flesh is thick, light green in color, and of rich, sweet flavor. Six melons of Champion Market will fill a market basket. The vines are very vigorous, remarkably healthy and *very productive*. The melons mature early and all ripen up finely. It is an *excellent shipper* and a most *popular variety for market*. Pkt., 5c.; oz., 10c.; ¼ lb., 30c.; lb., 90c.; 5 lbs., $4.00.

THE PERSIAN MONARCH. The fact of this grand new cantaloupe coming from Persia, the original home of the muskmelon, would probably be sufficient recommendation of itself to most customers who have never grown it, as some of our very finest and oldest varieties come from the same source. The Shah (as it is called in Persia) or Persian Monarch is decidedly the best of all foreign muskmelons, being much the richest in quality. The flesh is much thicker and the rind thinner than in any other, or, as a friend remarked in testing their quality: "There is three times as much eating in one of these melons as in any other, and good eating, too, fit for the gods." They grow to medium size, with very thick, rich salmon-colored flesh. Pkt., 10c.; 3 pkts., 25c.; oz., 75c.

"PRINCESS MELON IS THE MOST DELICIOUS AND SWEETEST OF ALL. FULLY UP TO REPRESENTATION." THOS. WHITEHEAD, BELTSVILLE, MD.

THE PRINCESS MUSKMELON.

We feel justly proud in having been, in 1889, the first seedsmen to offer to the public a new variety of such *extraordinary value*. IN THE PAST THREE YEARS OVER TWO THOUSAND MELON GROWERS HAVE PRONOUNCED THE PRINCESS TO BE THE FINEST AND SWEETEST OF ALL SALMON OR RED-FLESHED MELONS. It is quite distinct from all other varieties, and possesses so many strong points of superiority that it has speedily become the most popular variety for family and market purposes. The Princess is a chance seedling, discovered some years since by one of our customers, a large melon grower near Boston, who claims to have sold them as high as $2.50 each, to fancy restaurants in Boston, owing to their extremely *handsome appearance*, *wonderful weight and thick flesh* when opened. Our engraving, made from nature, shows their shape, which is nearly round, with heavily-netted, dark green skin; the flesh is of a rich salmon color, thicker than in any other melon, and in flavor is *sweet and luscious beyond description*. They ripen early and grow to good size, frequently weighing eight to ten pounds each and always command the very highest prices in market. The vines grow vigorously and are very productive and hardy. Pkt., 10c.; oz., 15c.; ¼ lb., 40c.; lb., $1.25.

GIANT OF COLORADO—The Largest of all Muskmelons.

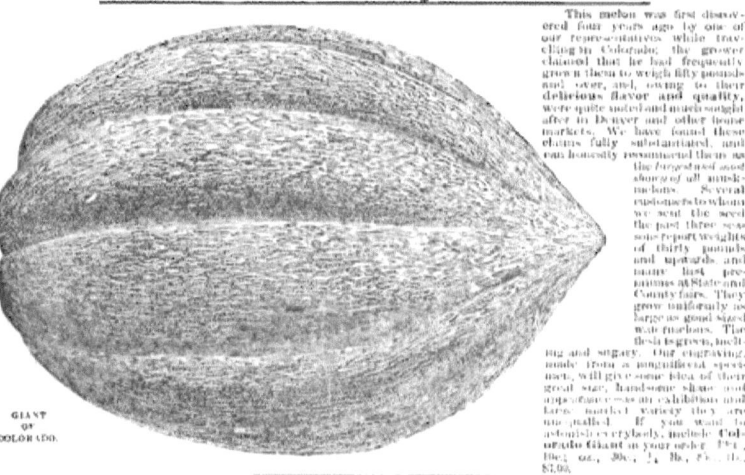

This melon was first discovered four years ago by one of our representatives while traveling in Colorado; the grower claimed that he had frequently grown them to weigh fifty pounds and over, and, owing to their **delicious flavor and quality**, were quite noted and much sought after in Denver and other home markets. We have found these claims fully substantiated, and can honestly recommend them as the *largest and most showy of all muskmelons*. Several customers to whom we sent the seed the past three seasons report weights of thirty pounds and upwards, and many last premiums at State and County fairs. They grow uniformly as large as good sized water melons. The flesh is green, inch thick and sugary. Our engraving, made from a magnificent specimen, will give some idea of their great size, handsome shape and appearance — as an exhibition and large market variety they are unequalled. If you want to astonish everybody, include Colorado Giant in your order. Pkt., 10c.; oz., 30c.; ¼ lb., $1.00; lb., $3.00.

GIANT OF COLORADO.

"COLORADO GIANT, LARGEST IN SIZE AND FINEST IN QUALITY; FIRST PREMIUM AT NIAGARA COUNTY FAIR." H. B. SIMONS & SON, WRIGHTS' CORNER, TEXAS.

JOHNSON & STOKES

EMERALD GEM MUSKMELON.

EMERALD GEM. This most excellent new muskmelon originated in Michigan. It is of superior flavor and quality; the skin is an unribbed green of moderately thick smoothness; they ripen early and profusely well in being about the size of our Gold melon, the flesh is light red or salmon, very thick, juicy and crystalline, and luscious in flavor. Pkt., 5c.; oz., 10c.; ¼ lb., 25c.; lb., 90c.; 5 lbs., $4.75.

OSAGE, or MILLER CREAM. After carefully testing these two varieties side by side on our Trial Grounds the past three seasons, we are unable to discover the slightest difference between them, although first introduced under the above two names.

No variety of muskmelon has ever advanced in popularity and become so widely known in such a short time as this variety. The past summer has been only the fifth season in the Chicago market, but it is now the favorite sort in all of the leading hotels and restaurants, and is also well known by all commission men and largely by the general public, being offered on the hotel and restaurant bills of fare under its own name of "OSAGE." It grows to medium size and is egg or globe-shaped. The skin is very thin, of dark green color, and well netted. The flesh is of a salmon color, remarkably sweet and spicy in flavor, extremely thick and delicious to the rind. The seed cavity is very small. All lovers and shippers of fine melons should grow the OSAGE, or MILLER CREAM. Pkt., 5c.; oz., 10c.; ¼ lb., 25c.; lb., 90c.

NEW SUPERIOR. A beautiful new round muskmelon originated in New Jersey, free from ribs and densely netted. Flesh light green and of the finest quality. Our customers will find it a very superior melon for either home or market garden. Pkt., 5c.; oz., 15c.; ¼ lb., 35c.; lb., $1.25.

HENDERSON'S BANQUET. In shape and size this new melon first introduced last spring resembles the New Superior, but has beautiful red flesh of superior flavor. Not a single customer who plants the New Banquet will be disappointed in having one of the best in quality. Pkt., 10c.; oz., 40c.; ¼ lb., $1.00; lb., $3.50.

THE DELMONICO. Another new melon of large size and oval in shape. The flesh is of a beautiful orange pink, and for excellence in quality, all lovers of good cantaloupes should try the Delmonico. Pkt., 5c.; oz., 10c.; ¼ lb., 30c.; lb., $1.00.

IMPROVED MONTREAL GREEN NUTMEG. This variety is largely grown by market gardeners in the neighborhood of Quebec and Montreal, Canada. The fruit is nearly round, slightly flattened at the ends, with a densely netted green skin. They grow to a very large, medium size, averaging from fifteen to twenty pounds in weight. The flesh is remarkably thick, and of splendid flavor. Owing to its large and handsome appearance, it sells rapidly in market at good prices. Pkt., 5c.; oz., 10c.; ¼ lb., 25c.; lb., 75c.; 5 lbs., and over, 65c. per lb.

PERFECTION. A new variety originated in Chenango County, N. Y. It has rich salmon-colored flesh of fine quality almost equal to that of Princess. In shape it is rounder than Princess and not so densely netted. It grows to large size, shape quite round, and distinct from all others. Pkt., 5c.; oz., 10c.; ¼ lb., 30c.; lb., 90c.

Hackensack, or Turk's Cap. A variety of the Green Citron; deeply netted, very large and productive, of excellent flavor, profitable and fine for market. Pkt., 5c.; oz., 10c.; ¼ lb., 25c.; lb., 75c.; 5 lbs. or over, by express, 60c. per lb.

CASABA PERSIAN. Of extraordinary size and delicious flavor, usual weight, from twelve to fifteen pounds; late oval and netted. Pkt., 5c.; oz., 10c.; ¼ lb., 25c.; lb., 70c.

BANANA CANTALOUPE. This variety originated in South Jersey, and is pronounced by many the most profitable variety they have ever grown. They are eagerly sought after in Philadelphia and New York markets, owing to their great oddity of shape, appearance and rich flavor, selling at very high prices. They grow from two to two and a quarter feet long, with deep salmon-colored flesh, of good quality; by many preferred to any other variety, and a great curiosity. Pkt., 5c.; oz., 10c.; ¼ lb., 30c.; lb., $1.00.

BAY VIEW. An early, vigorous growing and productive variety; large size, weighing twelve to fifteen pounds, and delicious flavor; desirable for market gardeners. Pkt., 5c.; oz., 10c.; ¼ lb., 25c.; lb., 70c.

Japan Coral-Fleshed. A new variety, of round shape and densely netted; flesh thick, coral color, of excellent quality. Pkt., 5c.; oz., 10c.; ¼ lb., 30c.; lb., 95c.

WHITE JAPAN. Early, of medium size, round, skin and flesh creamy white, orange centre, and of fine flavor. Pkt., 5c.; oz., 10c.; ¼ lb., 25c.; lb., 75c.; 5 lbs., $3.00.

CHOICE IMPORTED MUSKMELONS.

We offer seeds of each of the following varieties at 10 cents per packet, or 3 packets for 25 cents:

FRENCH De PASSY, ALGIERS, NEAPOLITAN WINTER, Hardy Ridge, or Prescott, Italian and French varieties mixed.

MANGO MELON, or VEGETABLE ORANGE. This new fruit belongs to the melon family, but has a flavor entirely peculiar to itself. When it first ripens it is quite hard, but soon it becomes mellow and sweet, and has a rich flavor, somewhat resembling the peach. When ripe the fruit falls from the vine, the flesh is very firm with a small cavity in the centre, and are easily peeled. For sweet pickles, pies or preserving, they are superb. A few pieces of sliced lemon, added to their flavor and is usually desirable. They are easily cultivated, wonderfully productive, and can be used in every way in which you would use a peach, except that they are not usually liked raw, although some consider them excellent simply sliced with a little sugar on. Pkt., 10c.; oz., 20c.; ¼ lb., 50c.; lb., $1.75.

MELON, WATER.

One ounce will plant about fifty hills, and four pounds will plant one acre.

JOHNSON'S DIXIE. An entirely new variety, surpassing the celebrated Kolb Gem in shipping qualities and without a peer in fine quality and productiveness. We first introduced this new melon in spring of 1890, and like all good things, it is being counterfeited. See Specialties, page 18, also colored plate on back of this book. Pkt., 10c.; oz., 25c.; ¼ lb., 70c.; lb., $2.25; 5 lbs. and over, $2.00 per lb.

JUMBO. The shape of this new melon is almost round. The skin is green, with faint stripes of lighter green. In form and habit of resting on the blossom end is like the **"Pride of Georgia,"** but is free from the ribs of that variety. As indicated by the name, they grow to a fine large size, with a very tough rind, making it a valuable shipping variety. Flesh red and very sweet. A melon introduced last spring, under the name of **"Fordhook Early,"** is so similar to as seem identical with it, and we can see no reason why two melons so near alike in all respects should be listed under separate names. Pkt., 5c.; oz., 15c.; ¼ lb., 40c.; lb., $1.25.

PHINNEY'S EARLY. Very thin rind, flesh scarlet, sweet, luscious; medium in size, oblong in shape and very early. Pkt., 5c.; oz., 10c.; ¼ lb., 30c.; lb., 65c.; 5 lbs., $2.50.

"JOHNSON & STOKES' CATALOGUES GIVE A STRIKING ILLUSTRATION OF THE ENTERPRISE AND PROGRESS OF SEEDSMEN." "RURAL NEW YORKER."

SEEDS FOR MONEY GROWERS 53

Three New Watermelons.

THE DELAWARE. A fine new variety, originated by Mr. Paynter Framo, of Delaware, the originator of the Iron Clad, being a cross of that variety, with Mountain Sweet. The shape is oblong, and skin striped light and dark green as shown in accompanying illustration. It is said to grow larger and ripen earlier than the Iron Clad, an excellent keeper and fine shipper. Pkt., 5c.; oz., 15c.; ¼ lb., 30c.; lb., $1.00; 5 lbs., $4.00.

WHITE GEM. A new round white-skinned variety, somewhat resembling the well known Russian Vodge, but said to have come originally from China. It is extremely hardy and productive, and thrives well in our climate; flesh pink and of delicious flavor, rind thin, but very tough and hard. Pkt., 5c.; oz., 15c.; ¼ lb., 35c.; lb., $1.25.

GREEN AND GOLD. This is a fine, new, large melon, with flesh of beautiful orange color, of delicious quality. We have tested this variety for two seasons and can recommend it as a fine, family melon, as well as a curiosity. Of course, the color of the flesh is against it as a market variety. Pkt., 5c.; oz., 10c.; ¼ lb., 30c.; lb., $1.00.

EARLY CALIFORNIA, or IMPROVED ODELLA. This is the most popular market variety grown in New Jersey, two weeks earlier than the Old Mountain Sweet, round to oval in shape, color light green, good quality and an excellent shipper; rind very tough and hard, grows to large size. Pkt., 5c.; oz., 10c.; ¼ lb., 20c.; lb., 60c.; 5 lbs., $2.25.

DARK ICING. This variety combines all the good qualities essential to perfection. They grow to medium size, averaging in weight from twenty-five to thirty pounds, although we have known them to reach fifty pounds. The skin is dark green and firm. The flesh is a deep rich scarlet, of *delicious flavor*, it is one of the best shipping and carrying melons grown. Pkt., 5c.; oz., 10c.; ¼ lb., 25c.; lb., 75c.; 5 lbs. or over, by express or freight, 60c. per lb.

JOHNSON'S CHRISTMAS WATERMELON.

JOHNSON'S CHRISTMAS. This melon, introduced by us a few years since has already become a most popular shipping melon for long distances. Hundreds of customers write us every year that they keep until Christmas in perfect condition. Their valuable keeping and shipping qualities are due to a peculiar, hard, tenacious coating or outside enameling of the skin, which also gives them an exceedingly handsome and fresh appearance, even after being kept or allowed to remain on the vines for months after ripening. The flesh is of a beautiful rich scarlet, *very solid and of delicious sugary flavor*. Its uniform size and handsome, fresh appearance at all times make it a *most suitable variety*. Pkt., 5c.; oz., 10c.; ¼ lb., 30c.; lb., 85c.; 5 lbs. and over, 70c. per lb.

VICK'S EARLY. Highly prized for its earliness, grows oblong, medium size, but somewhat irregular in color of outside skin. Flesh pink, very solid and sweet. Pkt., 5c.; oz., 10c.; ¼ lb., 20c.; lb., 65c.; 5 lbs., $2.50.

SCALY BARK. This variety originated in Georgia. The skin is dark green, quite smooth and is a peculiar scaly appearance. It is an unusually productive sort, the average weight of the melons being forty to fifty pounds, although it is not unusual for specimens to reach seventy pounds. The flesh is light crimson, solid, *tender and of exquisite flavor*; remains in choice *eating condition* long after being pulled. The rind, though quite thin, is remarkably tough. Pkt., 5c.; oz., 10c.; ¼ lb., 25c.; lb., 70c.

STOKES' EXTRA EARLY MELON.—EARLIEST OF ALL.

STOKES' EXTRA EARLY. This distinct melon, first introduced by us, is, without doubt, the *earliest of all.* Our illustration, made from a photograph, shows their shape, which is nearly round, dark green skin, slightly mottled with white. The flesh is deep scarlet, remarkably solid, and in *delicious, sugary flavor* is unsurpassed by any other melon. Their average weight is about fifteen pounds. The seed is very small, being only about half the size of other melon seeds. They are also much *more productive* than the larger sorts, and for family use are quite unequalled. Pkt., 10c.; oz., 20c.; ¼ lb., 60c.; lb., $1.25.

RUBY GOLD. This melon was introduced two years ago, under the claim of the flesh being veined with yellow and red. In our trials, however, we found many specimens bright red and others with intensely yellow flesh, but have never seen a particolored one. The originator's description does not therefore hold out with us; we think this statement due our customers, that those who purchase seed may not be disappointed. Pkt., 5c.; oz., 15c.; ¼ lb., 35c.; lb., $1.25.

"WE HAD A DELICIOUS CHRISTMAS WATERMELON JANUARY 20TH, AND HAVE A DOZEN MORE IN THE CELLAR. TRULY A WONDER."
M. E. POTTS, GLASCO, KANSAS.

JOHNSON & STOKES

THE BOSS. A distinct variety introduced a few years since. Skin is black green in color, and shape as shown in our illustration along side. Flesh deep scarlet, unusually sugary, crystalline and melting. The rind is very thin and tough, ripens early, and is enormously productive. This is considered by many the very best table melon for family use. Pkt., 5c.; oz., 10c.; ¼ lb., 25c.; lb., 75c.; 5 lbs. and over, 60c. per lb.

GRAYMONARCH, or LONG WHITE ICING. This distinct melon is, without doubt, one of the largest of all, frequently attaining a weight of ninety pounds and over. The skin is a mottled gray color, shape long, flesh bright crimson and of sweet, delicious flavor. It is also a fine shipper, carrying well long distances and bringing very high prices. Pkt., 5c.; oz., 10c.; ¼ lb., 25c.; lb., 90c.; 5 lbs., $3.50.

JERSEY BLUE. This variety has been grown with great profit by a few truckers in Northern New Jersey, where it originated a few years since. They grow to very large size, rather oval in shape, skin of deep blue color, slightly ribbed, with tough rind. Flesh deep scarlet and of fine quality. We recommend them highly as a shipping melon. Pkt., 5c.; oz., 10c.; ¼ lb., 25c.; lb., 75c.; 5 lbs., $3.50.

CUBAN QUEEN. Skin beautifully striped, dark and light green. Their flesh is *bright red, remarkably solid, luscious, crisp and sugary*; very solid and the best of keepers; excellent to ship to distant markets. They have been grown to weigh over one hundred pounds and are enormously productive. Pkt., 5c.; oz., 10c.; ¼ lb., 25c.; lb., 75c.; 5 lbs., $3.50.

HUNGARIAN HONEY. A new variety brought from Hungary a few years since. They grow round as a cannon ball, are very uniform in size and weight, running from ten to twelve pounds. The outside skin is dark green, rind very thin, flesh red and unusually sweet and luscious to the taste. Pkt., 5c.; oz., 10c.; ¼ lb., 30c.; lb., $1.00.

MAMMOTH IRON-CLAD. This melon grows to a very large *uniform size*, frequently weighing eighty pounds and over, and resembles in its markings the popular Cuban Queen. *In shape and seed, however, it is quite distinct*, being deeper and fuller at both ends, with seeds of drabwhite color. They are enormous yielders, flesh red, solid and of excellent flavor. The rind is extremely tough and hard—hence their name, Iron-Clad—rendering them valuable for shipping. Pkt., 5c.; oz., 10c.; ¼ lb., 25c.; lb., 50c.; 5 lbs., $2.75.

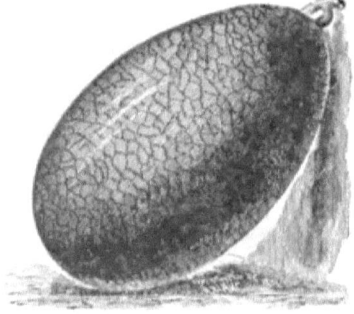

NEW RED-SEEDED VAUCLUSE

NEW RED-SEEDED VAUCLUSE. This is not only the best foreign watermelon we have ever grown, but is one of the most promising of all the many sorts lately introduced. It is of French origin, very early, of large size, elongated egg-shape, with stem end slightly inclined to a point. The flesh is a bright crimson, very sweet, not in the least stringy, and coming to within one-eighth of an inch of the skin; the seeds are also bright red. The rind, though thin, is very tough and the shell glossy, so that this melon is an excellent shipper. It is of dark green color, beautifully threaded with a still darker green. Pkt., 5c.; oz., 10c.; ¼ lb., 30c.; lb., $1.00.

Oz., 10c.; ¼ lb., 20c.; lb., 65c.; 5 lbs. and over, 50c. per lb.

KOLB GEM. This variety is more largely grown by Southern shippers than any other. It originated with B. F. Kolb, one of the largest melon growers of Alabama, and is a Hybrid of Scaly Bark and Rattlesnake. The rind, though quite thin, is very tough, standing handling and shipment long distances without breakage. The flesh is bright red and of fair quality. Pkt., 5c.; oz., 10c.; ¼ lb., 20c.; lb., 65c.; 5 lbs. and over, 50c. per lb.

AMONG THE NEW YEAR'S RESOLUTIONS WRITE THIS: "I WILL HAVE A GOOD GARDEN NEXT YEAR," AND THEN SIT DOWN AND WRITE OUT YOUR ORDER FOR JOHNSON & STOKES' SEEDS.

SEEDS FOR MONEY GROWERS

THE VOLGA. A Russian variety. Cultivated on the lower Volga, near the Caspian Sea, for shipment in barrels to St. Petersburg and Moscow. In form it is so nearly perfectly globular. In color it is so pale green as to be nearly white. The flesh is remarkably crisp, and when fully ripe, sweet, and red in color. Pkt., 5c.; oz., 10c.; ¼ lb., 25c.; lb., 80c.

OEMLER'S TRIUMPH. Originated on the borders of the Black Sea. The seeds are so small they can be swallowed without inconvenience. It is very early and productive. The color is a dark mottled green, and that of the flesh a dark red with an edging of orange yellow. Very sweet and delicious. Pkt., 5c.; oz., 15c.; ¼ lb., 50c.; lb., $1.50.

MUSHROOM SPAWN.

Mushrooms are much more easily cultivated than is generally supposed. They can be successfully grown in a cellar, under green-house benches, in sheds or in beds in open air, prepared in the same manner as hot-beds. Full directions for culture are furnished with each order for spawn.

KENTUCKY WONDER. This is a new red-seeded variety, and we have never known a red-seeded watermelon that was not a good one, this being the best we have ever grown. In shape it is oblong, as shown in above cut; skin dark green, marbled in stripes of lighter green; flesh a beautiful scarlet color, crisp, tender, rich and sugary flavor, always firm and never mealy. Attains an average weight of forty to sixty pounds. Not a mammoth variety, but a real good, old-fashioned Kentucky melon, that has few equals in quality. Pkt., 5c.; oz., 15c.; ¼ lb., 35c.; lb., $1.25.

SEMINOLE. This new watermelon comes from Florida. We find it one of the best of melons in quality, form long, growing to an extra large size, outside skin gray, slightly tinged with light green, extra early and very productive. Pkt., 5c.; oz., 15c.; ¼ lb., 30c.; lb., 90c.; 5 lbs., $4.25.

LIGHT ICING, or ICE RIND. Of round form, skin light color, thin rind and good quality, nearly or quite equal to the dark-skinned Sweet Icing, which it resembles in shape. Pkt., 5c.; oz., 10c.; ¼ lb., 25c.; lb., 75c.

GIRARDEAU'S FLORIDA FAVORITE. This variety is a hybrid of the Rattlesnake and Pierson, the latter being a celebrated home variety in Florida. It is pronounced one of the finest table melons extant; oblong in shape, growing to very large size; rind dark, with light green stripes; flesh light crimson, very crisp and deliciously sweet. It ripens about ten days earlier than Kolb Gem, Iron-Clad or Rattlesnake. We offer seed grown by the originator. Pkt., 5c.; oz., 10c.; ¼ lb., 25c.; lb., 75c.; 5 lbs., $2.75.

PRIDE OF GEORGIA. Originated in Monroe County, Georgia. The rind is dark green, shape nearly oval, and ridged like an orange; flesh rich scarlet, very sweet and crisp; attains a large size and a good shipper. Pkt., 5c.; oz., 10c.; ¼ lb., 25c.; lb., 75c.; 5 lbs., and over, 65c. per lb.

IMPROVED BLACK SPANISH. Large, round, very dark green skin, flesh red, sweet and delicious; an excellent market variety. Pkt., 5c.; oz., 10c.; ¼ lb., 25c.; lb., 65c.

GEORGIA GYPSY, or RATTLESNAKE. A superior early market variety, large, oblong; skin green, mottled and striped. Pkt., 5c.; oz., 10c.; ¼ lb., 25c.; lb., 65c.

IMPROVED MOUNTAIN SPROUT. Large, long, dark green skin, good quality; a good market variety. Pkt., 5c.; oz., 10c.; ¼ lb., 25c.; lb., 65c.; 5 lbs., $2.25.

IMPROVED MOUNTAIN SWEET. A general favorite for market; early, large, flesh red, solid, rich and sweet. Pkt., 5c.; oz., 10c.; ¼ lb., 25c.; lb., 75c.; 5 lbs., $2.25.

Mountain Sweet. An old standard variety, large size, good flavor. Pkt., 5c.; oz., 10c.; ¼ lb., 25c.; lb., 60c.

ICE CREAM, or PEERLESS. True, white seed, of medium size, early, green skin, very thin rind, flesh solid, scarlet, crisp and of a delicious flavor; an excellent variety. Pkt., 5c.; oz., 10c.; ¼ lb., 25c.; lb., 70c.

EXCELSIOR. Very large, skin striped; flesh sweet and solid. Pkt., 5c.; oz., 10c.; ¼ lb., 25c.; lb., 70c.

COLORADO PRESERVING. An improvement on the green preserving melon; enormously productive, and of better quality and making very clear, transparent preserves of fine flavor. Pkt., 5c.; oz., 10c.; ¼ lb., 25c.; lb., 75c.; 5 lbs., $3.00.

Green Citron. For preserving; small, round; flesh white and solid. Pkt., 5c.; oz., 10c.; ¼ lb., 25c.; lb., 75c.

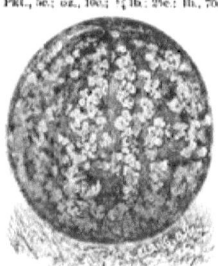

COLORADO PRESERVING MELON.

GROWING MUSHROOMS.

Best English Milltrack Mushroom spawn. In bricks of one and one-fourth pounds each, by mail, post-paid, each, 35c.; by express, 10 lbs., $1.25; 25 lbs., $3.00.

OKRA—Gumbo.

One ounce will plant one hundred hills.

IMPROVED DWARF PROLIFIC, or DENSITY. A distinct variety, growing about fourteen inches in height. Grown in competition with the ordinary dwarf, the stalks produced twice the number of pods, which are very smooth and beautiful. Pkt., 5c.; oz., 10c.; ¼ lb., 25c.; lb., 80c.

NEW WHITE VELVET. This distinct and beautiful new Okra was originated in Georgia. The pods are much larger than those of any other sort, perfectly smooth, never prickly, round, not ridged or square as in other okras. Pkt., 5c.; oz., 10c.; lb., 80c.

PERKINS' NEW MAMMOTH PODDED.

PERKINS' MAMMOTH LONG PODDED. This distinct new okra is by far the best. It was originated by M. B. Perkins, a well-known New Jersey trucker, after many years of careful study and selection. Its productiveness is simply wonderful, the pods shooting out from the bottom of the stalk within three inches of the ground, and the whole plant is covered with them to the height of a man's head, five to six feet. The pods are an intense green color, of unusual length, nine to ten inches, very slim, and do not get hard, as is the case with other okras. Mr. Perkins has always realized $3.00 to $4.00 per basket for his okra in Philadelphia markets; and it is also much sought after by canners, being the best of all green sorts for canning for winter use. Our seed is grown by the originator. Pkt., 5c.; oz., 10c.; ¼ lb., 25c.; lb., $1.00; 5 lbs. and over, 85c. per lb.

IT IS EASIER TO BUY GOOD SOIL THAN TO MAKE IT, AND CHEAPER TO BUY GOOD SEEDS THAN TO GROW THEM.

ONION.

One ounce will sow one hundred feet of drill. To grow large onions from seed, five pounds to the acre to grow small sets, fifty to sixty pounds to the acre is required.

There is no crop, perhaps, more sure than that of onions. Rich soil, with a good application of manure every year, and proper attention, will almost invariably insure a good crop. Five hundred bushels per acre is a medium crop, while from eight hundred to one thousand bushels are not unusual under the best cultivation. There are three varieties of onions commonly raised, namely: red, white and yellow. The yellow ones take the lead, as they are more hardy, grow larger, and bear handling better. Onions, unlike most other crops, may be raised on the same ground for an indefinite length of time.

Full information for Culture, Storage and Marketing of both onions and onion sets, will be found in our book of $100 Prize Essays. This book is sent by mail, postage paid, on receipt of price, 30 cents, or may be had free as a premium with all orders to the amount of $2.00 and over. See Book Premiums, page 21.

In comparing our prices with others, please remember that WE PAY THE POSTAGE, and if the seed is ordered by freight or express, at the expense of the purchaser, 8c. PER POUND may be deducted. For prices of onion seed in quantity, by freight or express, see page 43.

EXTRA EARLY RED. Ten days to two weeks earlier than the Large Red Wethersfield, of medium size and deep red color, an abundant producer, and of good form and flavor, keeping well. It is well adapted to the North, mainly soils of the North and Northwest, where other varieties fail to produce full-sized onions. Pkt., 5c.; oz., 20c.; ¼ lb. 50c.; lb., $1.85, postpaid ; 5 lb. lots, $1.70 per lb., not prepaid.

EARLY RED GLOBE. A new variety, maturing as early as the Extra Early Flat Red, but of a beautiful globe shape ; skin deep red, flesh mild and tender ; an excellent keeper and very desirable for market use. Pkt., 10c.; oz. 25c.; ¼ lb., 75c.; lb., $2.50.

TRUE AMERICAN EXTRA EARLY PEARL ONION. This is the largest and best of all the white varieties. It grows to enormous size and handsome round shape ; of pearly white color, the outer skin having a most showy waxy appearance, flesh of a pure, snow white, and flavor so mild that it can be eaten like an apple. It grows with wonderful rapidity, reaching the first season, from seed, the enormous size of six to seven inches diameter, frequently weighing three to four pounds each. A splendid keeper, succeeding everywhere, and requiring only thin soil. Our seed of this wonderful variety is Philadelphia grown, and should not be confounded with a cheap, imported variety offered by some dealers as Silver White King, or Early Pearl, which was entirely different onion, although somewhat resembling the American Extra Early Pearl in shape, being flatter, not so thick through, and it is vastly inferior in size and keeping qualities to the Genuine American Extra Early Pearl as grown by us. Pkt., 15c.; oz., 50c.; ¼ lb., $1.35 ; lb., $5.00.

THE GREAT KEEPING ONIONS
IVORY BALL and GOLDEN BALL.

Since our introduction of these valuable varieties three years since, the demand for the seed has been so great that we have been unable to fill all orders and we were obliged in many cases to return money for orders received late in the spring. They originated with one of the most successful onion growers of Ohio, Mr. John R. Williamson who has attained a large income from growing and keeping them until late in the spring, his onions frequently controlling the late markets and selling rapidly at high prices even long after new onions arrived from the South, owing to their excellent keeping qualities, fine appearance and handsome shape.

The accompanying engravings, made from Nature, show the shape and general appearance. These varieties are sure to bottom well ; in fact one hundred plants if cultivated properly, will produce one hundred fine, perfect, full proportioned onions, of much better quality for keeping or immediate use than the Southport Globe varieties. These extra qualities always insure extra prices to the growers.

GOLDEN BALL ONION.

The color of the skin is between a golden and a rich brown, flesh of exquisite whiteness, mild, well-flavored, and of unapproachable quality, and keeping the very first rank as a keeping variety. Pkt., 10c.; oz., 25c.; ¼ lb., 75c.; lb., $2.75.

IVORY BALL ONION.

In size, shape and keeping qualities, this variety is an exact counterpart of our Golden Ball. The skin and flesh, however, are of a pearly whiteness and so smooth, round and handsome that to a casual observer, they might easily be taken for billiard balls. It is just as easy to grow as the yellow varieties, and we recommend it to market growers in preference for the reason that white skinned usually command a higher price than yellow onions. Pkt., 10c.; oz., 25c.; ¼ lb., $1.00; lb., $3.50.

ROUND YELLOW DANVERS. Our superior stock of this celebrated variety is of fine shape, grows to good size, with thin yellow skin, white flesh, fine grained, mild flavor, and excellent quality. It ripens early, frequently producing from six hundred to eight hundred bushels to the acre ; keeps well and is considered a splendid sort. Pkt., 5c.; oz., 15c.; ¼ lb., 30c.; lb., $1.85, postpaid. By express or freight, in quantities of 10 lbs., and over, $1.70 per lb.

"AMERICAN EXTRA EARLY PEARL, THE LARGEST AND BEST EVER SEEN HERE. MANY WEIGHED OVER SIX POUNDS."
J. L. TRAVIS, CRESWELL, N. C.

PHILADELPHIA YELLOW GLOBE DANVERS ONION—PEDIGREE SEED

This **improved** variety is pronounced by all market gardeners and onion growers everywhere, who have tried it, the very best strain of Yellow Danvers in cultivation. It is the **earliest** yellow variety, **largest** in size, **uniformly perfect** in shape, the **largest cropper** and producing from seed 1,000 bushels to the acre with good cultivation. It is also the most reliable for bottoming and one of the **best keepers** of all American onions. In fact, it is everything that could be desired as a market or table onion. Prices of **our Pedigree Tested** seed crop of 1891, grown from selected, hand-picked bulbs, Pkt., 10c.; oz., 20c.; ¼ lb., 60c.; lb., $2.25, post-paid; 5 lb. lots, $2.10 per lb.; 10 lbs. and over, $2.00 per lb., by express.

PHILADELPHIA YELLOW DUTCH, or STRASBURG ONION.

THE GREAT SET ONION—OUR PEDIGREE SEED.

The most popular variety for sets, grown so extensively by market gardeners around Philadelphia. The sets of this variety grow round, plump and bright. Full size onions are somewhat flattened, flesh pure white, mild flavor and an excellent keeper. Skin bright yellow. Pkt., 10c.; oz., 20c.; ¼ lb., 60c.; lb., $2.00, post-paid; 5 lb. lots, $1.80 per lb.; 10 lbs. and over, $1.60 per lb., not pre-paid.

EXTRA LARGE RED WETHERSFIELD ONION.

Onion growers who prefer the red varieties will find this a magnificent strain, far surpassing the ordinary Red Wethersfield in size, productiveness and keeping qualities. It is of the finest form, skin deep purplish red, flesh purplish white, much finer grained than many of the red sorts. Immense crops of this onion are grown each season from our seed, by some of the largest growers in the United States, who realize the very highest prices for their crops. Admirably adapted to poor, dry soils. Pkt., 10c.; oz., 20c.; ¼ lb., 50c.; lb., $1.85; 5 lb. lots, $1.70 per lb.; 10 lbs. and over, $1.60 per lb., not pre-paid.

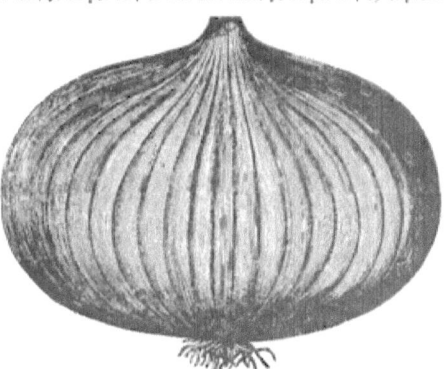

EXTRA LARGE RED WETHERSFIELD ONION.

"THE ENORMOUS YIELD AND FINE QUALITY OF YOUR PHILADELPHIA YELLOW GLOBE DANVERS SURPRISES US ALL." R. S. GEIBE, ROUGH-AND-READY, PA.

A LL plants grow splendidly in books, and some grow just as well in practice; but WHICH?—there's the rub. Have you time to test them all? Won't it pay better to buy from a house which is trying, testing, proving, all the time? You don't "try our seeds"—we have tried them. We sell what it PAYS to plant.

ONION—Continued.

SOUTHPORT LARGE RED GLOBE. This variety is very similar to the Southport Yellow Globe in shape and size, but ripens somewhat later, maturing a few days later than the Red Wethersfield. It is a splendid keeper and in quality is superior to most other red varieties. Pkt., 5c.; oz., 20c.; ¼ lb., 60c.; lb., $2.00; 4½ lbs, $3.50 per lb.

SOUTHPORT LARGE YELLOW GLOBE. This new American variety is entirely distinct from the Danvers. It is a very handsome, round or globe-shaped variety, of large size, with thin yellow skin, white flesh, fine-grained, mild, very firm and the best of keepers. It ripens early and sells readily at the highest prices in our markets. It is a most reliable variety for bottoming, and entirely free from scullions. Pkt., 5c.; oz., 20c.; ¼ lb., 60c.; lb., $2.00; 5 lbs. lots, and over, by express, $1.85 per lb.

NEW YELLOW EGG. A few gardeners who have grown and controlled this handsome onion for several years past, have made a profitable thing out of it. It is egg-shaped. The flesh is pure white, outside skin is a deep golden yellow. Pkt., 10c.; oz., 30c.; ¼ lb., 90c.; lb., $3.00.

PHILADELPHIA WHITE SILVERSKIN, or PORTUGAL. A good variety for family use; skin and flesh pure white, mild flavor and flat shape. The best white onion to grow largely for sets. Pkt., 10c.; oz., 30c.; ¼ lb., 90c.; lb., $3.25.

WHITE GLOBE. A large, firm, globe-shaped variety, with white skin; fine flesh, handsome in shape and a good keeper. Pkt., 10c.; oz., 25c.; ¼ lb., 80c.; lb., $3.00.

NEW WHITE BUNCH ONION. This variety is unquestionably the best onion for selling in bunches or using in a green state. It is a very early, vigorous grower and produces large, showy, white onions of the finest quality. Pkt., 10c.; oz., 20c.; ¼ lb., 60c.; lb., $2.25.

HARD ROUND SILVER SKIN FOR PICKLING. The best onion for pickling, producing uniform small, round handsome onions, with pure white skin, never turning green from exposure. Pkt., 5c.; oz., 20c.; ¼ lb., 60c.; lb., $2.00.

* ONION SETS, *

We are headquarters for Onion Sets, and have always in stock sets of the Yellow Dutch or Strasburg, Yellow Danvers, Extra Early Red and White Silver Skin, grown from our Pedigree Philadelphia Seed. Special prices will be quoted by the bushel or barrel. See page 65.

ITALIAN ONIONS.

The following varieties we have imported from the most reliable growers of Italy. They have all been tested and have proven a perfect success in every section of this country, and are largely grown for market, being milder in flavor than American varieties, and well adapted for early market and home garden use. They are of wonderful quick growth, forming fine large onions in a short time.

MAMMOTH SILVER KING. This mammoth variety is of attractive shape, with silvery white skin and flesh, of a most agreeable mild flavor. It matures a little later than our Extra Early Pearl, of flatter shape, reaching a very large size, and frequently measuring twenty inches in circumference, and weighing three to three and one-half pounds. Pkt., 10c.; oz., 25c.; ¼ lb., 70c.; lb., $2.30.

NEW WHITE ADRIATIC BARLETTA. The earliest, neatest and smallest onion grown; valuable for pickling or table use. Its great rapidity of growth will astonish everyone who tries it. Pkt., 10c.; oz., 25c.; ¼ lb., 75c.; lb., $2.50.

MAMMOTH POMPEII, or COPPER KING. Grows to enormous size; skin of a dark red color, flesh white and unusually mild in flavor. Fine exhibition and market variety. Pkt., 10c.; oz., 20c.; ¼ lb., 60c.; lb., $2.00.

NEW GIANT RED ROCCA. This magnificent variety resembles the popular Brown Rocca in shape and size, except that the skin is a beautiful bright red; flesh white, and mild in flavor. Pkt., 5c.; oz., 15c.; ¼ lb., 45c.; lb., $1.50.

GIANT ROCCA OF NAPLES. Large, of globular shape, bright brown skin, and delicate flavor, sometimes weighing three pounds and over. Valuable and remarkably handsome. Pkt., 5c.; oz., 15c.; ¼ lb., 50c.; lb., $1.75.

NEW GOLDEN QUEEN. This new Italian variety is a perfect model. Skin of a delicate golden straw color. It possesses all the characteristics of rapidity of growth and good keeping properties for which the White Queen is famous. Pkt., 10c.; oz., 25c.; ¼ lb., 75c.; lb., $2.50.

WHITE QUEEN. A rapid grower, white skin, of mild flavor, early, and remarkable for its keeping qualities. Pkt., 5c.; oz., 20c.; ¼ lb., 65c.; lb., $2.25.

GIANT WHITE ITALIAN TRIPOLI. (El Paso, or Large Mexican.) A large, white, flat onion of mild flavor and beautiful form. Pkt., 5c.; oz., 15c.; ¼ lb., 50c.; lb., $1.75.

NEW SPANISH ONION, MADRID GIANT.

This new variety, which we first introduced into America three years ago, is the largest and most popular onion grown around Madrid, the Spanish Capital, from whence we obtained the seed. It possesses the large size, mild flavor, excellent keeping, and all other good qualities of the celebrated Spanish King, but differs from that variety in its handsome red skin, which, in contrast with its pure white, fine grained flesh, attracts marked attention in market. Madrid Giant grows quicker and can be grown at least one-third larger than any other red onion. We believe there is a great future here for these Spanish varieties of onion, as instead of the tops dying down or running to seed, as is the case with American varieties, they keep on growing the entire season, thus attaining enormous weights and dimensions. A number of specimens sent in to us by customers, to whom we had sent seed, had attained a weight of five pounds and over. They are worthy of a trial from all market gardeners and onion growers. Pkt., 10c.; oz., 40c.; ¼ lb., $1.25; lb., $4.00.

The Spanish King, or Prize-Taker Onion.

We first introduced this handsome variety from Barcelona, Spain, five years ago, and have received hundreds of testimonial letters from growers, who all agree in pronouncing the Spanish King the largest, handsomest and most profitable variety they have ever grown. It is the large, beautiful onion that is seen every fall on sale at the fruit stores and stands in the large cities. The outside skin is of a rich, yellow straw color, while the flesh is white, sweet, mild and tender. They bottom well, are free from stiff necks, and have produced more bushels (1127) of marketable onions to the acre than any other variety known. In market it attracts marked attention, and although only offered to a limited extent has always been picked out and selected at three times the prices of any other sort on sale. Pkt., 10c.; oz., 30c.; ¼ lb., $1.50; lb., $5.00.

That well-known agricultural paper, Orchard and Garden, contained the following in its notes on onion tests:

"We grew twenty-three varieties from seed, side by side, the past season. Among all these, the Spanish King, introduced by JOHNSON & STOKES, was the only one with which we were entirely satisfied, and had we sowed the whole patch with this, the product would have been four times as large as it actually turned out. The bulbs were by far the largest of all, and among the rest we had Silver King and a number of other Mammoth sorts."

.˙. JOHNSON .˙. & .˙. STOKES .˙.

True Bermuda Onion Seed.

Our sales of this valuable early variety, the true stock of which is often difficult to obtain, have been increasing rapidly each year. We import it in very large quantities, and are consequently enabled to make our prices extremely low.

	Pkt.	oz.	¼ lb.	lb.
Bermuda Onion Seed, Pale Red,	10	20	60	$2 25
" " Pure White,	10	20	65	2 40

We grow each season large quantities of white, yellow and red onion sets from our Philadelphia onion seed, which being earlier, make sets of better quality for keeping or immediate use than that grown in any other section. Philadelphia-grown onion sets are everywhere recognized as the best and are annually supplied to dealers and gardeners in every market of the United States. As the price varies with the market, we shall be glad to quote prices by the bushel or barrel of three bushels when requested to do so.

Those desiring to grow onion sets will find full directions for growing, harvesting and storing in our book of $100 Prize Essays. Price, 30c., post-paid, or may be had free. See Book Premiums, page 21.

YELLOW DUTCH and DANVERS ONION SETS, each, per qt., 20c.; qt., post-paid, 30c.

EXTRA EARLY RED ONION SETS, per qt., 25c.; qt., post-paid, 35c.

WHITE ONION SETS, qt., 30c.; qt., post-paid, 40c.

POTATO ONION SETS, qt., 35c.; qt., post-paid, 45c.

TOP ONION SETS, qt., 30c.; qt., post-paid, 40c.

EGYPTIAN WINTER, or PERENNIAL TREE ONION SETS, per qt., 40c.; qt., post-paid, 50c.

NEW WHITE MULTIPLIER ONION SETS, per qt., 30c.; qt., post-paid, 40c.

WE ARE HEADQUARTERS FOR ONION SETS, and sell cheaper by the peck, bushel or barrel. We will quote special prices on application. We grow sets of the foreign onions for fall shipments only, as the sets are hard to keep over winter and should be planted in the fall.

PARSLEY.

One ounce will sow one hundred and forty feet of drill.

EMERALD, or DWARF EXTRA CURLED. Leaves tender, beautifully crimped; handsome bright green color, very ornamental. Pkt., 5c.; oz., 10c.; ¼ lb., 30c.; lb., $1.00.

EXTRA DOUBLE CURLED. A curled variety for garnishing. Pkt., 5c.; oz., 10c.; ¼ lb., 25c.; lb., 90c.

Plain or Single. Dark green with plain leaves; very hardy. Pkt., 5c.; oz., 10c.; ¼ lb., 20c.; lb., 65c.

MARKET GARDENERS' BEST. The best points yet obtained in parsley have certainly been reached in this sort. The plant is of very robust and free in growth and is greatly improved by severe cutting. The leaves are large and beautifully curled and of a very dark green hue and very fine for either open ground or frame culture. It stands heat, drought and cold better than any other sort. Pkt., 10c.; oz., 15c.; ¼ lb., 50c.; lb., $1.25.

CHAMPION MOSS CURLED. Leaves crimped and curls like a bed of moss, giving a most beautiful decorative appearance. Pkt., 5c.; oz., 10c.; ¼ lb., 30c.; lb., $1.00.

NEW FERN-LEAVED. Very early, of fine form and color; used for garnishing as well as for a decorative plant. Pkt., 5c.; oz., 15c.; ¼ lb., 25c.; lb., 90c.

Hamburg, or Turnip-Rooted. A very popular variety in Europe. Fine, fleshy, vegetable roots, which are used in soups, etc. Pkt., 5c.; oz., 10c.; ¼ lb., 25c.; lb., 90c.

PARSNIP.

One ounce will sow about two hundred feet of drill; five pounds will sow one acre.

NEW IDEAL HOLLOW CROWN. We offer a greatly improved and wonderfully fine strain of true Hollow Crown Parsnip. The roots do not grow as long as the old Hollow Crown variety, are of larger diameter and more easily gathered. It is a very heavy cropper. The roots are very smooth, flesh fine grained and of excellent quality, the best variety for the market or home garden. Pkt., 5c.; oz., 10c.; ¼ lb., 25c.; lb., 75c.; 5 lbs. and over, 60c. per lb.

A. D. PINKERTON, Cherry Valley, Wash., writes: "Ideal Hollow Crown Parsnip is a great improvement on the common varieties, being much smoother, of better shape, sweeter and richer, cooking as quickly as a potato. I have plenty of them, three feet in length and six inches in diameter at the crown."

Large Sugar, or Long Smooth. Roots long, white, smooth, tender, sugary, excellent flavor. Pkt., 5c.; oz., 10c.; ¼ lb., 15c.; lb., 50c.

"I have sold vegetables from your seeds when others were not wanted at all."—J. B. IRVIN, Trempealeau, Wis.

"SPANISH KING PRODUCED THE FINEST CROP OF ONIONS EVER GROWN IN THIS PART OF THE STATE. THEY TOOK FIRST PREMIUM AT NEW JERSEY INTERSTATE FAIR."
PERKINS BROS., KINGSTON, N. J.

∴ SEEDS ∴ FOR ∴ MONEY ∴ GROWERS ∴

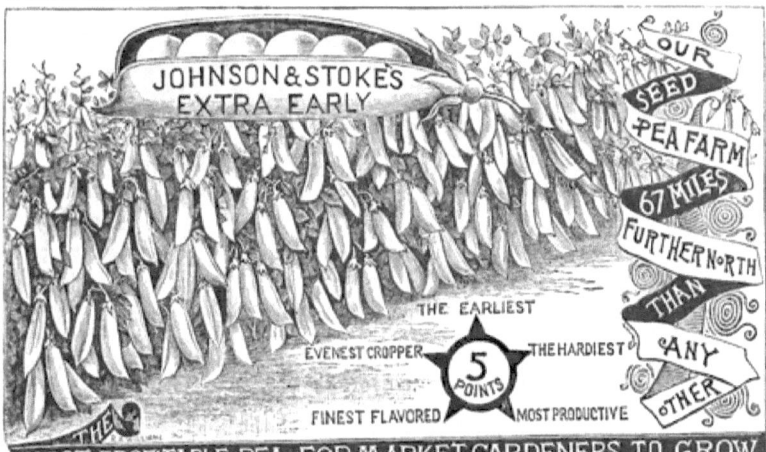

Johnson & Stokes' Selected Extra Early Peas.

This **Extra Early Pea**, bearing our brand, is a careful selection of our own, and will be found **entirely distinct and superior** to any other. Over 5,000 bushels of these peas are now annually sold by us to the market gardeners of the United States. No other pea grown has such a record as this. For several years past, we ourselves, and also many of the largest and most experienced truckers have made comparative trials with other leading brands of extra early peas, and in every case Johnson & Stokes' Extra Early was the first ready to pick by from three to five days. Our pea farm is situated in Ontario, Canada, sixty-seven miles further north than any other, which largely contributes to their extreme earliness and fine dwarf habit. The pod is of a dark green color, of a full round shape, and of strong texture, which especially fits it for shipping long distances. On average ground it will not exceed eighteen inches in height, and never more than two feet on the richest soil. It does not require stakes or brush of any kind for support. So evenly do the pods fill up, that frequently the entire crop can be gathered at one picking, never more than two pickings, which is a very valuable feature for the market gardener and trucker. All those requiring a pea to withstand extreme cold weather should not fail to plant this sort. The far northern point at which it is grown renders it almost proof against cold, and the best for early spring or late fall crop. While thousands of market gardeners have pronounced this pea **unequalled in earliness, yield and regularity of growth**, and in every sense a perfect truckers' pea, yet, at the same time, we know of no other variety more popular or better adapted to private gardens. Pkt., 10c.; pint, 25c.; qt., 45c., post-paid. Qt., 30c.; 2 qts., 50c.; 4 qts., 75c.; peck, $1.25; bush., $4.50; 5 bush., $21.00; 10 bush. and over, $4.00 per bush., by freight.

PEAS.

One quart will plant one hundred feet of drill. One and one-half to two bushels will plant one acre.

Please remember that our prices on all Peas by the pint and quart include prepayment of postage by us. If ordered to be sent by freight or express, 8c. per pint, or 15c. per quart may be deducted. **LARGE PACKETS OF ANY VARIETY, 10c. EACH.**

Early Varieties.

Those marked with a (*) are wrinkled varieties.

BLUE BEAUTY. This new sort, though not as early as our famous Johnson & Stokes' Selected Extra Early, still has many points of merit to recommend it. It is a blue, round pea, the pods are of medium size, are borne in great profusion and are well filled. In quality and flavor it cannot be surpassed by any other early smooth sort. Vines very uniform in growth, rarely reaching more than eighteen inches. Pkt., 10c.; pint, 25c.; qt., 45c.; peck, $1.15; bush., $4.25.

* **Laxton's Alpha.** The earliest blue wrinkled marrow; prolific, of fine flavor; pods large, height, two and one-half feet. Pkt., 10c.; pint, 20c.; qt., 40c.; peck, $1.25.

CLEVELAND'S ALASKA. The earliest blue pea, very uniform in growth. The dark green color of the pods makes it extremely desirable; as it can be carried long distances without losing color, which quality, combined with its earliness and uniformity of ripening, makes it a most desirable extra early pea for market gardeners; height, two feet. Pkt., 10c.; pint, 20c.; qt., 40c.; peck, $1.15; bush., $4.25.

Philadelphia Extra Early. (Carter's First Crop, or Early Kent.) An excellent variety, combining earliness and productiveness; height, two and one-half feet. Pint, 20c.; qt., 35c.; peck, $1.00; bush., $3.50.

* **AMERICAN WONDER.** This pea is a hybrid between the Champion of England and Little Gem, and possesses the merits of both. It is the earliest wrinkled variety, growing to the height of ten inches; very robust, producing large, well-filled pods; of fine flavor. Pkt., 10c.; pint, 25c.; qt., 45c.; peck, $1.60; bush., $6.00.

* **HORSFORD'S MARKET GARDEN.** This new wrinkled pea is the result of a cross between the Alpha and American Wonder. It requires no bushing, is extremely prolific, and bears its pods in pairs. Height, two feet. Pkt., 10c.; pint, 20c.; qt., 40c.; peck, $1.25; bush., $4.75.

* **McLEAN'S LITTLE GEM.** A first early, green wrinkled marrow, very prolific and of superior flavor; height, one foot. Pint, 20c.; qt., 40c.; peck, $1.25; bush., $4.75.

IT TAKES MORE RELIGION TO HOLD A MAN LEVEL IN A HORSE TRADE THAN IT DOES TO MAKE HIM SHOUT AT CAMP-MEETING.

Delicious New Pea—Sutton's Satisfaction.

A new pea from England, introduced by us three years ago, and which, according to the estimates of those who have tested it, promises to surpass the now celebrated Telephone and Stratagem. Their table qualities are the most **toothsome** and **delicious flavored** of any known variety of either American or foreign origin. This is **high praise**, but we believe does only justice to the **Satisfaction Pea**. The vine grows vigorously to height of about two and one-half feet, requiring no brush or sticks to hold them up, being very stocky and robust and literally filled with large **showy pods**, which almost hide completely their dark green foliage. They follow closely our best extra early sorts, being ready for the table **fifty-six days** from germination, and **continue in bearing longer** than any other early sort. The peas when green are unusually large, and of fine deep green color; when dry are very distinct in appearance, being much more wrinkled than any other sort.

WHAT THE LARGEST GROWERS OF PEAS AND BEANS IN THE WORLD THINK OF THEM.

MESSRS. N. B. KEENY & SON, who are well known as the largest pea growers in the world, write: "We are so much pleased with your Sutton's Satisfaction Pea that we want to report our test of same. The yield has been far greater than the average of all other varieties and the quality is first-class. They will be in brisk demand as soon as their fine qualities become known."

Sutton's Satisfaction has come to America to stay, not half-way up the ladder, but at the **very topmost round.** Pkt., 10c.; pint, 40c.; qt., 75c., postpaid. Qt. 60c.; 4 qts., $2.00; peck, $3.50, by express.

PREMIUM GEM. A fine, extra early variety; pods long and prolific; height fifteen inches; fine for forcing. Pkt., 10c.; pint, 25c.; qt., 40c.; peck, $1.35; bush., $5.00.

JOHNSON & STOKES' SECOND EARLY MARKET GARDEN PEA.

JOHNSON & STOKES' SECOND EARLY MARKET GARDEN. This valuable variety originated on our Canadian farm and is the best and most productive Second Early Pea on the market. Its fine medium-sized well-filled pods are ready for picking about a week after our Extra Early. The peas are larger and more wrinkled, when dry, than that variety, while in delicious flavor they are quite unsurpassed. It is also a prodigious bearer, having averaged seventy pods to the vine with ordinary field culture, and will produce more pods to the acre than any other pea in cultivation. The vines grow very uniformly to a height of two feet, and ripen up so evenly that the whole crop can be cleared off in two pickings. Pkt., 10c.; pint, 25c.; qt., 50c.; peck, $1.60; bush., $6.00.

McLEAN'S ADVANCER. A fine market variety, prolific, early, tender and of delicious flavor; height, two and one-half feet. Pint, 20c.; qt., 40c.; peck, $1.15; bush., $4.25.

BLISS ABUNDANCE. This new variety is claimed to be the most prolific variety known. Plant about eighteen inches high; foliage, large, thick, full and dark green. Pods three to three and one-half inches long, roundish and well filled, containing six to eight large wrinkled peas of excellent quality. Pint, 20c.; qt., 40c.; peck, $1.25; bush., $4.75.

Tom Thumb. Very dwarf, not exceeding ten inches in the richest soil, productive and of excellent quality. Pkt., 10c.; pint, 25c.; qt., 40c.; peck, $1.40.

McLean's Blue Peter. (Blue Tom Thumb.) One of the earliest and hardiest of the Tom Thumb varieties; blue seed, dark green pods, large peas of excellent quality; a capital bearer; height, nine inches. Pint 20c.; qt., 40c.

Improved Daniel O'Rourke. (First and best.) Seven to ten days later than Johnson & Stokes' Extra Early; very prolific; height, three feet. Qt., 35c.; peck, $1.00; bush., $3.40.

Late Varieties for General Crop.

Large pkts., 10c. each, postpaid.

LAXTON'S EVOLUTION. A new pea from England, growing about three feet in height, branching and bearing continuously the whole season; pods are very fine and large, containing eight to ten fine large wrinkled peas of unusually rich, sugary flavor. Pkt., 10c.; pint, 25c.; qt., 45c.

LONG ISLAND MAMMOTH (New). A favorite with the Long Island market gardeners, where it was originally introduced. An excellent cropper. Pods large size and well filled with peas of very good quality and earlier than the Champion of England. Seed green; height, three and one-half feet. Pkt., 10c.; pint, 35c.; qt., 50c.; peck, $1.75; bush., $6.50.

BLISS' EVERBEARING. This new pea is a cross between the Little Gem and the Champion of England; height, two feet; foliage large, firm and bright green; pods three to four inches long, each pod producing from six to eight large wrinkled peas; its habit of growth is of a peculiar branching character, forming as many as ten stalks from one root-stalk. Pint, 25c.; qt., 45c.; peck, $1.35; bush., $5.00.

CHAMPION OF ENGLAND. A most popular wrinkled variety of delicious flavor; a profuse bearer; height, five feet. Pkt., 10c.; pint, 20c.; qt., 40c.; peck, $1.10; bush., $4.00.

YORKSHIRE HERO. A large wrinkled, luscious and prolific variety; pods long, round and closely filled; for late crop it has few equals; height, three feet. Pkt., 10c.; pint, 25c.; qt., 45c.; peck, $1.25; bush., $4.50.

DWARF BLUE IMPERIAL. A favorite with market gardeners; a good bearer; fine flavor; height, two and one-half feet. Pint, 20c.; qt., 35c.; peck, $1.00; bush., $3.50.

A LEAD-PENCIL IS ONE OF THE VERY BEST OF FARM IMPLEMENTS FOR WINTER EVENING WORK.

SEEDS ∴ FOR ∴ MONEY ∴ GROWERS

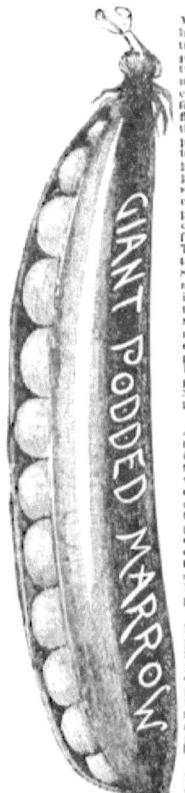

GIANT PODDED MARROW

PEANUT, OR GROUND PEA.

NEW GIANT PODDED MARROW. This new pea has given wonderful satisfaction to all who planted it the past two seasons. It grows about two feet high, and bears enormous handsome pods, seven to eight inches in length and well filled with large, deliciously flavored, deep green peas from the top to the bottom of the pod, as shown in our illustration. They are unequalled in productiveness, require no support, owing to their fine dwarf stocky habit, and are such heavy croppers that we know of no pea from which so large a bulk of produce can be obtained from a given number of vines. This variety is much harder than either the Telephone or Stratagem, and can be planted much earlier in consequence; it matures about ten days later than our famous Johnson & Stokes' Selected Extra Early, making it a valuable second early as well as our finest late pea. Your garden will not be complete without this grand pea. Pkt., 10c.; pint, 30c.; qt., 60c.; peck, $2.25; bush., $8.50.

CARTER'S STRATAGEM. A remarkably fine, new English variety, deserving the strongest praise. Height two feet, literally covered with large, handsome pods, often over six inches in length and containing from nine to ten very large, fine flavored peas. It is more sensitive to cold or wet weather than any other wrinkled sort, and on this account should not be sown until the ground is warm. Pkt., 10c.; pint, 30c.; qt., 50c.; peck, $1.75; bush., $6.75.

PRIDE OF THE MARKET. Another famous new pea from England, although introduced there but a few years since, has become one of the most popular of market peas. It bears very long pods, filled with fine large peas of superb quality. Height, one and one-half feet. Pkt., 10c.; pint, 30c.; qt., 50c.; peck, $1.75; bush., $6.50.

CARTER'S TELEPHONE. A very robust and productive English wrinkled variety, with long pods, containing ten to twelve very large, fine flavored peas. It is an enormous cropper; height, four and one-half feet. Pkt., 10c.; pint, 30c.; qt., 50c.; peck, $1.75; bush., $6.00.

ROYAL DWARF WHITE MARROWFAT. A large, delicious marrow pea; an excellent cropper and a favorite with market gardeners; height, two feet. Pint, 15c.; qt., 30c.; peck, 75c.; bush., $2.50; 5 bush., $2.25 per bush.

MELTING SUGAR. The best sugar pea, growing five feet in height, larger pods, more prolific and more delicious, in quality than the old varieties of sugar peas. The pods are without string, and snap equal to a wax bean and are used cooked in the same way. Pkt., 10c.; pint, 30c.; qt., 55c.

Dwarf Sugar. Edible pods when young; fine flavor; used like snap beans, also as a shelled variety; height, two feet. Pkt., 10c.; pint, 30c.; qt., 50c. post-paid.

Large White Marrowfat. A favorite late variety, with broad, well-filled pods; height, three feet. Qt., 30c.; peck, 65c.; bush., $2.10; 5 bush. and over, $2.00 per bush.

Black Eyed Marrowfat. This, as well as the White Marrowfat, is extensively grown as a field pea; hardy, productive, well-filled pods; height, three feet. Qt., 30c.; peck, 60c.; bush., $2.00; 5 bush. and over, $1.90 per bush.

PEAS—Field Varieties.

Write for special prices on large quantities.

Southern Black-Eye Cow Peas, (Whippoorwill,) The best for soiling. Qt., 30c.; bush., $2.00.

Canada Field Peas. Used as feed for pigeons, etc., and grown for canning; in a green state they are similar to the canned French peas. Qt., 30c.; bush., $1.75.

GEORGIA IMPROVED GROUND PEA, or PEANUT. This variety is much superior to the ordinary peanut, yielding fewer imperfect pods and containing each one more productiveness and size; yields on ordinary land over one hundred bushels to the acre. Full directions for planting, growing and harvesting printed on each packet. Large pkt., 15c.; pint, 30c.; qt., 50c., post-paid; peck, $2.00.

PEPPERS.

BELL, or BULL NOSE. A large, early, well-known variety, of mild flavor, rind thick and fleshy; the best for pickling. Pkt., 5c.; oz., 20c.; ¼ lb., 60c.; lb., $2.00.

NEW CARDINAL. This new pepper, offered for the first time last season, grows to a length of about six inches, very thick and sweet-fleshed and the most beautiful and brilliant vegetable grown. It would be worthy of cultivation for its beauty alone, there being no flower which can be grown in the North which equals it in depth, purity and brilliancy of color, appearing as though varnished in a bright cardinal. It will also be found a most useful variety, as it can be used for all purposes to which peppers are put. Pkt., 10c.; oz., 35c.; ¼ lb., $1.00; lb., $4.00.

RUBY KING PEPPER.

RUBY KING. This fine pepper grows to larger size than the Spanish Monstrous, and of different shape. The fruits are five to six inches long by about three and one-half inches through, of a bright red color. They are remarkably mild and pleasant in flavor, having no fiery taste whatever. Single plants ripen from eight to ten fruits, making them both productive and profitable. Pkt., 10c.; oz., 30c.; ¼ lb., 75c.; lb., $2.75.

PROCOPP'S GIANT. This new variety may be justly called the Goliath of all the pepper family. They grow uniformly to a very large size, measuring from eight to nine inches long, and three inches thick. They are of a brilliant scarlet color, flesh fully one-half inch in thickness. In flavor they are just hot enough to be pleasant to the taste. Each plant ripens from eight to twelve perfect fruits. Pkt., 10c.; 3 pkts., 25c.; oz., 5c.; ¼ lb., $4.00; lb., $3.50.

CORAL GEM BOUQUET. A wonderfully productive and handsome little pepper. The name given it was suggested by its handsome appearance, the whole plant resembling a "Bouquet of Corals," being literally covered with its small, bright, coral red fruits, which are quite hot and splendid for seasoning. Pkt., 10c.; oz., 40c.; ¼ lb., $1.00.

NEW DWARF EARLY RED SQUASH. A great improvement over the old Red Squash Pepper, being decidedly earlier and more prolific. It is of a dwarfer growth, while the fruit is rounder, smoother and milder in flavor; skin is also much thicker. Pkt., 10c.; oz., 25c.; ¼ lb., 75c.; lb., $2.50.

ALWAYS REMEMBER THE LARGEST ROOM IN THE WORLD IS THE ROOM FOR IMPROVEMENT.

JOHNSON & STOKES

Pkt., 10c.; 3 pkts., 25c.; oz., 40c.

MAMMOTH GOLDEN QUEEN. This is not only the best and most profitable mild pepper in cultivation, but is by far the *largest*, handsomest and most productive of *all varieties*, originated on our own grounds, growing to *twice the size* of Golden Dawn, and averaging a third larger than Ruby King. Of the most *perfect shape* and *uniform large size*. The above illustration is made from a photograph of a single fruit. They grow on a single plant from fifteen to twenty perfect fruits, from eight to ten inches long and four to five inches through. In color they are bright, waxy, golden yellow, and so mild in flavor they can be eaten like tomatoes, with pepper and vinegar. Our best market gardeners say they sell in market at *double the prices* of any other sorts, and are exceedingly valuable for stuffing as mangoes. Pkt., 10c.; oz., 40c.; ¼ lb. $1.00; lb., $3.75.

NEW CELESTIAL. A pepper marvel from China. It is not only a most useful pepper, but one of the *most beautiful plants in existence*. The plant begins to set in a pigmy early in the season, and continues until frost, branching freely and bearing profusely, single plants producing three hundred to four hundred perfect fruits. The peppers, up to the time they are full grown, are of delicate creamy yellow color, and when fully grown change to an intense vivid scarlet, making a plant when loaded with fruit—part one color and part another—an object of the most striking beauty and oddity, and worthy of a place in the flower as well as in the vegetable garden. The fruits are borne upright, two or three inches long, of clear, sharp flavor, and superior to any of the best sorts in which peppers can be put. Pkt., 10c.; 3 pkts., 25c.; oz., 50c.; ¼ lb., $1.50; lb., $3.75.

NEW OX-HEART. A small, heart-shaped pepper, of medium size, excellent for pickles; one of the best. Pkt., 5c.; oz., 25c.; ¼ lb., 75c.; lb., $2.75.

RED CLUSTER. This new pepper is undoubtedly a sport of the Chili, which it slightly resembles, the leaves and fruits are smaller, while it is much more productive, the fruits being curiously crowded together, making the plants extremely ornamental as well as useful. The peppers are very hot, long and very thin in shape, and of conspicuous coral red color. Pkt., 10c.; oz., 35c.; ¼ lb., 90c.; lb., $3.00.

Golden Dawn. In shape and size resembles the Bell. Color, bright yellow; very productive and entirely exempt from any fiery flavor; can be eaten as readily as an apple. Pkt. 5c.; oz., 25c.; ¼ lb., 75c.; lb., $2.50.

Sweet Mountain, or Mammoth. Similar to the Bull Nose in shape and color, but larger and milder. Pkt. 5c.; oz., 25c.; ¼ lb., 75c.; lb., $2.50.

LARGE SWEET SPANISH. Productive, mild flavor, fine top as King. Pkt., 5c.; oz., 20c.; ¼ lb., 60c.; lb., $2.25.

Long Red Cayenne. Three to four inches long, bright red color, very productive and hot. Pkt., 5c.; oz., 25c.; ¼ lb., 75c.; lb., $2.50.

Spanish Monstrous. A very large variety, very sweet, of good flavor. Pkt., 5c.; oz., 25c.; ¼ lb., 75c.; lb., $2.50.

Cheese. A large vines-shaped variety; used for pickling. Pkt., 5c.; oz., 25c.; ¼ lb., 75c.; lb., $2.50.

Cherry Red. A beautiful ornamental variety; fruit round, of a rich glossy color, and very hot; used for seasoning. Pkt., 5c.; oz., 25c.; ¼ lb., 75c.; lb., $2.50.

We make the selection of seed potatoes a specialty. Our stock as grown in the far North, by the most reliable growers, and for purity and superior quality cannot be excelled.

PLEASE NOTE.—As prices are subject to fluctuation, we would request that our customers send in their orders as soon as possible after receiving our Manual. All orders will be promptly acknowledged, and potatoes forwarded as soon as weather permits, in time for spring planting. Customers residing South can have them shipped at any time during the winter with little or no risk, but those residing North or West had better wait until the extreme freezing weather is over in March or early April, which will be in ample time for planting. To freeze potatoes, when packed in tight barrels, requires extremely cold weather. We ship each season several thousand barrels seed potatoes to nearly all sections, North, East and West, and rarely receive a complaint of freezing.

We pack our potatoes in **large round hoop barrels** of three bushels each and make no charge for bags, barrels or cartage. We will quote special prices on five barrels or one variety.

The following varieties have been tested in various parts of the country and have met with unqualified approval. They are selected, as those most worthy of consideration and tried excellency, and known to be good.

POTATOES BY MAIL. All potatoes will be sent by mail, postage prepaid, at 30c. per pound; 4 pounds for $1.00, carefully labelled and packed.

EARLY MAINE. This new variety was originated from a seed ball of the Early Rose, which it resembles. They grow very smooth, and are remarkably early and productive. Raised on a large scale, they yielded, in Massachusetts, as high as four hundred and ten bushels to the acre. Peck, 60c.; bush., $1.50; bbl., $3.25.

EARLY PURITAN. This new variety originated with Mr. E. L. Coy, of Washington County, N. Y., originator of the well-known and popular Early Beauty of Hebron. Mr. Coy says his Early Puritan far excels the Beauty of Hebron in productiveness and quality, which indeed is saying a great deal in its favor. The skin and flesh is very white; it cooks dry and mealy, even when half grown. It ripens with the Early Rose, greatly exceeds it in productiveness; the vines grow strong, fast and vigorous, standing up firm as a tree. Peck, 65c.; bush., $1.50; bbl., $3.25.

THE POLARIS. This potato originated in Northern Vermont. It is of long oval shape and creamy-white in color, cooking as white as the finest flour; is hardy, prolific, handsome, early and a good keeper. With the originator it has yielded at the rate of six hundred bushels per acre. It has made for itself a wonderful record during the past few years wherever grown. Peck, 65c.; bush., $1.60; bbl., $3.40.

LEE'S FAVORITE. This new potato is said to be a week earlier than Beauty of Hebron, resembling the Early Rose in shape, but with lighter skin. It has yielded over four hundred bushels to the acre, and its quality is all that can be desired. Peck, 60c.; bush., $1.50; bbl., $3.25.

PEARL OF SAVOY. This new variety is a cross of Clark's No. 1 and Extra Early Vermont. Quite as early as the Early Rose, very productive and vigorous in growth. The tubers are oblong, fair and of large size, the flesh is pearly-white. Peck, 60c.; bush., $1.50; bbl., $3.25.

PRINCE EDWARD ISLAND EARLY ROSE. Our stock of this popular variety is imported direct from Prince Edward Island, where we find them in their original purity, most of the stock of Early Rose now grown in the States being mixed and inferior. Peck, 60c.; bush., $1.50; bbl., $3.25.

IF YOU WANT YOUR BOY TO LOVE YOU, DON'T MAKE HIM HOE POTATOES IN THE BACK YARD WHILE A BRASS BAND IS PASSING THE HOUSE.

∴ SEEDS ∴ FOR ∴ MONEY ∴ GROWERS ∴

The Crown Jewel Potato.

The Crown Jewel Still Leads as the Earliest and Best of all Extra Early Sorts.

Every claim we have made for it has been fully substantiated by more than five hundred of our largest potato growers and truckers for early market, all of whom vote it as the very earliest and finest they have ever seen. It is a seedling of the Early Ohio. The seed-balls were found in a large field of that well-known variety, and it partakes of all the pure and unadulterated qualities of its excellent parent, without any admixture of baser blood. Its skin is white and smooth, eyes shallow, but strong; flesh pure white and floury, cooking evenly throughout. The vines grow vigorously, the roots extend very deeply into the soil, thus resisting drought, and its keeping qualities are equal to the best. Its extreme earliness makes it the most profitable potato for early market or home consumption. Lb., 30c.; 4 lbs., $1.00, post-paid; peck, 65c.; bush., $1.75; bbl. of 3 bush., $4.00; 5 bbls., $19.00; 10 bbls. and over, $3.75 per bbl.

Bliss' Triumph, or Improved Bermuda Potato.

This beautiful variety combines the wonderful productiveness of the Peerless with all the good qualities of the Early Rose, is much more productive, and matures its crop at least a week in advance of the Early Rose. Tubers are of medium size, round and uniform in shape, with but a very few small ones; eyes slightly depressed; color a beautiful light red; flesh fine grained and excellent flavor.

The tubers grow compactly in the hill and are easily harvested. It is an excellent keeper, not inclined to sprout early. Its great beauty, productiveness and fine quality will make it one of the best market varieties in cultivation. It is now being planted on the Island of Bermuda to the exclusion of nearly all others, having supplanted almost entirely the old Bermuda potato, and is the first potato to reach our markets from the Bermudas. It has become so popular in some sections of the South that, notwithstanding we grew large crops the past two seasons, the entire stock was exhausted before the selling season was half over, obliging us to return many orders. Lb., 30c.; 4 lbs., $1.00, post-paid; peck, 65c.; bush., $1.75; bbl., 3 bush., $4.00; 10 bbls. and over, $3.75 per bbl.

Rural New Yorker, No. 2, Potato.

This, the best intermediate and main crop potato, originated on the experimental grounds of the *Rural New Yorker*, where more than five hundred varieties have been tested practically during the past twelve years. It has been tried there and elsewhere for several years with much care, and critically watched by its experienced originator for the development of weak points, any of which would have caused it to be promptly discarded. So far it may well lay claim to being a perfect potato, and is so pronounced by hundreds of our largest potato growers, who are now planting their whole crops with it.

The "Rural New Yorker, No. 2," is a potato of most distinct appearance, and could readily be distinguished among a hundred others. It is very large and unusually smooth, with few and shallow eyes; in form it is oblong, inclining to round, the skin is white, as is the flesh, which is of superior quality. In maturity the variety is intermediate, and its solidity and vigor are such that it has rotted less in very wet seasons than any of the numerous sorts grown with it. The vines are heavy and strong and the yield of handsome tubers of great uniformity of size is unusually large—less than ten per cent. of the potatoes dug have been of unmarketable size. Lb., 30c.; 4 lbs., $1.00, post-paid; peck, 65c.; bush., $1.75; bbl., 3 bush., $4.75; 10 bbls. and over, $3.50 per bbl.

Something New—Potato Eyes by Mail, Postage Paid

To Save Our Customers Money Owing to the heavy expense of sending potatoes long distances, by express and freight, we last season adopted a plan of sending out potato eyes by mail to any part of the world, which will enable our customers (no matter how far away) to test the new and choice varieties of northern-grown seed potatoes we offer, at trifling cost. The way we do this is to cut out the eye with a piece of the potato attached, and a sufficient depth to insure its vitality after being transported thousands of miles. After the eyes are cut out they are carefully packed with damp moss in boxes made thin and strong, carefully labelled and sent to their destination. When received they should be carefully removed from the boxes, care being taken to note the labels on different varieties. If too soon to be planted out-doors, they should be placed with damp earth in a box where there is no danger of freezing. We send out none but the strongest and best eyes, which will produce crops as good as if the whole tubers were planted. Owing to the amount of labor attached to preparing and packing the eyes for safe shipment, we can only offer the eyes of the newest varieties, described above. For $1.00 we will send, all postage paid, 60 good strong eyes of either **Crown Jewel, Bliss' Triumph**, or **Rural New Yorker, No. 2**; 100 eyes for $1.50, or 200 for $2.00. For $3.00 we will send 100 eyes each, post-paid, of all three of the new potatoes, **Crown Jewel, Bliss' Triumph** and **Rural New Yorker, No. 2**. This collection of three hundred eyes will produce thirty to forty bushels of nice potatoes.

"CROWN JEWELS PLANTED APRIL 7TH, DUG JUNE 14TH—67 DAYS. OVER 200 BUSHELS TO AN ACRE."
JOHN KERNS, CLARKSBORO, N. J.

POTATOES—Continued.

NEW LATE PURITAN. Identical with the Early Puritan in color, appearance and quality but later and more productive. Peck, 60c.; bush., $1.25; bbl., $3.00.

THE SUPERIOR, or COY'S SEEDLING, No. 88. A seedling of the White Star, which it strongly resembles. Skin and flesh very white, of excellent quality. They ripen medium late. Peck, 60c.; bush., $1.50; bbl., $4.25.

The following STANDARD POTATOES are so well-known that we do not give them a detailed description.

EARLY SUNRISE. Peck, 65c; bush; $1.50; bbl., $3.25.
CLARK'S No. 1. Peck, 65c; bush., $1.50; bbl., $3.25.
AMERICAN MAGNUM BONUM. Peck, 65c.; bush., $1.05; bbl., $3.46.
STRAY BEAUTY. Peck, 65c.; bush., $1.60; bbl., $3.10.
EARLY OHIO. Peck, 65c.; bush., $1.50; bbl., $3.00.
EARLY BEAUTY OF HEBRON. Peck, 50c; bush., $1.40; bbl., $3.00.
EXTRA EARLY VERMONT. Peck, 50c.; bush., $1.40; bbl., $3.00.
MAINE, or HOULTON EARLY ROSE. Peck, 60c; bush., $1.40; bbl., $3.25.
MAMMOTH PEARL. Peck, 60c.; bush., $1.50; bbl., $3.25.
QUEEN OF THE VALLEY. Peck, 60c.; bush., $1.50; bbl., $3.25.
RURAL BLUSH. Peck, 60c; bush., $1.50; bbl., $3.25.
EMPIRE STATE. Peck, 60c.; bush., $1.50; bbl., $3.25.
MAMMOTH PROLIFIC. Peck, 60c.; bush., $1.50; bbl., $3.00.
WHITE STAR. Peck, 50c; bush., $1.40; bbl., $3.00.
WHITE ELEPHANT, or LATE BEAUTY OF HEBRON. Peck, 60; bush., $1.50; bbl., $3.25.
BELLE. Peck, 50c; bush., $1.50; bbl., $3.25.
BURBANK'S SEEDLING. Peck, 50c.; bush., $1.40; bbl., $3.00.
PEERLESS. Peck, 65c; bush., $1.40; bbl., $3.00.

✦ ✦ POTATO SEED. ✦ ✦

MIXED. From the best hybridizers. Pkt., 25c.; 5 pkts., $1.00.

THE CONCAVE AND CURVED SEED POTATO KNIFE is thin and right shape to cut to one, two or three eye pieces fast and not crush the tuber or injure the germs. Endorsed by planters everywhere; thousands now in use.

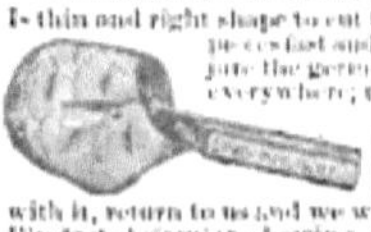

Give this knife a fair trial and if you are not satisfied that it will pay you to cut your potatoes with it, return to us and we will refund your money. Illustrated circular, showing structure and full directions for cutting, with each knife. Price, **30c. each, post-paid**.

SEED SWEET POTATOES.

We make a specialty of seed sweet potatoes, growing our stock exclusively in New Jersey, about nine miles from our Philadelphia warehouse, where we have unequalled facilities for handling and storing. We pack them for shipment in boxes and barrels, with the greatest care; but as they are very susceptible to climatic changes, we cannot hold ourselves responsible for their condition on arrival after long journeys of several hundred miles.

EXTRA EARLY CAROLINA—THE EARLIEST SWEET POTATO.

SWEET POTATO—EXTRA EARLY CAROLINA. This wonderful variety originated in North Carolina, and is far superior to all other varieties in earliness, productiveness and quality. Of a bright yellow color, shape nearly round, and shorter than the ordinary varieties. Will produce fine edible tubers in ten weeks from planting slips. Owing to its extreme earliness, it is better adapted to cultivation in the Northern States than any other variety. Does well on any ordinary soil, and is the best of keepers. Price per peck, $1.00; bush., $2.00; bbl., $5.00. Price of plants, ready May 1st, 85c. per 100, by mail, post-paid; 50c. per 100; $4.50 per 1,000, by express.

NEW JERSEY SWEET AND EARLY NANSEMOND. The justly celebrated Philadelphia Sweet Potatoes universally grown for Philadelphia and New York markets. Peck, 75c.; bush., $2.50; bbl., $4.00.

Plants of the above varieties ready May 1st, 75c. per 100, by mail, post-paid; 50c. per 100, $2.50 per 1,000, by express.

PUMPKIN.

One pound will plant two hundred to two hundred and fifty hills; four to six pounds are required to plant one acre.

LARGE CHEESE PUMPKIN.

LARGE CHEESE. One of the best for table use; very productive; skin orange; flesh yellow and sweet. Shape as shown in above cut. Pkt., 5c.; oz., 10c.; ¼ lb., 25c.; lb., 60c.

NEW JAPANESE PIE PUMPKIN. This remarkable variety comes from Japan, and has proven a valuable addition to our pie and cooking pumpkins. The flesh is very thick, and of a rich salmon color, nearly solid, the seed cavity being very small in one end of the pumpkin, unusually fine grained, dry and sweet, having much the same taste and appearance as sweet potatoes, making pies as rich without eggs as other varieties do with. They ripen early, keep well and produce largely. The seeds are peculiarly marked and sculptured in Japanese characters. Pkt., 5c.; oz., 10c.; ¼ lb., 30c.; lb., $1.00.

DUNKARD WINTER PUMPKIN. This hybrid variety originated with the religious sect of Dunkards in Bucks County, Pa., where it has had a local reputation for a few years past. They are oblong in shape and frequently attain weights of twenty to twenty-five pounds. The outside skin is a rich, deep orange color, lightly striped. The flesh is very thick and of a beautiful golden-yellow color, very rich and sweet in flavor. Their most wonderful property is their great keeping qualities, having been kept for a period of two years in perfect condition. The vines are very hardy and productive. They sell in Philadelphia markets at double the prices of other varieties. Owing to the hybrid origin of the variety, they as yet vary some in shape, there being a tendency to sport back to the original parents. All specimens, however, are equally good in quality. Pkt., 10c., oz., 20c.; ¼ lb., 60c.; lb., $1.50.

NEW GOLDEN OBLONG PUMPKIN. A very fine, new and productive variety, growing oblong to a length of sixteen to eighteen inches and seven to eight inches in diameter. The outside skin is dark green when young, changing to a deep golden color as it ripens. Flesh rich yellow, very sweet, dry and excellent for pies. Its keeping qualities are almost if not quite equal to our best winter squashes. All lovers of fine pumpkins should try the Golden Oblong. Pkt., 5c.; oz., 10c.; ¼ lb. 20c.; lb., $1.00.

GOLDEN MARROW. A splendid pie pumpkin. They are slightly ribbed, skin is of a deep orange color, flesh fine and of excellent flavor, cook soft and tender, and are excellent keepers. The vines are very productive and hardy. Pkt., 5c.; oz., 10c.; ¼ lb., 25c.; lb., 70c.

CASHAW. Long, yellow crookneck; splendid for table use or feeding stock; flesh yellow, solid, fine grained and sweet. Pkt., 5c.; oz., 10c.; ¼ lb., 25c.; lb., 75c.

NEW BANANA, or CUSTARD. A splendid little pumpkin of finest quality for pies and custards. They grow rather oblong in form, and have ten prominent ridges their entire length; flesh rich yellow, sweet and delicious. They produce largely, and are great keepers. Pkt., 5c.; oz., 15c.; ¼ lb., 35c.; lb., $1.25.

JONATHAN PUMPKIN. This new pumpkin is pronounced by a veteran pumpkin grower one of the finest varieties he has ever grown. It is a good keeper, of large size, very prolific, smooth and even fleshed; very sweet and fine for pies. Pkt., 5c.; oz.; 10c.; ¼ lb., 30c.; lb., $1.00.

"BY HONESTY AND LIBERALITY YOUR FIRM HAS GAINED THE HIGHEST ESTEEM AND CONFIDENCE OF ALL MARKET GARDENERS HERE."
C. W. HILDEBRAND, POUGHKEEPSIE, N. Y.

∴ SEEDS ∴ FOR ∴ MONEY ∴ GROWERS ∴

The Great Prize Pumpkin, King of the Mammoths.

✦ ✦ ✦ $50.00 CASH FOR HEAVIEST GROWN IN 1892. ✦ ✦ ✦

Our attention was first called to this truly colossal variety while visiting France, in 1884, where we first secured seed, and distributed it among our customers. The results have been astonishing. No other pumpkin ever introduced has reached such enormous weights, and been awarded as many prizes. In competition for our cash prizes the past seven seasons, hundreds of our customers have raised specimens weighing over one hundred and fifty pounds each, the heaviest ever grown being two hundred and fifty pounds, in 1889. The heaviest weights attained in 1891, and for which our cash prizes were awarded are as follows: First prize, one hundred and ninety-five pounds, to H. S. Vetter, Stockholm, N. J.; second prize, one hundred and eighty and one-half pounds, to Thomas McAlowan, Ambler, Pa.; third prize, one hundred and seventy-two pounds, to Jonas F. Yost, Tohickon, Pa. The prize-winning specimens are at this writing on exhibition in front of our store, and being located on the principal business street of Philadelphia, it is needless to say they are constantly surrounded by an admiring crowd, our fall pumpkin show having become quite a feature of the town. We offer

∴ ∴ $50.00 IN THREE CASH PRIZES FOR HEAVIEST SPECIMENS GROWN IN 1892. ∴ ∴

$25.00 for heaviest; $15.00 for second heaviest; $10.00 for third heaviest. All reports of weights to be sent in by October 15th, at which time the prize-winning specimens will be ordered sent to us (at our expense), and cash forwarded to the successful competitors. With one of these pumpkins you would also be sure of a first prize at your county fair. The flesh and skin of a bright golden-yellow color, very fine grained, of excellent quality, and notwithstanding its enormous size, it is one of the very best pie or table pumpkins ever grown, and a splendid keeper.

PRICES FOR 1892: Seeds saved from specimens selected from our patch, weighing one hundred pounds and over, pkt., 25c.; 5 pkts., $1.00. Seeds saved from general crop, all good, large, uniform specimens, pkt., 10c.; oz., 30c.; 2 oz., 40c.; ¼ lb., 90c.; lb., $3.00.

OTHER FOREIGN PUMPKINS.

GRAY BOULOGNE. Grows to very large size, and although quite new, is already very popular. It is large, round and slightly flattened on the ends, skin of a grayish-green color, growing to a weight of sixty to seventy-five pounds with ordinary culture, and with special culture will reach enormous size. Pkt., 10c.; oz., 18c.; ¼ lb., 40c.; lb., $1.25.

MAMMOTH ETAMPES BRIGHT RED. This giant variety, also from France, is quite celebrated, and has been grown in this country to enormous size; it is of a bright glossy red color, a splendid variety to grow for exhibition purposes. Pkt., 10c.; oz., 15c.; ¼ lb., 46c.; lb., $1.25.

MAMMOTH TOURS. A French variety, which grows to an immense size, often weighing over one hundred pounds. Pkt., 5c.; oz., 10c.; ¼ lb., 25c.; lb., 75c.

JOHNSON ∴ & ∴ STOKES ∴

IMPROVED GREEN STRIPED CASHAW PUMPKIN.

GREEN STRIPED, or IMPROVED CASHAW. This is a great improvement on the well-known Yellow Cashaw Pumpkin in very many respects, and those who have tried the Yellow Cashaw entirely. They are much more beautiful in appearance, being a distinct growth, green and white striped, as shown in the above cut. The flesh is a rich yellow color, solid, fine grained, very thick, sweet and excellent for pies, and equally good for baking. They are very hardy, bugs seldom bother them, can be grown among the corn, and yield a much heavier crop than Yellow Cashaw, and better for stock feeding. They are hard to beat. Try them. Pkt., 5c.; oz., 10c.; ¼ lb., 25c.; lb., $1.00.

TRUE TENNESSEE SWEET POTATO. A splendid pie and cooking pumpkin. They grow to medium size, slightly ribbed; skin is a creamy white, lightly striped with green; flesh very thick, creamy white, dry and fine grained, keeping well until late in the spring; when cooked resembles sweet potatoes, but much more delicious in taste. The vines are hardy and enormously productive. Pkt., 5c.; oz., 10c.; ¼ lb., 30c.; lb., 60c.

QUAKER PIE PUMPKIN. A distinct variety from New York State, where it has been grown for many years by a family of "Quakers" or Friends. The shape is nearly oval, tapering slightly towards the ends. Color, creamy white, both inside and out; flesh is sweet and rich, and an excellent keeper. Pkt., 5c.; oz., 10c.; ¼ lb., 20c.; lb., 65c.

SMALL SUGAR. A very handsome little pumpkin with deep orange-colored skin, and flesh of unusually fine sugary flavor; fine grained; very productive, and keeps well. Pkt., 5c.; oz., 10c.; ¼ lb., 20c.; lb., 65c.

NANTUCKET SUGAR. This great pie pumpkin is comparatively unknown outside of a few of the far Eastern States, where it is used exclusively in making the celebrated Yankee Pumpkin Pies. The skin is very dark green, almost black, flesh thick and of a rich orange yellow. They weigh from twelve to fifteen pounds, and will keep for a year. Pkt., 5c.; oz., 10c.; ¼ lb., 25c.; lb., 75c.

TRUE POTIRON. Another wonderful variety from France, somewhat resembling our celebrated "King of Mammoths" in shape. They, however, do not grow so large and weigh so heavy, so their flesh is thin and watery. Pkt., 10c.; oz., 25c.; ¼ lb., 60c.; lb., $2.00.

Common Yellow Field. Very productive and grown for feeding stock. Pkt., 5c.; oz., 10c.; lb., 35c.; 10 lbs., $2.00.

SPECIAL ▲

We offer a **CASH PRIZE** of **$50.00** to the growers of the largest Pumpkins in 1892.

As an extra inducement for competition, and that our customers may give all our Mammoth varieties a trial, we will send, free by mail, **one packet each, King of Mammoths, Mammoth Bright Red Etampes, Gray Boulogne, and Mammoth Tours**, giving a magnificent collection of mammoth pumpkins, **for 25 cents.**

RHUBARB. Pie Plant.

One ounce will produce about one thousand plants.
Large Victoria. An excellent cooking variety. Pkt., 5c.; oz., 20c.; ¼ lb., 60c.; lb., $1.75.
Rhubarb Root. Each, 30c.; doz. $1.75; 100, $8.00. By mail, post-paid, 30c. each, or $1.75 per doz.

SORREL.

Large-Leaved Garden. Cultivated for its acidity and much used in salads. Pkt., 5c.; oz., 20c.; ¼ lb., 50c.

One ounce will sow one hundred feet of drill; nine pounds will sow one acre in drills.

THE STARTLE, or TWENTY-DAY FORCING. The earliest half-long red forcing radish, selected by a Philadelphia market gardener. See Specialties, page 19. Pkt., 5c.; oz., 10c.; ¼ lb., 30c.; lb., $1.00.

FELTON'S MODEL WHITE BOX. The best early white radish. Truly a model. See Novelties and Specialties, page 19. Pkt., 10c.; oz., 15c.; ¼ lb., 35c.; lb., $1.25.

EARLY SCARLET GLOBE. For forcing in the greenhouse, hot-beds or cold frames and for sowing in open borders early in the spring there is no other red variety more desirable. It is entirely distinct and one of the earliest; in flavor it is mild, crisp, juicy and tender. It forms a small top and will stand a great amount of heat without becoming pithy. Pkt., 5c.; oz., 10c.; ¼ lb., 25c.; lb., 90c.; 5 lbs. and over, 75c. per lb.

ROSY GEM, or RAPID FORCING (White Tipped Scarlet Ball). Since we first introduced this wonderful new radish it has won golden opinions in all sections of the country. It is one of the very earliest in cultivation, being a week earlier than Scarlet Turnip White Tipped, which it somewhat resembles in form and color. Their shape is perfectly globular, with rich deep scarlet top, blending into pure white at the bottom, exceedingly tender, crisp and delicious, never becoming hollow or pithy, very desirable for forcing, being fit to pull in three weeks from sowing, and should be planted by everybody. Pkt., 5c.; oz., 10c.; ¼ lb., 30c.; lb., $1.00.

NEW FIREBALL. The shape of this exceedingly valuable variety is well shown in the above illustration, although it grows nearly twice the size. It is the finest red forcing turnip variety ever introduced; has a very small, short top. Color, brilliant scarlet, crisp, solid, tender and of fine flavor. It is alike valuable for out-door planting early in the spring or in the autumn, and will always command ready sale at good prices throughout the year. It will not disappoint a single market or family gardener who sows it. Pkt., 5c.; oz., 10c.; ¼ lb., 30c.; lb., $1.00.

"MY KING OF MAMMOTHS TOOK FIRST PREMIUM AT THE COUNTY FAIR; ALSO SPECIAL PRIZE OF PAIR BOOTS OFFERED BY AN OSHKOSH SHOE FIRM." THOS. DAVIS, OSHKOSH, WIS.

∴ SEEDS ∴ FOR ∴ MONEY ∴ GROWERS ∴

PHILADELPHIA GARDENERS' LONG SCARLET. This very excellent new strain is the result of years of patient and careful selection. There is just as much difference between this strain and the European as generally sold, as there is between the American and European grown potato. Briefly stated, the improvements are these: it is fully six days earlier, has a shorter and more compact top, will remain in the ground longer without becoming jelly or going to seed. In shape it is somewhat shorter and thicker, thus enabling it to withstand transportation better, which is a very desirable feature. In color the upper portion is of an unusually deep brilliant red, which gradually shades to a deep waxy pink towards the tip. Owing to its handsome shape, brilliant color and fine eating qualities, it invariably commands a higher price, and more ready sale than any other Long Scarlet. Gardeners everywhere should plant this fine strain. No other can equal it. Pkt., 5c.; oz., 10c.; ¼ lb., 25c.; lb., 80c.; 5 lbs. and over, 65c. per lb.

NEW WHITE LADY-FINGER RADISH. This is unquestionably the finest long white radish in cultivation. Shape most attractive and handsome, as shown in our illustration, while in color it is a beautiful snow white. It is of very rapid growth and its fine white flesh is remarkably crisp, brittle and tender, equally desirable for the market or home garden. Sow Lady-Finger once and you will sow it always. Pkt. 5c.; oz., 10c.; ¼ lb., 25c.; lb., 75c.

PHILADELPHIA WHITE "BOX." This variety, previous to our introduction of Felton's Model White Box, which is superseding it, was the most popular Early White Radish grown by Philadelphia gardeners. Its short top and rapid growth especially fits it for growing under glass, in frames or "boxes," hence its name; as well as for early sowing on squares or borders in the open ground. Owing to its very few short leaves, it can be sown very thickly without causing the leaves to "draw." Pkt. 5c.; oz., 10c.; ¼ lb., 25c.; lb., 85c.

Extra Early White Turnip. Pure white, of very quick growth and small top. Pkt., 5c.; oz., 10c.; ¼ lb., 20c.; lb., 60c.

SCARLET TURNIP, WHITE TIPPED. Resembling the above in shape, except of a deep scarlet color, with white tip; very handsome. Pkt., 5c.; oz., 10c.; ¼ lb., 20c.; lb., 60c.

Early Deep Scarlet, Olive-Shaped. Flesh rose-colored and very tender. Pkt., 5c.; oz., 10c.; ¼ lb., 20c.; lb., 60c.

PARIS BEAUTY. Demi-long Deep Scarlet. This handsome variety is the most popular early radish sold in the markets of Paris. In shape they are intermediate between the popular Long Scarlet and Scarlet Olive. They are of rapid growth, with rich deep scarlet skin, white flesh, very tender and crisp. Pkt., 5c.; oz., 10c.; ¼ lb., 25c.; lb., 80c.

Early Long Scarlet, or Salmon. The old standard family and market gardeners' variety. Long, bright scarlet, with small top. Pkt., 5c.; oz., 10c.; ¼ lb., 20c.; lb., 50c.

JOHNSON & STOKES' NEW SCARLET OLIVE. A decided improvement on the ordinary deep scarlet olive-shaped radish, of better shape, and handsomest in color of all deep red sorts; very popular in the South for shipment to Northern markets and although only introduced by us three years since, is now largely grown. Pkt., 5c.; oz., 10c.; ¼ lb., 30c.; lb., $1.00.

Extra Early Scarlet Turnip. A round, deep scarlet, turnip-shaped, small-top variety, of quick growth; mild and crisp when young. Pkt., 5c.; oz., 10c.; ¼ lb., 20c; lb., 60c.

EARLIEST ROUND DARK RED (Scarlet Button). An improved strain of the Extra Early Scarlet, of deeper color and handsomer appearance; very early, firm, crisp and of extra fine quality. Pkt., 5c.; oz., 10c.; ¼ lb., 25c.; lb., 75c.

NEWCOM. This new radish, introduced by us four years ago, has already taken a leading place with our market and family gardeners. It is the earliest, largest white radish known. Owing to their beautiful half-long shape and fine appearance, they readily sell at double the prices of ordinary varieties. Quality very superior and they hold their fine eating condition four or five weeks after being fit to pull. They stand heat and cold to a remarkable extent; small top. Pkt., 5c.; oz., 10c.; ¼ lb., 25c.; lb., 75c.

Early White, Olive-Shaped. Of fine olive shape; skin and flesh white, crisp, tender and of very quick growth. Pkt., 5c.; oz., 10c.; ¼ lb., 20c.; lb., 60c.

WOOD'S EARLY FRAME. A splendid forcing variety, earlier than the Long Scarlet, shape not quite so long and has a smaller top. Pkt., 5c.; oz., 10c.; ¼ lb., 20c.; lb., 60c.

Early French Breakfast. Of quick growth, very tender and beautiful, oval shape; scarlet, tipped with white; a great favorite. Pkt., 5c.; oz., 10c.; ¼ lb., 20c.; lb., 60c.

RADISH. Summer Varieties.

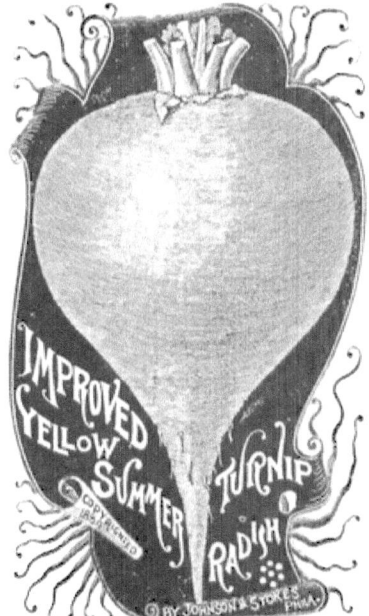

NEW IMPROVED YELLOW SUMMER TURNIP. This exceedingly fine type of yellow summer radish, is the result of hybridizing and many years' continued selection by an experienced Philadelphia market gardener. The neck is much smaller, leaves finer, flesh whiter and of a much better shape, as shown in above cut, than the old Yellow Summer, and always commands a readier sale at a higher figure, and withstands the summer heat better. Market and private gardeners will find it a most valuable acquisition. Pkt., 5c.; oz., 10c.; ¼ lb., 30c.; lb., $1.00.

THE CENTRE LEAVES OF A RADISH SHOULD BE EATEN ALONG WITH THE RADISH, AS THEY RENDER EASIER THE DIGESTION OF THE RADISH ITSELF.

RADISH (Summer Varieties)—Continued.

NEW WHITE STRASBURG. This valuable variety was introduced by us eight years ago, and is now the most popular summer radish grown. Of handsome oblong shape, tapering beautifully to a point, both skin and flesh are pure white and almost translucent, very tender and of a delightful pungent taste. It can be pulled five weeks from time of sowing the seed and continues to grow without losing its fine quality, and remains in a tender condition longer than any other summer sort. There is much cheap and spurious seed being offered. Procure your stock direct from the introducers, and have it reliable. Pkt., 5c.; oz., 10c.; ¼ lb., 25c.; lb., 75c.; 5 lbs. and over, 60c. per lb.

LARGE WHITE SUMMER TURNIP, or GLOBE. A general favorite; of large turnip shape and beautiful form, pure white skin and flesh, very crisp. Our strain of this variety is the finest known to Philadelphia and New York truckers. Pkt., 5c.; oz., 10c.; ¼ lb., 20c.; lb., 60c.; 5 lbs., $2.75.

CHARTIER, or SHEPHERD RADISH. A variety of the Long Scarlet, originated in Western Pennsylvania. It is exceedingly handsome and attractive, being of a deep crimson color at the top and blending off to almost white at the bottom. It is very tender, and remains so for a long time after attaining its growth, an important feature to the market gardener. Pkt., 5c.; oz., 10c.; ¼ lb., 20c.; lb., 65c.

OLIVE-SHAPED GOLDEN YELLOW. This is a fine new German radish, equally well adapted as an early forcing or summer radish. It is of very rapid growth and fine quality, flesh white, tender, crisp and brittle. The outside skin is a bright, fresh yellow, and has a very small top. Pkt., 5c.; ¼ lb., 20c.; lb., $1.20.

Long White Naples. A long, clear, white radish; crisp, tender and mild. Pkt., 5c.; oz., 10c.; ¼ lb., 20c.; lb., 70c.

WHITE GIANT STUTTGART. Will produce roots of excellent quality and as large as a winter radish, in six to eight weeks after sowing. Pkt., 5c.; oz., 10c.; ¼ lb., 20c.; lb., 70c.

NEW SURPRISE. A variety from Spain, very early, light brown skin, pure white flesh, crisp and tender keeps in fine eating condition without getting pithy for a long time. Pkt., 5c.; oz., 10c.; ¼ lb., 20c.; lb., 60c.

NEW CELESTIAL, or WHITE CHINESE. Has been grown for a few years past by California gardeners, who obtained it direct from China. It is an "All-seasons Radish," being ready for use when three inches long and continues until nearly six inches long. Flesh firm, solid and pure white. Pkt., 5c.; oz., 10c.; ¼ lb., 25c.; lb., 60c.

RADISH—Winter Varieties.

CHINA ROSE WINTER. One of the best winter varieties, bright rose-colored; flesh white, firm and of superior quality. Pkt., 5c.; oz., 10c.; ¼ lb., 20c.; lb., $1.00.

ROUND BLACK SPANISH. A fine globe-shaped radish, very popular with the Germans known as Rettig; good quality and flavor. Pkt., 5c.; oz., 10c.; ¼ lb., 25c.; lb., 85c.

Long Black Spanish. A large winter variety; one of the hardiest, with dark green leaves; firm in texture, keeping until spring. Pkt., 5c.; oz., 10c.; ¼ lb., 25c.; lb., 75c.

CALIFORNIA MAMMOTH WHITE. A winter variety growing twelve inches long; white fleshed, firm and of excellent quality. It is the largest radish grown, called by some the Mammoth Russian. Pkt., 5c.; oz., 10c.; lb., $1.00.

SPINACH.

One ounce will sow one hundred feet of drill. Twelve pounds will sow one acre.

Market Gardeners desiring to purchase by the bushel will be given special prices on application.

AMERICAN ROUND-SEEDED SAVOY, or BLOOMSDALE SPINACH. Our Celebrated Philadelphia Stock. Our entire stock of this very superior variety is Pennsylvania grown, of 1891 crop, and we guarantee it to possess every important quality that makes this valuable sort so popular. The leaves are large, thick, finely curled, heavy, are produced in great numbers, and stand handling and transportation better than any other sort. By far the best and most productive spinach in cultivation. Pkt., 5c.; oz., 10c.; lb., 40c.; 5 lbs., $1.25; 10 lbs. and over, 20c. per lb.

ENKHUIZEN, LONG STANDING. This genuine long standing spinach was first imported and introduced by us several years ago. We have often seen it stand so long that the leaves actually turned yellow before shooting to seed, hence its great value for spring sowing. The leaves are round, large, unusually thick, deeply curled and of a fine dark-green color. Our stock is grown in Holland especially for us. This variety is superior to the ordinary Long Standing offered in many catalogues. Pkt., 5c.; oz., 10c.; ¼ lb., 15c.; lb., 40c.; 5 lbs., $1.25.

NORFOLK SAVOY. A large, curled variety, with thick, fleshy leaves. Pkt., 5c.; oz., 10c.; ¼ lb., 15c.; lb., 35c.

NEW THICK-LEAVED ROUND. Produces large, thick, dark green, crumpled leaves; does not run to seed quickly. Pkt., 5c.; oz., 10c.; ¼ lb., 15c.; lb., 40c.

NEW LONG STANDING PRICKLY SPINACH.

NEW LONG STANDING PRICKLY. This new variety, now offered for the first time, is the Largest, Thickest Leaved and Best Keeping spinach we have ever seen. It is very hardy and a wonderful improvement on the old prickly spinach. It is one of the best for spring sowing, and is equally desirable for summer. It gives the largest weight of thick, tender leaves of any sort and remains a long time in condition for use. Pkt., 5c.; oz., 10c.; ¼ lb., 20c.; lb., 60c.

NEW ZEALAND SPINACH (Tetragonia Expansa). Produces leaves in great abundance throughout the entire summer, succeeding when the ordinary spinach would not even grow. Sow in May, where the plants are to stand. Pkt., 5c.; oz., 10c.; ¼ lb., 25c.; lb., 90c.

SALSIFY—Oyster Plant.

One ounce will sow about sixty feet of drill.

MAMMOTH SANDWICH ISLAND. This new Salsify first introduced from the Sandwich Islands, grows fully double the size of the Long White, and is superior in quality. It is pure white in color and is invaluable to market gardeners. Pkt., 10c.; oz., 20c.; ¼ lb., 50c.; lb., $1.75.

Long White. The old favorite variety; the tops can also be used in the spring, dressed like asparagus. Pkt., 5c.; oz., 15c.; ¼ lb., 40c.; lb., $1.25.

Scorzonera, or Black. Pkt., 10c.; oz., 25c.; lb., $2.50.

SQUASH.

One ounce will plant twenty to forty hills, according to size of seed. Four to six pounds will plant one acre.

Summer Varieties.

NEW SWEET NUT. See Novelties, page 15. Pkt., 10c.; oz., 50c.; ¼ lb., $1.50.

NEW MAMMOTH WHITE BUSH SQUASH.

NEW MAMMOTH WHITE BUSH, SCOLLOPED. An improved strain of the well-known White Bush, or Patty Pan Squash growing uniformly to twice the size. They ripen early; skin a handsome white color, and wonderfully productive. Pkt., 5c.; oz., 10c.; ¼ lb., 25c.; lb., 80c.

EARLY WHITE SCALLOP BUSH, or PATTY PAN. A popular variety, grows to large size, and bears an abundant crop. Pkt., 5c.; oz., 10c.; ¼ lb., 20c.; lb., 60c.

Early Golden Bush. Similar to the preceding, but of a deep orange color. Pkt., 5c.; oz., 10c.; ¼ lb., 20c.; lb., 65c.

SQUASH (Summer Varieties)—Continued.

NEW GOLDEN CUSTARD BUSH. The largest of all the scalloped sorts, attaining a diameter of two feet under good cultivation, and very productive. Color deep golden-yellow, unsurpassed in quality. Pkt., 5c.; oz., 10c.; ¼ lb., 30c.; lb., $1.00.

GOLDEN SUMMER CROOKNECK. Early, productive, of good quality; skin yellow. Pkt. 5c.; oz., 10c.; lb., 60c.

NEW GIANT, or MAMMOTH SUMMER CROOKNECK. This new squash is not only earlier than the common variety, but grows uniformly to twice the size, frequently two feet long. What few have been grown for market thus far, have realized the growers a handsome profit, selling "three to one" compared with the old sorts. Pkt., 5c.; oz., 10c.; ¼ lb., 20c.; lb., $1.00.

EGG-PLANT SQUASH. A new early variety with white flesh, quite equalling the Egg Plant when fried, and used as a substitute for it. Pkt., 5c.; oz., 10c.; ¼ lb., 35c.; lb., $1.25.

WHITE PINEAPPLE. This new variety has attracted much attention, owing to its peculiar shape. The skin and flesh are of a pure, creamy-white color, flesh fine grained and of excellent flavor, resembling the cocoanut when made into pies or custards. They can be used any time during growth, and after maturing make an excellent autumn and winter sort. They are remarkably strong growers, each vine producing generally from ten to fifteen perfect fruits. Pkt., 5c.; oz., 10c.; ¼ lb., 25c.; lb., 75c.

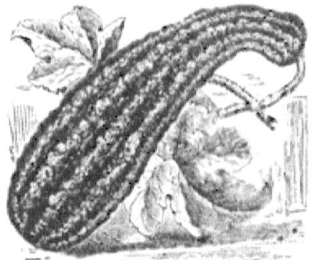

LONG GREEN CROOKNECK SQUASH.

LONG GREEN SUMMER CROOKNECK. It seems strange that this valuable squash should be so little known outside of Philadelphia market gardeners, who grow it largely with great profit, as it is preferred to all other summer squashes in our markets. We have had the above engraving made of one of these squashes, which shows the shape. They have a dark green skin, striped with lighter shades of green and yellow, are very productive and of the finest quality. As a squash for frying they are unequalled, being superior in flavor to eggplant. They are also delicious when made into fritters. Customers who have never grown this excellent squash will be fully repaid by giving it a trial. Pkt., 5c.; oz., 15c.; ¼ lb., 40c.; lb., $1.25.

Fall or Winter Squashes.

ISLAND PRIZE. Dryest and sweetest of all squashes. See Specialties, page 15. Pkt., 15c.; 2 pkts., 25c.; 5 pkts., 60c.

MEDITERRANEAN. We were the first seedsmen in America to offer this very valuable new fall and winter squash, which, from its numerous excellent qualities, has proven a most valuable acquisition. Our attention was first called to it by a sea captain plying between this port and the Mediterranean, who, on one of his voyages brought a few of these squashes with him for our inspection and trial. They grow about the same size as the Hubbard, but perfectly round and smooth, and owing to their very thick flesh, will weigh much heavier. The outside skin is quite smooth and of a pleasing red, salmon color, while the flesh is of a beautiful rich yellow, very sweet, fine and floury. The vines grow vigorously, are extremely hardy and very productive. Pkt., 5c.; oz., 10c.; ¼ lb., 30c.; lb., $1.00.

EARLY PROLIFIC ORANGE MARROW. This variety ripens two weeks ahead of the Boston Marrow, and excels it in productiveness and keeping qualities. Of very handsome color, medium in size, sweet flavor, with thick, high-colored orange flesh, fine grained and dry when cooked. Growing very quickly, it does well when planted as a second crop, following early peas, potatoes, etc. Pkt., 5c.; oz., 10c.; ¼ lb., 25c.; lb., 75c.

NEW WHITE CHESTNUT. The shape of this very distinct new variety is well shown in the above cut. The outside skin is creamy white, while the flesh is lemon-yellow, fine grained, sweet and most excellent in quality, suggesting the flavor of a boiled chestnut. The size and form so much like the good old original Hubbard, fully equalling it in great productiveness and keeping qualities. This squash is now creating quite a furore in the Eastern States, where gardeners pronounce it the very best squash they have ever grown. It is a good one. Try it. Pkt., 5c.; oz., 10c.; ¼ lb., 30c.; lb., $1.00.

FORDHOOK. A new winter squash, of excellent quality for winter use, the flesh being very sweet and dry. Ripens early and is well adapted to the far North. Pkt., 5c.; oz., 10c.; ¼ lb., 30c.; lb., $1.00.

SIBLEY, or PIKE'S PEAK. The shell of this valuable new and distinct squash is pale green in color, very hard and flinty, but so very thin and smooth as to occasion the least possible waste in baking. The flesh is solid and thick; a vivid brilliant orange color, dry and of a rich delicate flavor. They range in weight from eight to eleven pounds. Vine remarkably vigorous and ripens its fruit simultaneously with the Hubbard. In productiveness, the new Sibley Squash has decidedly the advantage of either the Hubbard or Marblehead; it moreover ripens its fruit so evenly that nearly the whole crop may be gathered at one picking. In its keeping qualities it excels, remaining in a good dry cellar, perfectly sound, until the last of March. Pkt., 5c.; oz., 10c.; ¼ lb., 25c.; lb., 75c.

BAY STATE. This variety comes from the same origin as the popular Essex Hybrid. The exciting features are its extreme solidity, heavy weight, fineness and dryness of grain, and sweetness of flavor. It is earlier than the Essex Hybrid, the crop averaging smaller in size and more in number. It has an extremely hard, flinty shell, and is an excellent keeper. The color of the shell is distinct from anything we have among the present varieties grown, being a blue shade with a peculiar greenish tinge. The flesh is of a beautiful, bright golden-yellow, and exceedingly sweet. Their average weight is ten pounds. Pkt., 5c.; oz., 10c.; ¼ lb., 25c.; lb., 90c.

HUBBARD. A general favorite and one of the best table varieties; of large size, flesh fine grained, dry and of excellent flavor. Pkt., 5c.; oz., 10c.; ¼ lb., 25c.; lb., 75c.

ESSEX HYBRID, or AMERICAN TURBAN. This variety is one of the finest grained and sweetest of the squash family. Specimens kept until June as sound and good as when gathered in the fall. The flesh is very thick, rich colored and solid. It ripens early and is one of the most productive. Pkt., 5c.; oz., 10c.; ¼ lb., 25c.; lb., 70c.

BOSTON MARROW. Extensively grown and most profitable for winter use and canning. Flesh orange, fine grained; splendid for pies and as a winter keeper. Pkt., 5c.; oz., 10c.; ¼ lb., 20c.; lb., 60c.; 5 lbs. and over, by express, 45c. per lb.

MAMMOTH CHILI. The largest of the squash family, specimens often weighing two hundred pounds and over. Flesh is a rich orange yellow, very thick and of good quality, very nutritious and profitable for stock feeding. Pkt., 10c.; oz., 20c.; ¼ lb., 50c.; lb., $1.50.

The following squashes are each 5c. per pkt.; 10c. per oz.; 25c per ¼ lb.; 75c. per lb.: **New Olive, Brazil Sugar, Perfect Gem, Marblehead, Cocoanut, Long White Marrow, Yokohama, Red China, Valparaiso and Butman.**

FOR CUT WORMS: LAND PLASTER FIVE PARTS AND PYRETHRUM POWDER ONE PART. SPRINKLE ON THE GROUND AROUND AND ON THE STEM OF THE PLANT.

TOMATO SEEDS FROM SELECTED FRUIT.

One ounce will produce about thirteen hundred plants.

For years we have made a careful study of growing the very best tomato seed. All tomatoes showing the slightest variation from the standard type are rigidly discarded. Thus we obtain the purest possible seed. Our long experience and great care enable us to furnish a prime article of this important seed to market gardeners, and to retain the patronage of all who deal with us.

CUMBERLAND RED. A matchless new tomato. See Novelties and Specialties, page 16. Pkt., 15c.; 2 pkts., 25c.; oz., 60c.; ¼ lb., $1.75; lb., $6.00.

JOHNSON & STOKES' EXTRA EARLY TROPHY. This variety was first discovered in a patch of the well-known Trophy, where it ripened nearly two weeks ahead of others. Its shape resembles the well-known Trophy, but it ripens much earlier and is remarkably productive, of a deep red color, growing to a good size and does not show the least trace of rotting in its early stage of growth, as the Acme and Paragon sorts do. The tomato is firm, slightly lobed, has very few seeds and has the happy feature of ripening its entire crop at one time, which is a very important thing to a market gardener whose profit depends upon getting his crop into market early. Pkt., 10c.; oz., 30c.; ¼ lb., 80c.; lb., $3.00.

EXTRA EARLY ADVANCE. A cross between Alpha and Perfection, of bright scarlet color, medium size and good quality. It surpasses the Alpha in wonderful early ripening qualities and equals Perfection in beautiful form and productiveness. The vines bear heavily, frequently one hundred to one hundred and twenty-five fruits to a vine. Our market garden friends will find the Extra Early Advance a valuable variety with which to strike the earliest markets. Pkt., 10c.; oz., 25c.; ¼ lb., 75c.; lb., $2.50.

VOLUNTEER. This tomato originated on Long Island with Messrs. Reed and Fumph, the well-known growers, who procured it by crossing Trophy and Canada Victor, and the result of that crossing with Perfection, combining their good qualities without retaining any of their objectionable features. They grow to large size, averaging six to ten ounces, very smooth and perfect in form, color bright red, with little core and very early. The quality is very superior for table-use and canning. Enormously productive, ripening well to the stem. Pkt., 10c.; oz., 25c.; ¼ lb., 75c.; lb., $2.50.

EARLY OPTIMUS. A very fine new variety, somewhat resembling Favorite, but earlier and more uniform in size. Fruit medium sized, oval, very smooth, exceedingly bright, rich, crimson-scarlet color, free from cracks and rot. The flesh is of a crimson-scarlet color, quite distinct and beautiful. It is also a splendid keeping and shipping variety. Pkt., 10c.; oz., 25c.; ¼ lb., 75c.; lb., $2.50.

IGNOTUM TOMATO.

THE IGNOTUM (Unknown). This new tomato was first discovered at the Michigan Agricultural College, in 1887, by Prof. L. H. Baily, being a sport from a foreign variety under test at that station. In our tests we find it earlier than Dwarf Champion, growing to very large size and remarkably smooth, regular in size and very solid. It is of handsome, deep red color, ripening to the stem and free from crack or rot. It will become one of the finest market sorts. Pkt., 10c.; oz., 30c.; ¼ lb., 80c.; lb., $3.00.

NEW STONE. The fact of this tomato coming from Mr. Livingston, the well-known originator of such excellent varieties as the Paragon, Favorite, Beauty, Acme and Perfection, is of itself sufficient recommendation to strongly endorse it. In describing it we cannot do better than to quote the following from Mr. Livingston, who writes: "The New Stone Tomato ripens for main crop; is very large, and of bright scarlet color; very smooth, with occasionally a specimen very slightly octagon-shaped; ripening evenly to the stem without a crack; exceedingly solid and firm-fleshed (as its name indicates); is an excellent shipper; quality the very best; fine for canning; a good keeper; without hard core; not subject to rot; its appearance on market remarkably attractive; a heavy variety; its vines and foliage rank and robust, heavily loaded with very uniform specimens of fruit." In our tests the past two seasons we have found all the above claims fully substantiated. Pkt., 10c.; oz., 40c.; ¼ lb., $1.25; lb., $4.00.

DWARF CHAMPION. A very distinct variety of upright growth. After Atlantic Prize and our Extra Early Trophy, it is probably the earliest tomato grown. Its close upright growth allows it to be planted closer together than other varieties. The fruit resembles the Acme, is of a purplish pink color and always smooth and symmetrical in form. It is of medium size and attractive in appearance; the skin is tough and the flesh solid and of fine quality. A very shy seeder. Pkt., 10c.; oz., 30c.; ¼ lb., 80c.; lb., $3.00.

MITCHELL'S IMPROVED, No. 1. This new tomato comes from Canada having been originated by Mr. Mitchell, who is well known as the originator of the Canada Victor some years ago. In our tests the past season we find it one of the best on trial, very early, smooth, beautiful red in color, and in quality hard to beat. Pkt., 10c.; oz., 35c.; ¼ lb., $1.25; lb., $4.50.

LIVINGSTON'S BEAUTY. A popular variety. The color is a glossy crimson, with a purple tinge; it grows in clusters of four and five, retaining its large size late in the season; very solid, with a tough skin, making it very desirable for shipping. Pkt., 10c.; oz., 25c.; ¼ lb., 75c.; lb., $2.50.

THE MIKADO, or TURNER HYBRID. This new variety, also called the $1,000 Tomato, originated in Iowa, and is entirely distinct from all known varieties. The foliage differs from other tomatoes, the large leaves being entire and not cut. It is a rank grower, with thick stalks, and enormously productive. The fruit is extra large in size, round, smooth, very thick through and remarkably solid. The average weight of the tomatoes is from twelve to eighteen ounces. They ripen up evenly and are entirely free from core. They make the handsomest sliced tomatoes, and have been pronounced by all who have tried them, unequalled in fine flavor and table qualities. The skin is thick, but rather tough, consequently the tomatoes keep in fine condition much longer than most other varieties. Color is a deep brilliant red. Our stock has been carefully selected and is unsurpassed. Pkt., 10c.; oz., 30c.; ¼ lb., 80c.; lb., $3.00.

LIVINGSTON'S POTATO LEAF. A fine market tomato, remarkable for its great firmness and solidity. It is named Potato Leaf, in consequence of its having such a very peculiar leaf, being whole, not cut or serrated like the leaves of ordinary kinds. In this respect it resembles the Mikado, or Turner Hybrid, but while the fruit is not quite so large as these, but large enough for all purposes, it is far smoother, and ever-bearing until killed by frost. Pkt., 10c.; oz., 25c.; ¼ lb., 75c.; lb., $2.50.

THINKING AND PLANNING IN WINTER WILL DO MUCH TO FACILITATE AND LIGHTEN THE LABOR OF SPRING.

ATLANTIC PRIZE. THE VERY EARLIEST OF ALL TOMATOES.

This new tomato ripens fully two weeks ahead of all others and is the result of many years' careful selection by one of the most successful tomato growers of Atlantic County, New Jersey. The vines grow strong, stiff and very rapidly, setting the crown fruit when quite young, the buds appearing before the plant is four inches high. The fruit is borne in immense clusters. Each vine produces from sixty to eighty large, perfect fruits, very solid and of the finest quality, being unusually free from core and seeds. Another great feature, beside extreme earliness, about this wonderful tomato, and one which must prove of great advantage to all tomato growers and market gardeners, is that when first fruiting it ripens more evenly and abundantly than any other tomato grown. It is by far the most valuable market variety ever introduced, and is so pronounced by every gardener who has grown it the past three seasons. Pkt., 10c.; oz., 40c.; ¼ lb., $1.25; lb., $4.50.

THE BRANDYWINE TOMATO.

Nothing we have ever introduced has excited so much comment in so short a time as this magnificent tomato. It has brought us in hundreds of unsolicited testimonials from customers who all agree in pronouncing it the most productive, continuous in bearing, and attractive in both color and form.

It is unquestionably one of the very best second early and late tomatoes, owing to its large size, beautiful bright red skin, uniformly smooth and handsome appearance, and great productiveness.

With two such handsome varieties as the **Atlantic Prize** for early and the **Brandywine** for second early and late, no private or market gardener could fail to have a bountiful supply of most delicious tomatoes the entire season. Pkt., 10c.; oz., 40c.; ¼ lb., $1.25; lb., $4.50.

EARLY MARKET CHAMPION TOMATO.

This valuable tomato originated with a prominent Philadelphia market gardener, who has for many years made the selection and improvement of the tomato a specialty. He has always had extremely fine, large tomatoes in the market very early and realizing handsome prices for his crop. His aim has always been to combine earliness with large size and perfect, smooth shape. There is no other purple tomato cultivated that will ripen so early or produce more bushels of large, handsome fruit to the acre than the **Market Champion**. Pkt., 10c.; oz., 30c.; ¼ lb., 80c.; lb., $3.00.

"WE PLACE THE ATLANTIC PRIZE AND BRANDYWINE AT THE HEAD OF THE TOMATO LIST."
W. F. MASSEY, HORTICULTURIST OF NORTH CAROLINA AGRICULTURAL EXPERIMENT STATION.

TOMATOES—Continued.

MATCHLESS. A new variety, of large size and red color; grown quite extensively in some sections of New Jersey for shipping. The great objection being the deep indentation of the fruit around the stem. Pkt., 10c.; oz., 25c.; ¼ lb., 75c.; lb., $2.50.

THE PEACH TOMATO. Almost identical with some forms of peaches, both in shape and color. The fruit is produced in clusters, is very solid, with red interior, and red, pinkish and green blush on the outside skin, which can be easily peeled, like the skin of a peach. Vines compact in habit and very productive. For preserving, Peach Tomato is hard to beat. Pkt., 10c.; oz., 25c.; ¼ lb., $1.00.

LIVINGSTON'S PERFECTION. This valuable variety comes from the same source as the Acme and Paragon. It is shaped like the Acme, larger, fully as early, perfectly smooth, blood-red in color, very solid and a heavy cropper. Pkt., 5c.; oz., 20c.; ¼ lb., 60c.; lb., $2.00.

SELECTED EARLY PARAGON. Very solid, dark red color, heavy foliage, a favorite market variety; excellent for canning. Pkt., 5c.; oz., 15c.; ¼ lb., 60c.; lb., $2.00.

SELECTED EARLY ACME. Ripens evenly, of medium, uniform size, round, very solid, and of a pink purplish color; very productive, bearing until killed by frost. Pkt., 5c.; oz., 20c.; ¼ lb., 60c.; lb., $2.00.

THE CARDINAL. The fruit is uniformly smooth and free from ridges, and is of a brilliant cardinal red. The flesh is of the same brilliant color, having no green core and very few seeds. Its evenness of ripening—so many tomatoes in the same stage at the same time—is a marked feature in this variety, as is also the uniformity of the same large size throughout the entire season. It keeps well and is a fine shipper. Pkt., 5c.; oz., 25c.; ¼ lb., 60c.; lb., $2.25.

LIVINGSTON'S FAVORITE. An early variety somewhat smoother than the Paragon. Does not crack after ripening, is of a darker red than the Perfection, and is larger than either. Pkt., 5c.; oz., 15c.; ¼ lb., 60c.; lb., $2.00.

Trophy. This well-known variety has become a favorite family and market tomato; large size, fine flavor, fruit solid. Pkt., 5c.; oz., 25c.; ¼ lb., 75c.; lb., $2.50.

THE SHAH, or GOLDEN MIKADO. A beautiful yellow tomato, a sport from the celebrated red variety, **Turner Hybrid, or Mikado,** and is identical with it in every respect except in color (which is a dark, waxy yellow). Pkt., 10c.; oz., 30c.; ¼ lb., 75c.; lb., $2.50.

The following varieties of Tomatoes are each 5 cents per packet, 25 cents per ounce, $2.50 per lb:

Horsford's Prelude, Lorillard, Station Upright, Queen, Scoville's Hybrid, Golden Queen, Early Ruby, King of the Earlies, Mayflower, Essex Hybrid, Climax, Hathaway's Excelsior, General Grant, Feejee Island, Large Smooth Red, Cook's Favorite, Canada Victor, Tree Tomato, Golden Trophy, Large Yellow, Pear-shaped, and Red Cherry.

TOBACCO SEED.

ROSE MUSCATEL TOBACCO.

PERSIAN ROSE MUSCATEL. Imported from Hungary, where it is regarded as the very best. It possesses a delicious Turkish or Rose perfume. Leaves are of medium size and regular. Pkt., 10c.; oz., 30c.; lb., $4.00.

CONNECTICUT SEED LEAF. Saved from selected plants. Pkt., 5c.; oz., 20c.; ¼ lb., 60c.; lb., $2.00.

HAVANA. Imported seed. Pkt., 10c.; oz., 40c.; lb., $4.00.

General Grant, Primus, Pennsylvania, or Lancaster (Broad Leaf), Maryland and Virginia (Broad Leaf), Yellow Oronoko, Gold Leaf, Medley Pryor, each, pkt., 10c.; oz., 25c.; ¼ lb., 60c.; lb., $2.25.

TURNIP.

One ounce will sow one hundred and fifty feet of drill; one to one and one-half pounds will sow an acre.

EXTRA EARLY PURPLE-TOP MILAN (Strap-Leaved). This new variety has proven to be the earliest and handsomest flat turnip in cultivation. No other variety can equal it for spring sowing. It is of medium size and flat shape, with bright purple top; pure white flesh, of excellent flavor, never bitter, small top, and a good keeper. It is a very shy seeder, hence true stock must be always high in price. Pkt., 5c.; oz., 10c.; ¼ lb., 25c.; lb., 80c.

EXTRA EARLY PURPLE-TOP MUNICH. This handsome turnip is entirely distinct from any other variety, growing entirely above ground, pure white, with a bright, purplish-red top and few leaves, flesh fine and of good flavor when young. Pkt., 5c.; oz., 10c.; ¼ lb., 20c.; lb., 60c.

EARLY RED-TOP WHITE GLOBE. A very early and attractive variety; very productive, white flesh, of fine quality. Pkt., 5c.; oz., 10c.; ¼ lb., 15c.; lb., [illegible]

POMERANIAN WHITE GLOBE. Useful for table as well as feeding stock; productive, hardy and a splendid autumn turnip. Pkt., 5c.; oz., 10c.; ¼ lb., 15c.; lb., [illegible]

BUDLONG TURNIP.

BUDLONG, or BREAD-STONE. This new strain is the result of years of careful selection made by Mr. Budlong, one of the most extensive market gardeners of New England, and while of Ruta Baga form, it well deserves to be classed with the best table turnips, owing to its fine texture and extra high quality. It is of half-long shape, as shown in our illustration, with a beautiful purple crown, pure white skin and flesh. Medium in size and of very quick growth. This new turnip has had a great local reputation for several years in a few towns of New England, where gardeners would pay almost any price to obtain seed in seasons when scarce. From our own experience with it we pronounce it the very best table turnip for spring and winter use that we have ever seen grow. Pkt., 5c.; oz., 10c.; ¼ lb., 25c.; lb., 90c.

EARLY WHITE FLAT DUTCH. An early white-fleshed variety, usually sown early in the spring; of quick growth, juicy, mild flavor and excellent quality; also grown for a fall crop. Pkt., 5c.; oz., 10c.; ¼ lb., 15c.; lb., 50c.

PURPLE-TOP FLAT (Strap-Leaved). This variety is similar to the above, excepting it is red or purple above ground. Pkt., 5c.; oz., 10c.; ¼ lb., 15c.; lb., 50c.

GOLDEN BALL, or ORANGE JELLY. A rapid grower, of excellent flavor, bright yellow, a good keeper, a superior table variety. Pkt., 5c.; oz., 10c.; ¼ lb., 15c.; lb., 50c.

YELLOW, or AMBER GLOBE. Flesh firm and sweet; grows large, excellent for either table use or feeding stock; keeps well. Pkt., 5c.; oz., 10c.; ¼ lb., 15c.; lb., 50c.

IMPROVED PURPLE-TOP YELLOW RUTA-BAGA. The leading market variety, and largely grown for stock as well as family use; hardy, productive, flesh yellow, solid, sweet, fine grained, good flavor. Pkt., 5c.; oz., 10c.; ¼ lb., 20c.; lb., 50c.; 5 lbs., $2.00.

Large White Ruta-Baga. Differs from the yellow only in color. Pkt., 5c.; oz., 10c.; ¼ lb., 20c.; lb., 60.

The following varieties of Turnips are each 5c. per packet; 10c. per oz.; 15c. per ¼ lb.; 50c. per lb.

White Egg, Large White Norfolk or Globe, Large Cow Horn or White French, Purple-Top Yellow Aberdeen, Seven-Top or Forrester, Carter's Swede.

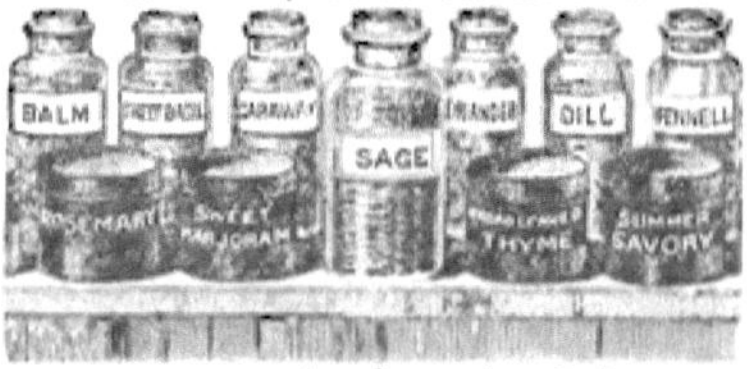

SEEDS OF POT AND SWEET HERBS.

Those marked with an * are perennial, and when once obtained in the garden may be preserved for years.

Anise. Pkt., 5c.; oz., 10c. ***Balm.** Pkt., 10c.; oz., 25c. **Basil, Sweet.** Pkt., 5c.; oz., 20c. **Borage.** Pkt., 5c.; oz., 20c. **Catnip.** Pkt., 10c.; oz., 40c. **Coriander.** Pkt., 5c.; oz., 10c.; ¼ lb., 25c. ***Caraway.** Pkt., 5c.; oz., 10c.; ¼ lb., 25c. **Dill.** Pkt., 5c.; oz., 10c.; ¼ lb., 25c.; lb., 80c. ***Lavender.** Pkt., 10c.; oz., 25c. **Marigold, Pot.** Pkt., 5c.; oz., 15c. ***Fennel.** Pkt., 5c.; oz., 10c. **Hyssop.** Pkt., 10c. ***Horehound.** Pkt., 10c.; oz., 30c. ***Marjoram, Sweet.** Pkt., 5c.; oz., 20c.; lb., $2.00. **Opium Poppy.** Pkt., 5c.; oz., 25c. ***Rosemary.** Pkt., 10c.; oz., 40c. ***Rue.** Pkt., 5c.; oz., 15c. **Saffron.** Pkt., 10c. **Sage.** Pkt., 5c.; oz., 15c.; lb., $1.50. **Savory, Summer.** Pkt., 5c.; oz., 15c.; ¼ lb., 35c. ***Savory, Winter.** Pkt., 5c.; oz., 20c. ***Tansy.** Pkt., 10c.; oz., 30c. **Thyme.** Pkt., 10c.; oz., 30c.; lb., $3.00. ***Wormwood.** Pkt., 5c.; oz., 25c.

SELECTED FARM SEEDS

Fully appreciating the great importance to the farmer of GOOD FIELD CROPS, we have given particular attention to this department of our business, and have made the SELECTION AND IMPROVEMENT OF FARM SEEDS a specialty, exercising great care to secure the best varieties, thoroughly cleaned and of the finest possible quality.

☞ At prices given, we make no charge for bags, and deliver free to any freight depot or express in Philadelphia.

AMERICAN BEAUTY OATS.

This grand new oat was obtained by a continued selection for several years, by O. H. Alexander, of Vermont, of a new variety sent him from Moscow, in Russia. He writes: "It is one of the heaviest croppers known, having yielded eighty-two bushels per acre here in Vermont when the average yield of other good varieties was fifty-two bushels, and I find, after testing over twenty varieties in the past few years, the straw is far more valuable for foddering purposes than any that I know of." This variety was also tested at the Experimental Station, Geneva, N. Y., the report being as follows: "Alexander's No. 26 (American Beauty) Oats, being long and taper pointed; average height, three feet three inches; culm very erect and stout, leaves often exceeding sixteen inches in length; average length of panicle, nine inches; berry, large. This variety is destined to become very popular and is one of the most prolific varieties known." Progressive farmers, try it. Prices, per large pkt., 15c.; lb., 30c.; 3 lbs., $1.00, postpaid; peck, 75c.; bush., $2.00; bag of 2½ bush., $4.50; 10 bush. and over, $1.75 per bush., sacks included.

AMERICAN BEAUTY OATS

BALTIC WHITE OATS.

This new and distinct oat comes from the borders of the Baltic Sea, in Sweden, where it is considered the very best of all Swedish varieties. We have sold it now for the past two seasons and hear nothing but praise from it. Well-cleaned samples will weigh fifty pounds per bushel. Aside from its extraordinary weight, it ripens earlier and will produce more weight of grain to the acre than ordinary oats. The straw is straight, stiff, of good height, crowned with long, beautiful branching, well-filled heads, twenty to twenty-four inches long, and free from any tendency to lodge. If you want to double the yield of your oat crop, you must sow either American Beauty or Baltic, as there is nothing to equal them in productiveness and quality. Pkt., 10c.; lb., 30c., 3 lbs., 75c., post-paid; by freight or express, peck, 60c.; legal bush. of 32 lbs., $1.50; 10 bush. and over, $1.35 per bush., bags included.

WELCOME, CLYDESDALE, Pringle's Progress, Wide-Awake, American Triumph, White Belgian, White Russian, Probsteir, Surprise, Excelsior, and other well known and popular varieties of seed oats at bottom prices. Each, 30c. lb., or 3 lbs. for 75c., post-paid; by freight or express, bags included, per legal bush., 32 lbs., $1.20; 10 bush. and over, $1.00 per bush.

JERUSALEM ARTICHOKE ROOTS.
THE GREATEST HOG FOOD KNOWN.

This variety is not produced from seed. They are sometimes used as a table vegetable when pickled, but their greatest value is for feeding stock. They are the best hog food known and are now attracting much attention on account of their great fattening properties, great productiveness (over one thousand bushels having been grown on one acre) and ease with which they can be grown. They need not be dug in the fall; the hogs should be turned in on them, and will help themselves by rooting for them. One acre will keep from twenty to thirty head in fine condition from October until April, except when the ground is frozen too hard for them to root. They are also said to be a preventative of cholera and other hog diseases, and they are also highly recommended for milch cows, increasing the yield of milk and at the same time improving their condition. They are well adapted to any soil where corn or potatoes can be grown. Three bushels will seed an acre, and they should be cut the same as potatoes, one eye to a cutting sufficient, planted in April or May, in rows three feet apart and two feet in the rows, and covered about two inches deep. To destroy them, they should be plowed under when the plant is about a foot high, at which time the old tuber has decayed and new ones are not yet formed. They can be shipped at any time during the season, as they are not injured by freezing. Lb., 25c.; 3 lbs., $1.00, postpaid; by freight or express, peck, $1.00; bush., $1.00; bbl., of 5 bush. (enough for one acre), $7.50.

SEED CORN.

We make it an invariable rule to test our seeds carefully before sending out, and our customers may depend on getting Seed Corn that will grow perfectly. A sample ear is put in each sack with all orders of one bushel and over.

JOHNSON & STOKES' NEW GIANT BEAUTY FIELD CORN.

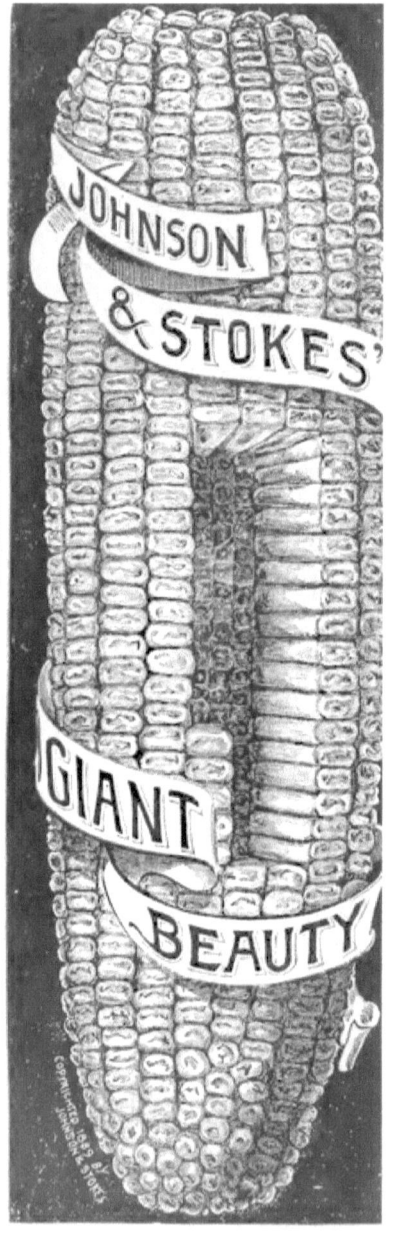

In the new Giant Beauty we have a very valuable and long sought for variety, viz.: A very large ear and grain, yet a very early Yellow Dent Corn. Giant Beauty is a cross between Cloud's Early Dent and Golden Beauty, possessing the earliness and deep grain of the former, with the handsome deep yellow color and breadth of grain of the latter. It is absolutely the largest grained of all yellow corn. Its small red cob and great depth of grain are well shown in the accompanying illustration made from an average ear. Its rich deep golden color and fine quality of grain make it very superior for grinding into meal, and indicate its strong nutritive qualities. It is a very vigorous grower, taking strong hold in the ground and averaging eight feet in height, producing two large ears well filled to the extreme ends of the cobs, even on light and poor land. Giant Beauty presents the most perfect type of Yellow Field Corn yet introduced, in every respect, and should be planted by all farmers who want to be abreast of the times. Pkt., 10c.; ear, 25c.; lb., 40c.; 3 lbs., $1.00, post-paid by mail. By express or freight, peck, 80c.; bush., $2.50; sack of 2 bush., $4.50.

IMPROVED LEAMING
THE EARLIEST YELLOW DENT

The True Improved Leaming Corn is a pure, fixed and distinct variety, first introduced by us ten years ago. Our strain has been selected and improved each year since its introduction, and is the **Earliest Yellow Dent Corn in Cultivation**, ripening in ninety to a hundred days from time of planting, surpassing the Yellow Canada and Flint varieties in earliness, productiveness and quality.

It is not a hard, flinty corn, but sweet and nutritious, making excellent feed and the finest meal. The ears are large and handsome, with deep large grain, of deep orange color and small red cob. Stalks grow to medium size (not large) with few suckers, tapering gradually from root to top, producing two good ears to each stalk, husks and shells easily. One hundred and thirty-six bushels shelled corn have been grown to the acre on good corn ground. It is also adapted to a greater variety of soils than other varieties, producing unusually well on light and heavy land, where other varieties would not thrive. Prices by mail, post-paid, pkt., 10c.; lb., 30c.; 3 lbs., 75c. By freight or express, bags included, qt., 25c.; peck, 60c.; bush., $1.75; bag of 2 bush., $3.25; 10 bush. and over, $1.50 per bush.

FARMERS' FAVORITE DENT.

This is an improved variety of the Golden Dent Gourd Seed, which it resembles in some respects, ripening earlier. The ears are of good size, with very small cob and very large, deep grains, of a beautiful bright golden yellow color. The corn meal made from this corn is very superior in quality and appearance. It produces well even on light land, frequently yielding from ninety to one hundred bushels shelled corn to the acre. Lb., 30c.; 3 lbs., 75c., post-paid; qt., 25c.; peck, 60c.; bush., $1.75; bag of 2 bush., $3.25; 10 bush. and over, $1.50 per bush.

CLOUD'S EARLY YELLOW DENT.

This corn was originated some years ago by Jas. Cloud, a prominent Chester County farmer. It has taken first premiums whenever it has been exhibited. It has a fine, rich appearance, weighs well, starts early and with a strong stalk; as soon as it comes out of the ground grows vigorously, though the stalk only range from seven to nine feet in height. It withstands severe droughts to a remarkable degree. Ears, set low, are of large size, well filled, very deep grained; sixty to seventy ears will yield a bushel of shelled corn. Matures early and very productive. Lb., 30c.; 3 lbs., 75c., post-paid; qt., 20c.; peck, 75c.; bush., $2.00; bag of 2 bush., $3.75; 10 bush. and over, $1.75 per bush., bags included.

∴ SELECTED ∴ FARM ∴ SEEDS ∴

EARLY MASTODON CORN.

A new early Dent variety, originated in Ohio. The ear is very large, and grain deep. It grows strong, rank quick, and makes the finest appearing shelled corn, being purely Dent, of two shades of white and yellow. In the American Agriculturist corn contest of 1889 it outyielded all others, making the wonderful record of two hundred and thirteen bushels shelled corn to the acre. Pkt., 10c.; lb., 40c.; 3 lbs., 75c.; post-paid. Qt., 20c.; peck, 60c.; bush., $1.75; bag of 2 bush., $3.25; 10 bush. and over, $1.50 per bush., bags included.

GOLDEN BEAUTY CORN.

The Golden Beauty is a large and broad-grained yellow corn. The ears of perfect shape, with from ten to fourteen straight rows of bright golden yellow grains, filled out completely to the extreme end of the cob. The cob is very small in comparison with the size of the ear, and when broken in half the grains will reach across. The richness of color and fine quality of grain makes it vastly superior for grinding into meal. The stalks take strong hold in the ground, grow vigorously to a height of eight to nine feet. Golden Beauty matures in one hundred and ten days from planting. We have many favorable reports from customers who planted this corn, yielding in many cases at the rate of one hundred and twenty-five bushels to the acre. Prices by mail, postpaid, large pkt., 10c.; lb., 30c.; 3 lbs., 75c. By freight or express, qt., 15c.; peck, 65c.; bush., $1.75; bag of 2 bush., $3.25; 10 bush. and over, $1.50 per bush.

CHESTER COUNTY MAMMOTH.

Wherever introduced has given universal satisfaction, both on account of its **large yields**, **fine quality of grain** and **superior fodder**. The ears are large and well formed, grain very large, deep, and of a bright yellow color; the stalk is large, averaging from ten to fourteen feet producing a larger quantity of fodder than any other yellow corn. Our stock has been improved each year by the most careful and skilful selection of the largest and earliest ears. By mail, post-paid, pkt., 10 cts.; lb., 30 cts.; 3 lbs., 75 cts. By express or freight, bags included, qt., 15c.; peck, 60c.; bush., $1.75; bag of 2 bush., $3.25; 10 bush. and over, $1.50 per bush.

HICKORY : KING : CORN.

This is unquestionably **the largest grained and smallest cobbed pure white Dent corn in cultivation**. The grain is so large and cobs so small, that by breaking an ear in half, **one grain will cover the entire end of the cob**. The ears grow seven to nine inches in length, are generally borne three to a stalk. It ripens medium early, yet we do not recommend it as an entirely safe crop north of the latitude of Pennsylvania. It is particularly adapted to and will yield more on thin soil than any other White Field Corn. By mail, pkt., 10c.; lb., 30c.; 3 lbs., 75c. By express or freight, qt., 20c.; peck, 75c.; bush., $2.00; bag of 2 bush., $3.75.

RED COB ENSILAGE CORN.

This new and superior ensilage corn we can recommend, from experience, as being the **heaviest cropping variety** in cultivation, producing fifty to seventy-five tons per acre. It has been thoroughly tested in all dairy sections of the country with the best results. It is a pure white Dent corn of large size and handsome appearance, growing on a red cob. The fodder is sweet, tender, juicy, and said to contain more nourishment than any other variety. It grows thirteen to fourteen feet in height, taking strong hold in the ground, standing up well and resisting storms of all kinds to a remarkable degree. Peck, 50c.; bush., $1.50; 10 bush. and over, $1.40 per bush.

BLUNT'S WHITE PROLIFIC, or MAMMOTH ENSILAGE CORN. Produces three to eight good ears to a stalk. It is also much used for ensilage, and has been known to produce seventy tons of fodder to the acre. Peck, 50c.; bush., $1.50; 10 bush. and over, $1.40 per bush.

LONGFELLOWS AND EARLY YELLOW CANADA. These well-known eighteen-rowed yellow flint varieties ripen very early, and are well adapted to the North and for late replanting. Qt., 20c.; peck, 65c.; bush., $2.00.

SUGAR CORN FOR GREEN FODDER. Profitable as green feed for milch cows, being sweeter and more nutritious and eaten more readily than fodder from Field Corn. Bush., $1.50; 5 bush. and over, $1.40 per bush.

MAMMOTH RUSSIAN SUNFLOWER.

THE GIANT OF ALL SUNFLOWERS. Growing to double the size of the common sunflower, and the yield of seed is twice as great. One hundred and twenty-five bushels to the acre have been grown at a less expense than corn. It is highly recommended for poultry; the best egg-producing food known. The leaves make splendid fodder, much relished by all kinds of stock. The seed is good feed for horses, and yields a fine quality of oil. The strong, thick stalks are used for fuel. Oz., 5c.; qt., 20c.; qt., post-paid, 30c.; peck, 75c.; bush., $2.50; sack, 2 bush., $4.00.

WEBER'S IMPROVED EVERGREEN.

BEST AND PUREST BROOM CORN IN CULTIVATION.

This is the best and purest in cultivation, originated and selected by Mr. Geo. Weber, one of the largest growers of Montgomery County, Pa., who has for many years had the reputation of having the best in the State, having made his stock famous by selection and improvement for length, strength and straightness of brush. It is of a very bright green color without the slightest reddish tinge. It makes by far the best brooms of any other grown; height seven to eight feet. Qt., 20c.; peck, $1.00; bush., $3.00; 2 bush., $5.50.

Dwarf Evergreen Broom Corn. Grows three to four feet high, straight, smooth brush. Qt., 20c.; peck, 80c.; bush., $2.25.

MANSBURY BARLEY. The earliest and most productive. Qt., 20c.; peck, 60c.; bush., $2.00.

SPRING BARLEY. Qt., 15c.; peck, 50 cts.; bush., $1.50.

Spring Tares, or Vetches. Qt., 15c.; bush., $3.50.

SPRING RYE.

Distinct from the winter rye, grain of finer quality and more productive; can be successfully grown in any latitude. Lb., 35c.; 3 lbs., $1.00, post-paid; peck, 65c.; bush., $2.00.

SPRING WHEAT.

FRENCH IMPERIAL. This wheat has proven itself a most desirable variety. It possesses the quality of filling out plump, hard, extra No. 1 wheat, weighing sixty-two to sixty-four pounds per measured bushel. It is well adapted to rather poor soils, producing good crops of No. 1 hard wheat. The wheat is vigorous and strong in its growth and yielded the past season from forty to fifty bushels per acre. By mail, pkt., 10c.; lb., 35 cts.; 3 lbs., $1.00. By express or freight, peck, 60c.; bush., $2.75.

SASKATCHEWAN FIFE. This wheat comes originally from Manitoba, and is pronounced by the great milling kings of the Northwest the best. It frequently weighs sixty-five pounds to the bushel, and it is said fifty bushels to the acre is not an uncommon yield. It is ten days earlier than the common fife, straw growing about a foot taller, standing stiff and strong; highly recommended. Pkt., 10c.; lb., 35c.; 3 lbs., $1.00, post-paid. Peck, 65c.; bush., $2.75.

SEED BUCKWHEAT.

NEW JAPANESE. In 1885 a gentleman travelling in Japan sent to a friend in New Jersey about a thimbleful of this new variety. It was carefully planted and enough seed raised to sow one-half bushel in 1886, from which the crop was forty bushels. A few bushels of this were given out for trial among neighboring farmers who were delighted with the enormous yields it produced. Sown at the same time with silver-Hull it proved two weeks earlier and yielded twice as great. The kernels are twice the size of any other buckwheat; of a rich dark brown color and manufacture a superior flour. Owing to its branching character only one-half as much seed is required per acre, while the straw is much stiffer and stands up better. This new buckwheat is rapidly displacing all others. Pkt., 10c.; lb., 30c.; 3 lbs., 75c., post-paid; qt., 20c.; peck, 60c.; bush., $2.50; 5 bush. and over, $1.40 per bush., sacks included.

SILVER HULL. Sown at the same time as the common buckwheat, this variety continues in bloom longer, matures earlier, and yields nearly double. The flour produced from it is whiter and more nutritious. Lb., post-paid, 25c.; qt., 20c.; peck, 50c.; bush., $1.50.

COMMON BUCKWHEAT. Qt., 15c.; bush., $1.25.

OSAGE ORANGE. Lb., 50c.; peck, $2.00; bush. of 33 lbs., $7.00.

FLAX SEED. Qt., 15c.; bush., 56 lbs., about $2.50.

SOJA HISPIDA (Soja Bean). Grown largely for forage crops and valuable for green manuring. Pkt., 10c.; lb., 30c., post-paid; peck, $1.25; bush., $4.00.

JERUSALEM CORN.
A NEW FORAGE AND GRAIN PLANT.

The JERUSALEM CORN belongs to the non-saccharine sorghums, and was brought a few years since from the arid plains of Palestine. It is pronounced, by all who have grown it, the best and surest grain crop for dry countries and seasons, even better than Kaffir Corn and Milo Maize. It grows about three feet high, makes one large head on main stalk, and several smaller heads on side shoots, often as many as eight heads on one stalk. The grains are pure white and nearly flat. Three pounds will plant an acre.

The cultivation is the same as for Kaffir Corn and other forage plants. We hope all our customers who are interested in this class of plants, and have not already tried it, will give the new Jerusalem Corn a trial. Pkt., 10c.; lb., 75c.; 3 lbs., $2.00, post-paid. Lb., 25c.; 10 lbs., $2.00; bush., 60 lbs., $9.00, by freight or express.

KAFFIR CORN

Is now successfully cultivated for both forage and grain in all sections of the United States. It is the best general purpose plant of all the varieties of sorghum yet offered, unless it be the new **Jerusalem Corn**, described above, and will make a paying crop on land that will not yield five bushels of corn or wheat. It is early as Amber Cane. It will make a fine crop of forage if cut in early bloom, and the shoots that then follow will mature a full crop of seed and forage. Both grain and fodder are excellent, the whole stalk tender to the full maturity of seed. There is no fallacy about it, as it possesses the quality that all the tribe possesses, of waiting for rain without any loss of capacity to yield. The grain makes a flour that is like wheat. It can be cultivated the same as our common Indian Corn, requiring four to five pounds of seed per acre. By mail, postage paid, pkt., 10c.; lb., 30c.; 3 lbs., 75c.; by freight or express, qt., 20c.; peck, $1.00; bush. (60 lbs.), $3.00.

WHITE MILLO MAIZE, or DHOURA. A grain of South American origin, which we have distributed largely in past seasons. It can be cut repeatedly for green feed or for fodder. It stools or branches freely; the mass of foliage it produces is enormous, and it stands dry weather well. Plant in April, in rows three or four feet apart, five to eight seeds in a hill, requiring two pounds to the acre, and cultivate as corn. Post-paid, pkt., 10c.; lb., 30c.; 3 lbs., 75c.; by express or freight, qt., 20c.; peck, $1.00; bush., $3.00.

YELLOW MILLO MAIZE, or YELLOW BLANCHING DHOURA. Another new variety of sorghum, valuable for both forage and grain. Its growth is tall nine to twelve feet, shooting from the ground like the White Millo Maize. It sends out shoots also from the joints. The seed heads grow to great size, often weighing a full pound after being fully ripe. The heads are set close and solid, with a large, plump grain, double the size of White Millo, and of deep golden-yellow color. In shape, the seed head is thick, well shouldered, solid, never long and narrow, and by reason of size and weight, each head is the full equal in grain to a fine ear of corn. The heads begin to turn down usually as soon as formed, and when ripe hang on short goose-neck stems. The grain makes most excellent feed for horses, cattle, chickens or human food. It will mature its main head in one hundred days and will go on maturing others until cut down by frost. Pkt., 10c.; lb., 30c.; 3 lbs., 75c.; post-paid; qt., 20c.; peck, $1.00; bush., $4.00.

TEOSINTE (REANA LUXURIANS). The gigantic Grammeæ of Central America, somewhat resembles Indian Corn. It produces a great number of shoots, growing twelve feet high, very thickly covered with leaves, yielding an abundance of forage. Oz., 15c.; ¼ lb., 50c.; lb., $1.50.

LARGE AFRICAN MILLET. A variety of sorghum used for forage, growing stalks ten feet high, with heads of grain twelve to fourteen inches long. Pkt., 10c.; qt., 30c.; peck, $1.00; bush., $4.00.

SUGAR CANE—EARLY AMBER. This is by far the best variety for sugar as it matures quickly, and has been cultivated as far north as St. Paul, Minn. The seed is valuable also as food for horses and cattle, and is greedily eaten by poultry, increasing the egg production. For ensilage or fodder it possesses important advantages. By mail, post-paid, lb., 30c.; 3 lbs., 75c.; by express or freight, qt., 20c.; bush. of 56 lbs., $1.75; 10 bush. or over, $2.50 per bush.

SAINFOIN, or ESPARSETTE (Onobrychis Sativa). An excellent new perennial Fodder Plant, growing to the height of about three feet, and flowering in June and July. If broadcasted it will require about five to six bushels per acre; if drilled, four to five bushels. It will crop from seven to ten years, according to the quality of the soil. Lb., 25c.; 10 lbs., $1.50; bush. of 25 lbs., $3.00.

RAMIE Silver China Grass (Urtica nivea). This is the variety now so extensively cultivated in the South for its fibre. Pkt., 20c.; oz., 50c.; lb., $10.00.

Grasses for the North and South.

This little work contains a complete list, with descriptions and illustrations, of all the desirable grasses now grown in the United States. Will be mailed free to all who write for it.

Thank God for grass! No other glory vies
With the refreshing glory of the grass;
Not e'en the blue of the o'erbending skies
Nor feeling upheaveth when the daylight dies,
Can this sweet smile of living green surpass.

Our grass and clover seeds are extra cleaned and of the highest quality. We take great care to have them absolutely free from all noxious weed seeds.

POSTAGE ON GRASS SEEDS.

Remit, in addition to price, 8c. per lb., and 15c. per qt. except on light varieties, which do not weigh over 14 lbs. per bush., on which remit 5c. per qt., to prepay postage.

VARIETIES OF CLOVER.

ALSIKE, SWEDISH or HYBRID CLOVER (Trifolium Hybridum). This valuable variety is the hardiest of all the clovers and is sometimes called "Giant White Clover." It is a perennial, therefore adapted for permanent pastures or for hay crop.

Its superior pasturage is much liked by cattle. Blossom heads round, flesh-colored, sweet and fragrant, much liked by bees. Sow six pounds per acre in spring or fall. Lb., 30c.; 10 lbs., $2.50; 25 lbs. and over, 20c. per lb.; bush. of 60 lbs., $14.00.

LUCERNE, or ALFALFA CLOVER. A perennial forage plant, and when once properly seeded in suitable soil will produce fine crops for several years. It has a remarkable strong growth, occasioned by its roots penetrating the ground to a great depth, ten to twenty feet, until they are altogether out of reach of drought. Seed can be sown with any grain crop in the spring, or as a separate crop, at the rate of ten to twelve pounds to the acre. Lb., 25c.; 10 lbs., $2.00; 25 lbs. and over, 15c. per lb.; bush., 60 lbs., $8.00.

BOKHARA CLOVER. Excellent for bee food, growing well on poor soil. Lb., 35c.; 10 lbs., $3.00.

CRIMSON, or CARNATION CLOVER. The most attractive of the clovers by its bright scarlet flowers, giving a desirable succession of green food. Lb., 25c.; 10 lbs., $2.00.

WHITE DUTCH CLOVER. The best to sow with lawn grass and valuable in permanent pastures. Oz., 5c.; lb., 45c.; 25 lbs. and over, 30c. per lb.; bush., 60 lbs., $12.00.

Clover, Common Red. Lowest market prices.
MAMMOTH PEA VINE, or SAPLING CLOVER. Market variable. Lowest market prices.
Japan Clover. Valuable for the South. Lb., 50c.

.·. EXTRA .·. CLEANED .·. GRASS .·. SEEDS .·.   79

OUR SPECIAL GRASS MIXTURE
FOR HAY AND PERMANENT PASTURES.

PRICE, $2.50 PER BUSHEL; 10 BUSHELS AND OVER, $2.25. SOW 2 TO 2½ BUSHELS TO THE ACRE.

In the preparation of these mixtures for Permanent Pasture and Mowing, the greatest care is exercised in selecting such varieties as are suited to the soil to be laid down and are likely to realize the object in view. To facilitate this, a description of the soil, whether light, medium or heavy, also climate, the range of temperature, and the purpose for which sown, and if with or without a crop, should accompany each order.

Johnson & Stokes' No. 1 Mixture for Permanent Pasture. Contains blended in proper proportions for the purpose, the following grasses: Orchard Grass, Sheeps Fescue, Meadow Fescue, Hard Fescue, Canadian Blue, Sweet Vernal, Meadow Foxtail, Tall Meadow Oat, Red Top, Kentucky Blue, Italian Rye Grass, Perennial Rye Grass, Rhode Island Bent, Timothy, Wood Meadow, Rough-Stalked Meadow, Alsike Clover, White Clover, Mammoth Clover. Bush., $2.50.

Johnson & Stokes' No. 2 Mixture for Permanent Mowing. Contains, properly blended: Red Top, Perennial Rye Grass, Orchard Grass, Timothy, Red Clover, Mammoth Clover, White Clover, Fine-Leaved Fescue, Rhode Island Bent, Rough-Stalked Meadow, Meadow Fescue, Meadow Foxtail. Bush., $2.50.

JOHNSON & STOKES' NEW EVERGREEN LAWN GRASS SEED.

The most beautiful thing that can be placed about a home is a well-kept lawn. It is the soul of the surroundings of a house. Not only is it one of the most beautiful, but also useful features of the landscape. Grass is the carpet of the earth, and like the carpet of the house it should be used.

OUR EVERGREEN LAWN MIXTURE will insure a beautiful dwarf, green, compact sward, and remain green and fresh during our hot dry summer months, even when sown on Lawns, Tennis, Croquet and Ball Grounds in constant use, and has become widely known, and is exclusively used on the finest public and private grounds around Philadelphia, New York and other cities. A quart will sow about three hundred square feet. Three to four bushels are required to sow an acre. Instructions how to prepare and sow a lawn are printed on each package. Prices, qt., 25c.; 2 qts., 40c.; qt., post-paid, 30c.; peck, $1.00; bush., 16 lbs., $4.00.

CANADIAN BLUE GRASS (Poa Compressa). The hardiest grass in cultivation, should not be confounded with the Kentucky Blue Grass. Qt., 25c.; bush., 14 lbs., $3.50.

KENTUCKY BLUE GRASS (Fancy, triple cleaned.) Valuable for pasture when mixed with other varieties. Qt., 15c.; bush., $1.25; 5 bush. and over, $1.00 per bush.

ORCHARD GRASS. One of the most desirable pasture grasses. Qt., 15c.; bush., 12 lbs., about $1.75.

Timothy. Qt., 20c.; bush., 45 lbs., about $2.25.

HERD, or RED TOP GRASS. A valuable native permanent grass, as a mixture in meadows or pastures. Qt., 10c.; bush., 10 lbs., 75c.; in sacks of 50 lbs., about $2.75.

East India, or Pearl Millet. Cultivated for fodder. Lb., 30c.; 10 lbs. and over, 25c. per lb.

Hungarian Millet Grass. One of the most valuable annual forage plants. Qt., 10c.; bush., 48 lbs., about $1.50.

German, or Golden Millet Grass. Will grow in almost any climate of soil; the yield in hay or seed is larger than any other variety. Qt., 10c.; bush., 50 lbs., about $1.75.

Common Millet. Qt., 10c.; bush., 50 lbs., about $1.50.

Johnson Grass (Sorghum Halapense). Qt., 20c.; bush., 25 lbs., $3.00.

Sweet Vernal Grass. True Perennial. Lb., 60c.; bush., 10 lbs., $5.00.

Natural Green Grass. Qt., 20c.; bush., $3.00.

Meadow Fescue, or English Blue. Qt., 20c.; bush., $4.00. Sow two bushels to the acre.

Tall Meadow Oat Grass. A valuable grass for permanent pasture, on account of its early, luxuriant growth. Makes splendid hay. Qt., 20c.; bush., 14 lbs., $2.50.

English Rye Grass. A nutritious permanent grass, for meadows and pastures. Qt., 20c.; bush., 24 lbs., $2.50.

Italian Rye Grass. Qt., 20c.; bush., 20 lbs., $2.50.

Wood Meadow Grass. Adapted for pleasure grounds, under trees; fine for pastures under close feeding. Sow twenty-eight pounds to acre. Lb., 48c.; bush. of 14 lbs., $4.50.

Meadow Foxtail, Crested Dogstail, Fine Leaved Fescue, Water Meadow, Rough-Stalked Meadow, Water Fescue, each per lb., 40c.; 10 lbs. and over, 35c. lb.

Rhode Island Bent, Meadow Brome, Tufted Hair, Creeping Bent, Wood Hair, Hard Fescue, Sheep Fescue, Meadow Soft, each per lb., 30c.; 10 lbs. and over, 25c. per lb.

Novelties AND Choice Specialties IN

Flower Seeds.

Two new Exquisite Asters.

New White Plume, OR Comet Aster.

This is, we believe, the grandest floral novelty of the year. The flower, which resembles very closely a pure white, large-flowered Japanese Chrysanthemum, is larger and more double than that of the other colors, the petals being much longer and more twisted; each petal is ribbed, thus giving to the flower a quite peculiar and elegant appearance. The color is the purest possible glossy satiny-white.

345. **NEW WHITE PLUME.** (See cut.) Price per pkt., 25c.

346. **NEW CARMINE PLUME, or COMET ASTER.** Similar in shape and style of flower to the above, but of a beautiful rich carmine color. Price per pkt., 25c.

347. **NEW "QUEEN OF THE EARLIEST" ASTER.** Last season at our "Floracroft" Trial Grounds this Aster, sown and of course, bloomed ahead of plants that had been started under glass six weeks before. They are dwarf plants with fine large flowers of beautiful form. They are without doubt the very earliest Aster listed. (See cut.)

If weather is propitious, they may be had in bloom by the beginning of July.

Queen of the Earliest, pure white, 25c per pkt.
" " " mixed colors, 15c. "

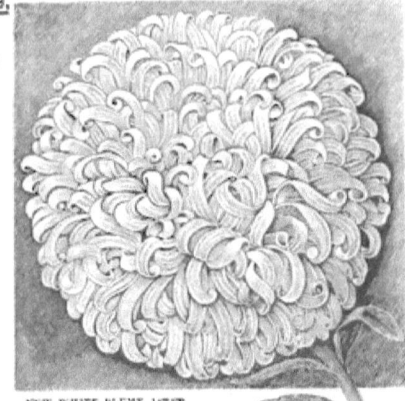
NEW WHITE PLUME ASTER.
Pkt., 25c.

425. **BEGONIA CREDNERI.** A perfectly distinct new variety originated by hybridizing B. Schertliana and Metallica. Its graceful habit is similar to the former species, while in shape and coloring of the foliage it resembles the B. Metallica. The flowers hanging in large umbel-like clusters, by far excel both parents. The plants attain a height of two to three feet, and produce a profusion of bloom that is astonishing; the leaves are dark green of a metallic gloss and hairy on surface, dark red underneath, six inches broad by eight inches in length. The color of the individual flowers is a snowy white on the inside of the petals, while the reverse is thickly set with fine red hairs, thus forming a most striking and beautiful contrast. Per pkt. 25c.

NEW QUEEN OF THE EARLIEST ASTER.

426. **BEGONIA SEMPERFLORENS ATROPURPUREA.** (Vernon.) This beautiful new Begonia is similar in habit to the old and well-known B. semperflorens, but surpasses the latter by far by its brilliant orange-carmine flowers and by its glossy, deep brown-shaded foliage, the deep red tint growing in intensity as the season advances. The beauty of the male flowers is still enhanced by the bright yellow stamens, which contrast admirably with the brilliant red flowers and the dark metallic leaves. Blooming in the greatest profusion throughout the summer and autumn, it cannot be too highly recommended for flowering beds or for pot culture. Per pkt. 25c.

BEGONIA CREDNERI. Pkt. 25c.

*"In all places, then, and in all seasons,
Flowers expand their light and soul-like wings;
Teaching us, by the most persuasive reasons,
How akin they are to human things." —LONGFELLOW.*

TESTED FLORAL NOVELTIES

NEW SCARLET SAGE.

2521. **Salvia Splendens Ingeniour Clevenard.** A new and splendid variety of this old favorite, blooming some two months earlier than the old sort, and producing flowers in the greatest profusion, of a splendid brilliant scarlet red. Very distinct and magnificent for beds. Pkt., 25c.

1065. IPOMŒA "HEAVENLY BLUE."

This wonderful new annual climber originated from seeds of Mina Lobata (see below), which grew near Ipomœa Leari. All summer humming birds flitted back and forth between the two. That season, the fall of 1888, the latter gave no seeds, the former but few which were planted in the spring. Among the seedlings appeared these, with large cordage, light green leaves, smooth and firm in texture, with reddish brown vine, and stems like Mina Lobata, but with flowers shaped like I. Leari. Color, in and out and out sky blue, the lovely blue so rarely seen in flowers, resembling Salvia Patens but lighter; centre of flower shaded lighter, delicately rayed with a glow of yellow deep in the throat. In the morning about nine o'clock no lovelier sight can be imagined than this climber, which is completely covered with bloom, so much so as to almost cover the foliage. Undoubtedly the humming birds were match-makers and this beautiful hybrid the result. It is a rampant grower, and blooms till very late fall. Will do well in the conservatory as well as outside. Every one who sees it, with its cloud of airy blossoms, measuring four to four and one-half inches across, exclaims: "That is the loveliest thing I ever saw! I must have it." Plant very early in the spring, in the house to insure quick bloom. Pkt., 15c.

NEW IPOMŒA, "HEAVENLY BLUE." Pkt., 15c.

MINA LOBATA.

3080. Half-hardy Mexican climbing annual. The buds are, at first, of a vivid red, but turn to orange yellow immediately before they open, and when fully expanded the flowers are of a creamy white shade. They are freely produced from the base to the summit of the plant, which attains a height of from eighteen to twenty feet, and constitutes a strikingly beautiful object. Seed should be sown in January or February. (See cut.) Pkt., 15c.

NEW WHITE TOM THUMB AGERATUM. "WHITE GEM."

104. A charming new very dwarf and compact growing Ageratum, attaining only four inches in height, and profusely covered with nice white flowers. Like all Ageratums this blooms continuously, and for beds in the flower garden, either as edgings, ribbon planting or for masses—it is very effective until frost—and is equally as desirable for pot culture, or as a basket or vase plant. Pkt., 5c.

MINA LOBATA, A BEAUTIFUL VINE. Pkt., 15c.

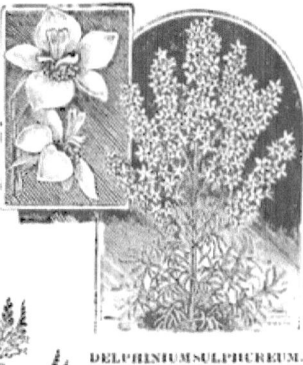

DELPHINIUM SULPHUREUM.

1068. A most beautiful sulphur yellow Delphinium. One of the most beautiful hardy perennials grown. Flowers resemble the finest orchids. Pkt., 15c.

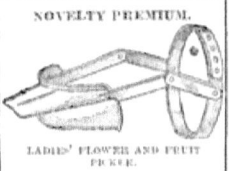

NOVELTY PREMIUM.

LADIES' FLOWER AND FRUIT PICKER.

A very pretty little nickel plated Flower Picker. Fits any though, by mail, 25c., or will send it free with orders of flower seed novelties amounting to $1.00 or over when requested.

NEW MARGUERITE CARNATIONS.

CARNATIONS THE YEAR ROUND.

Flowers Four Months from Seed.

TRY AND JUDGE YOURSELF.

By sowing in the autumn you will have flowers in spring.

Early sowing in the year will give you a profusion of sweet-scented flowers in July.

Sow in May, take off the tips of the branches, pot in August, keep the plants in a cold frame, and you will have beautiful flowers in the winter.

By a proper method of growing you will have flowers throughout the year.

Though not strictly a **Novelty** this year the Marguerite Carnations have met with such deserved success, that we desire to give them a prominent position, so that all our customers will try them. Per pkt., 15c.; 7 pkts., $1.00.

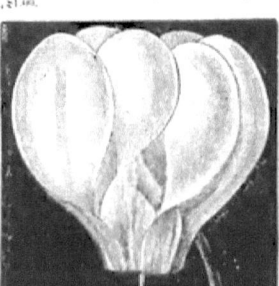

NEW CYCLAMEN, MT. BLANC. Pkt., 25c.

962. **Pure White Perpetual Blooming, Large Flowering, Fragrant Cyclamen, Mt. Blanc.**—This charming cyclamen, unlike other sorts, blooms the year around; it throws its snowy white exquisitely fragrant flowers high above the foliage; one good sized bulb will frequently have fifty to one hundred buds and blooms at one time. Flowers are from one and one-fourth to one and one-half inches long, and as it blossoms summer or winter, can be brought out any time desired. Bulbs have been known to bloom fifteen months without resting. Per pkt., 25c.

NICOTIANA COLOSSEA.

2173. Amongst all ornamental foliaged plants coming to perfection the first season from being sown, this novelty ranks foremost. It is an annual (perennial when grown under glass) attaining a height of five to six feet in the open ground. The leaves, of about three feet in length by eighteen to twenty inches in breadth, are erect at first, gracefully bending downward successively. When young, they are downy, and of a reddish tint, changing to a glossy dark green later on, this lovely green contrasting beautifully with the reddish brown ribs. The plants being of branching habit and of robust growth, and the leaves being very tough, are never damaged by wind or rain. It is well adapted for subtropical gardening, either as single specimens or for groups with other ornamental-leaved plants. Pkt., 25c.

MANDAVILLA SAVEOLENS.

An exquisite summer climber, with graceful foliage and great clusters of large, waxy star-shaped blossoms, exquisitely fragrant, resembling the single Tuberose in shape, but larger. Per pkt., 15c.

NICOTIANA COLOSSEA. Pkt., 25c.

2170. **Nicotiana Affinis.** It produces splendid, pure white Bouvardia-like flowers on long terminal tubes. When its large flowers are fully expanded in the evening and early morning, it has a most striking effect, and so fragrant that a small bed will perfume the whole surrounding atmosphere. Pkt., 15c.

Fresh air and sunshine, flowers, health, and love,—
These are endowments, if we learn to prize them;
The wise man's treasure—better far than gold,
And none but fools and wicked men despise them.

THE GORGEOUS ANNUAL POINSETTIA.

"Mexican Fire Plant," or "Fire on the Mountain."

(*Euphorbia heterophylla.*)

1221. This glorious novelty is an annual of the easiest culture, forming bushy plants three to four feet high, with glossy green table-shaped leaves, which form at the ends of the branches into large whorls and bracts, among which small green flowers appear in summer, and immediately after the leaves commence to color up. The smaller bracts among the flowers are of a brilliant orange-scarlet, and the large surrounding leaves soon become blazed with a darker fiery scarlet so that only a tip of green is left. As these colored bracts almost cover the plant, the effect is indescribably grand. The seeds grow easily if sown in the open ground as soon as it is warm enough, but if they can be started early in the house or hotbed the brilliant scarlet color will appear much earlier in the season, and is always retained until frost. Pkt., 20c.

POPPY "WHITE SWAN." Pkt., 20c.

WHITE SWAN POPPY.

2187. The introducer describes this poppy as probably one of the finest novelties of this year's introduction. The plant forms a dense, freely branching bush two feet in height; above this are elevated on strong, slender stems, the very large flowers. These are of immense size, very double, with beautifully laciniated petals, and of the purest possible white. It lasts much longer in bloom than any other poppy. Its luxuriant green foliage and pure white flowers will make it a conspicuous object when planted in groups or as single specimens in the garden. Pkt., 20c.

2188. **Papaver Glaucum, Tulip Poppy.** A glossy new annual poppy from twenty to twenty-four inches high, with beautifully shaped large flowers four inches across, of a most brilliant dark scarlet. The two outside petals are double the size of the inner ones, and each pair forms by itself a round cup of flower which nearly resembles a single tulip. The flower will stand well for several days, and the plant is therefore always in full bloom. Pkt., 20c.

EUPHORBIA HETEROPHYLLA. Pkt., 20c.

PIGMY ZINNIA.

2944. The plants of this excellent little novelty are of candelabra form, close and vigorous in habit, and when fully developed are only five to seven inches high and are nearly covered with pretty flowers extraordinarily double and of an intense orange-yellow. As each plant bears from ninety to one hundred and twenty-five flowers, it is consequently nearly covered. It continues in bloom throughout the season, and is very suitable for edging or bedding as well as of much value for pot culture. Pkt., 20c.

SULPHUR GEM SUNFLOWER.

1813. A novel and beautiful sunflower, growing about five feet high, of very branched, tree-like form, each branch bearing flowers of a delicate primrose or sulphur yellow with a black centre. The flowers are borne from within two feet of the ground to the summit, and come out in succession until killed by frost. Its rare color in a sunflower, added to its effectiveness for garden decoration, make it very desirable. Pkt., 10c.

PIGMY ZINNIA. Pkt., 20c.

"*Hurry* and *Worry* were too busy men,
They worked and worked till the clock struck ten,
They gained high station, power and wealth,
But lost their happiness, youth and health.*"

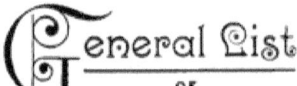 eneral List of Flower Seeds.

All flower seeds are sent free by mail on receipt of price.

Full cultural directions will be found on each packet.

Numbers. To save our customers the trouble of writing out names, we have attached a number to each variety; therefore, **please order by the numbers.**

Premiums. In ordering Flower and Vegetable Seeds in packets, purchasers sending $1.00 may select packets to the amount of $1.25. Those sending $2.00, to the amount of $2.50. Those sending $4.00, to the amount of $5.25, and so on.

*"Upon the wild old Winter King,
And shook his head of snow.
'I hear the first piercing bluebell ring,
'Tis time for me to go.'
Northward o'er the icy rocks,
Northward o'er the sea,
My daughter runs with sunny locks,
This land's too warm for me."*

LITTLE MISS COSMOS AND HER COUSIN MISS DAHLIA.

ABOBRA.

A rapid growing and climbing gourd, with beautiful dark green foliage and bright scarlet fruit; half-hardy perennial.
50. **A. Viridiflora.** Flowers fragrant and of a pale green color. 10 ft. Pkt., 10c.

ABRONIA.

A beautiful trailing plant from California, producing clusters of sweet-scented verbena-like flowers, remaining in bloom a long time; very pretty for beds, rock-work or hanging baskets; half-hardy annual.
40. **A. Umbellata.** Rosy lilac the most showy sort; ½ ft. Pkt., 5c.

ROYAL PRIZE ABUTILON.

ABUTILON.

Few lovers of these beautiful flowers are aware how easily they can be raised from seed and how beautifully they flower all summer the first season. To get them in bloom early, the seed should be started in the house and the young plants set out in the garden when the weather is warm and settled. The *Royal Prize Abutilons* here offered embrace the most elegant colors both selfs and streaked and veined varieties. Half-hardy perennial.
45. **A. Royal Prize Mixed.** Pkt., 25c.
46. **A. Fireball.** Dwarf; compact habit; large deep crimson flowers. Pkt., 25c.

ACROCLINIUM.

Elegant summer flowering plants for beds, etc.; also a good everlasting for winter bouquets; half-hardy annual.
50. **A. Choice Mixed.** Pkt., 5c.

ADLUMIA.

(*Mountain Fringe, or Allegheny Vine.*)

A pretty climber, with pale green foliage, of very graceful habit; hardy biennial.
60. **A. Cirrhosa.** Small, flesh-white flowers; 15 ft. Pkt., 10c.

ADONIS.

Very showy and popular border flower, remaining in bloom a long time; hardy annual.
80. **Æstivalis** (*Flos Adonis*). Fine scarlet; 1 ft. Pkt., 5c.
81. **A. Autumnalis** (*Pheasant's Eye*). Pkt., 5c.

AGERATUM.

This plant is a continual bloomer from early summer until the ensuing spring, and highly prized as a pot and bedding plant; half-hardy annual.
100. **A. Mexicanum Nanum.** Lilac-blue; 1½ ft. Pkt., 5c.
101. **A. Lasseauxii.** Beautiful rose color. A perennial, if given green-house protection in the winter; 1½ in. Pkt., 5c.
102. **A. Ageratum.** Choice mixed. Oz., 25c; pkt., 5c.
103. **A. Imperial Dwarf**; white. Pkt., 5c.
104. **A. White Gem**, Novelty. See page 81. Pkt., 20c.

AGROSTEMMA.

Showy for beds and borders; they are also known as "Rose of Heaven," "Rose Campion," etc. Hardy annual.
110. **A. Fine Mixed.** Pkt., 5c.

ALONSOA (*Mask Flower*).

A beautiful cut-leaved plant from Chili; flowers very showy and attractive, produced on spikes. Half-hardy annual.
120. **A. Warscewiczii.** Rosy scarlet; 1½ ft. Pkt., 5c.

ALYSSUM.

A well-known favorite, with delicate flowers of a honey-like fragrance; much prized for bouquets, baskets, rockeries and bedding; a continual bloomer.
140. **A. Sweet.** Flowers white; 1 ft. Hardy annual. Oz., 25c; pkt., 5c.
141. **Little Gem** (*Benthami Compactum*). A new and very compact growing sort, thickly studded with spikes of pure white flowers; ½ ft.; hardy annual. Oz., 50c; pkt., 5c.
142. **Saxatile Compactum.** Golden-yellow flowers; ½ ft. hardy perennial. Pkt., 5c.

"It is only by labor that thought can be made healthy, and only by thought that labor can be made happy, and the two cannot be separated with impunity."—JOHN RUSKIN.

AMARANTHUS.

Plants are grown entirely for their richly colored foliage and long racemes of curious-looking flowers. Half-hardy annuals.

160. **A. Caudatus** (*Love-lies-bleeding*). Blood-red, drooping; 3 ft. Pkt., 5c.
161. **Tri-Color** (*Joseph's Coat*). Handsome red, yellow and green foliage; 3 ft. Pkt., 5c.
162. **Cruentus** (*Prince's Feather*). Erect flowering; bright scarlet. Pkt., 5c.
163. **Salicifolius** (*Fountain Plant*). Of a pyramidal drooping habit; leaves willow-shaped, changing to magnificent hues; 4 ft. Pkt., 5c.
164. **Bi-Color.** Rich brown and yellow. Pkt., 5c.
165. **Marguerite.** Charming dwarf plant; a free bloomer, commencing to flower in a month after the seeds are up; long, graceful shafts of flowers of purple color, see cut. Pkt., 10c.

AMPELOPSIS (*Japanese or Boston Ivy*).

180. **A. Veitchii.** Clings firmly upon any surface, and can be continued to any limit by pruning. Leaves olive green, which turn to scarlet in the autumn; the best kind of a plant for covering unsightly objects; 50 ft. Hardy perennial. Oz., 35c.; pkt., 10c.

ANAGALLIS (*Pimpernel*).

Very desirable for small beds, edgings, rock work, baskets or borders; a constant and profuse bloomer. Half-hardy annual.

200. **A. Grandiflora Mixed.** White, blue and deep vermilion red; ½ ft. Pkt., 5c.

ANTIRRHINUM (*Snap-Dragon*).

One of our very best perennials; blooms abundantly the first summer until after frost. Flowers are large, finely shaped and of the most brilliant colors. Hardy perennial.
220. **A. Nanum, Mixed.** Finest dwarf Tom Thumb; very rich colors; 1 ft. Pkt., 5c.
221. **Majus, Mixed.** Tall varieties; fine assortment; 2 ft. Pkt., 5c.

AQUILEGIA (*Columbine*).

This plant blooms early in the spring and summer and produces beautiful, curiously-formed and variously colored flowers; hardy perennials.
240. **A. Single.** All colors mixed; 2 ft. Pkt., 5c.
241. **A. Double.** All colors mixed; 18 in. Pkt., 5c.
242. **A. Chrysantha.** (Golden Spurred Columbine.) This is one of the finest perennials for the border evergrown. Flowers of the most intense primrose yellow throughout, with long slender spurs; fragrant and exceedingly showy. Pkt., 15c.
243. **A. Chrysantha Alba.** (New Pure White Spurred Columbine.) This pure white variety has flowers of the largest size, pure snow white, with long spurs of elegant shape, and borne in lavish quantity; charming for groups in the garden and an excellent pot plant. Pkt., 25c.
244. **A. Skinneri.** A magnificent columbine, with crimson sepals, lined with light green, and light green petals and long, straight, *crimson* spurs. One of the finest. Pkt., 15c.
245. **A. Cærulea.** Flowers are very large, violet blue, and inner petals pure white; 2 ft. Pkt., 10c.

One pkt. each of these 4 magnificent columbines for 50c.

AURICULA. Pkt., 25c.

AMARANTHUS MARGUERITE. Pkt., 10c.

ARGEMONE (*Prickly Poppy*).

Grows well in any garden soil; plants bear large flowers resembling a single poppy; the foliage is large, of a bright green color, sparsely covered with slender prickles. Hardy annual.
280. **A. Grandiflora.** White; very handsome; 2 ft. Pkt., 5c.
281. **Argemone.** Fine mixed. Per pkt., 5c.

ARMERIA (*Sea Pink*).

290. **A. Maritima.** A very handsome, compact growing plant, well adapted to rock-work, edgings, etc.; flowers rosy pink. Hardy perennial; ½ ft. Pkt., 10c.

ASPERULA.

A profuse blooming plant, bearing many clusters of small sweet-scented flowers; very pretty for bouquets. Hardy annual.
300. **A. Orientalis.** Sky blue; ¾ ft. Pkt., 5c.
301. **A. Setosa.** Sky blue. Pkt., 5c.

ARISTOLOCHIA.

(*Dutchman's Pipe.*)

An attractive, quick growing, hardy perennial, with large heart-shaped leaves and flowers of singular formation, resembling a pipe; 30 ft.
260. **A. Sipho.** Flowers brownish purple. Pkt., 10c.
261. **A. Elegans.** A rapid growing climber with very novel flowers; color, externally, white veined with purple; internally, rich purplish brown, irregularly marked with white. It grows rapidly from seed, flowering the first year if sown early and is a very pretty vine for outside decoration in summer and the greenhouse in winter. The blossoms are borne profusely, even on small plants. (*See cut.*) Pkt., 20c.

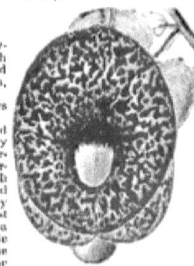

ARISTOLOCHIA ELEGANS. Pkt., 20c.

AURICULA.

A dwarf growing plant, bearing umbels of fragrant flowers of many rich and beautiful colors. A great favorite in Britain, where flower shows are held of this plant alone. Hardy perennial; ½ ft.
350. **A. Extra Choice, Mixed.** From a prize collection. Pkt., 25c.

BALLOON VINE (*Love in a Puff*).

340. **Cardiospermum Halicacabum.** A climbing plant, useful for either inside or out-door decoration; succeeds best in a light, warm situation. Flowers white; 6 ft. Half-hardy annual. Pkt., 5c.

BARTONIA.

Plants of a succulent nature, flowers expanding after the middle of the day, and very fragrant towards evening. The leaves are thistle-like in appearance, and somewhat downy. Should be watered freely during dry weather. Hardy annual.
360. **B. Aurea.** Flowers very bright yellow; 2 ft. Pkt., 5c.

"An ounce of keeping your mouth shut is better than a pound of explanation after you have said it."

NEW DOUBLE BALSAMS ROYAL CAMELLIA PRIZE.

BALSAM (*Lady Slipper, or Touch-me-not*).

Our collection embraces all the most improved kinds, and there have certainly been great improvements made in varieties within the last few years. The largest and best double flowers are secured by first sowing in a seed bed and then transplanting them where they are to grow. Hardy annuals; 2 ft.

  B. Extra Double, White. This is the handsome, double, white balsam so much grown by florists. Very choice. Pkt., 10c.
  The King. Brilliant scarlet, very double. Pkt., 10c.
  New Challenger Prize. The flowers are of wonderfully large size and perfect shape, colors brilliant and varied, comprising pure white, lemon, salmon, rose, crimson, deep pink, purple, mottled and striped. Pkt., 20c.
  Camellia Flowered. Very double and beautiful colors; perfect form. Pkt., 10c.
  Double. Extra choice, mixed. Pkt., 5c; oz., 40c.
  Double Solferino. Very beautiful, white ground, striped and streaked with lilac and scarlet. Pkt., 10c.
  Royal Camellia Prize. This is the most magnificent strain of perfectly double Balsams ever introduced. The flowers are wonderfully large size and perfect shape, of exquisite shades of pure white, white shaded with pale lemon, cream white, salmon, rose, rich crimson, deep pink, violet, bright purple, and a great variety of superbly mottled varieties. Price, pkt., 25c.
  Peach Blossom. Beautiful. Pkt., 10c.

GIANT FLOWERED TUBEROUS-ROOTED BEGONIA.

As bedding plants there is nothing to equal the New Tuberous Rooted Begonia. They bloom equal to the geranium but with a form and variety of colors and shading equal to the rose. The flowers are borne upright on stout stiff stalks, showing the full beauty of the flowers. These are immense in size, frequently measuring five to seven inches across. The seed should be sown as early as possible. A single packet will produce bulbs by the fall the first season.

  B. Tuberous-Rooted, Single. Mixed. Containing the greatest variety of shades, from pure white through all the tints of cream, yellow, orange, pink, red and scarlet. Pkt., 25c.
  B. Tuberous-Rooted, Double, Mixed. Exquisite double kinds. Pkt. 25c.
  B. Rex Hybrida, Mixed. Beautiful varieties with variegated foliage. Pkt. 25c.
  B. Crednerii. See Novelties, page 80. Pkt. 25c.
  B. Semperflorens Atropurpurea. See Novelties, page 80. Pkt. 25c.

BEGONIA REX. Pkt. 25c.

BRACHYCOME IBERIDIFOLIA.

BRACHYCOME.

  B. Iberidifolia. (*Swan River Daisy.*) An erect growing plant, covered the entire season with pretty flowers about one inch in diameter; mixed colors of blue and white with a dark centre; 1 ft. Half hardy annual. Pkt., 5c.

BROWALLIA.

The Browallia is valuable, alike for blooming during the winter in the house as well as for bedding out during the summer. Remarkably free and attractive bloomers. Half-hardy annual.

  B. Elata Cœrulea Grandiflora. Pale blue; 1½ ft. Pkt., 5c.
  B. Elata Alba. Pure white; 1½ ft. Pkt. 5c.
  Rozeli, Mixed. An exceedingly pretty species, flowers double the size of the preceding varieties, and forms a dense compact bush; flowers azure blue and white with a yellow centre; 2 ft. Hardy annual. Pkt., 10c.

CACALIA (*Tassel Flower*).

Small pretty plants with tassel-like flowers, keeping in bloom from early summer until autumn; 1½ ft. Hardy annual.

  C. Mixed. Golden yellow and scarlet. Pkt., 5c.
  C. Coccinea. Scarlet. Pkt., 5c.

*"My Grandfather's rule was safer 'n 'tis to crow.
Don't never prophesy, unless ye know."* —LOWELL.

SUCCESSFUL ∴ FLOWER ∴ SEEDS ∴

CALAMPELIS (*Eccremocarpus*).

440. **C. Scabra.** A quick-growing evergreen climber, bearing profusely clusters of orange-colored tube-like flowers. Half-hardy perennial; 10 ft. Pkt., 10c.

CALANDRINIA.

Pretty plants, with succulent stems and fleshy leaves; splendid for edgings and rockeries.

500. **C. Grandiflora.** Beautiful rose; 1½ ft. Hardy annual. Pkt., 5c.

501. **Umbellata.** Dazzling magenta crimson; 1 ft. Half-hardy biennial. Pkt., 5c.

CALCEOLARIA.

Now recognized as one of the grandest plants in existence, producing masses of pocket-like flowers; a universal favorite for decorating the green-house and conservatory early in the spring.

520. **C. Hybrida Grandiflora.** Tall Mixed. The finest large flowering and most floriferous sort, of the richest colors; ½ inch. Pkt., 25c.

521. **C. Hybrida Grandiflora Pumila Compacta Mixed.** A new strain of dwarf, compact and strong-growing sorts, producing large and brilliant self-colored and spotted flowers; 1 ft. Pkt., 10c.

522. **C. Rugosa.** Small flowering varieties for bedding, of the finest colors; 2 ft. Pkt., 10c.

CALENDULA (*Marigold*).

Very free and attractive bloomers, growing well in almost all situations. Hardy annuals.

540. **C. Officinalis Meteor.** A splendid large flowering variety, double striped, of a deep orange on a pale yellow ground; 1 ft. Pkt., 5c.

541. **Prince of Orange.** A novelty surpassing in beauty C. Meteor, the florets being striped with a more intense shade of orange; 1 ft. Pkt., 5c.

542. **Ranunculoides.** Fl. Pl. (Cape or Garden Marigolds). Deep orange color, 1 ft. Pkt., 5c.

543. **CALENDULA.** Fine mixed. Pkt., 5c.

CALCEOLARIA.

COREOPSIS LANCEOLATA. Pkt., 10c.

COREOPSIS, or CALLIOPSIS.

Very showy free-flowering plants, natives of this country; fine for borders and beds, easily cultivated. Hardy annuals.

560. **C. Drummondi.** Yellow, with a circle of rich crimson brown; 1 ft. Pkt., 5c.

561. **Atrosanguinea.** Dark crimson; 2 ft. Pkt., 5c.

562. **Mixed.** Embracing the most showy colors. Oz., 50c.; pkt., 5c.

563. **Coreopsis Lanceolata.** The most charming hardy perennial sent out for many years. It grows easily, flowers the first season from seed and continues in bloom during the entire summer. The flowers are borne on long stems, are of a lovely bright golden-yellow color, remain in perfection a long time when cut, and are a charming flower for ladies' wear. Pkt., 10c.

564. **Golden Wave.** For a mass of bright color, this is probably the most effective of all annuals. Plant very bushy and compact, reaching two feet in height, and covered from July to October, with hundreds of beautiful golden blossoms, with small dark centres. It is indeed a wave of gold. Pkt., 10c.

CALLIOPSIS GOLDEN WAVE. Pkt., 10c.

CALENDULA, PRINCE OF ORANGE. Pkt., 5c.

CALLIRHOE.

580. **C. Involucrata.** Flowers beautiful crimson, begin to bloom when quite small and continue in bloom the entire summer and autumn. ½ ft. Hardy perennial. Pkt., 10c.

COLLECTIONS OF FLOWERS.

A fine collection of ten Choice Annuals, ... $0 25
A fine collection of ten Floral Novelties, ... 50
A fine collection of Summer Flowering Bulbs, ... 50
A larger collection of Summer Flowering Bulbs, ... 1 00
A fine collection of Wonderful Cacti, ... 1 00

*"Joy and temperance and repose
Shut the door on the doctor's nose."*

CAMPANULA
(Bell Flower).

Very attractive plants with pretty bell-shaped flowers; of very easy cultivation.

650. **C. Speculum** (Venus Looking Glass). Pretty blue; 1/2 ft. Hardy annual. Pkt., 5c.

651. **Media, Single Mixed** (Canterbury Bells). Beautiful large, bell-shaped flowers; handsome for border or pot culture; 2 1/2 ft. Hardy biennials. Pkt., 5c.

652. **Media, Double Mixed.** All the finest double varieties; 2 1/2 ft. Hardy biennials. Pkt., 5c.

653. **Carpatica, Mixed.** Free flowering, blue and white, bloom the whole season; 3/4 ft. Hardy perennial. Pkt., 5c.

654. **THE "CUP AND SAUCER" CAMPANULAS** are a very striking and beautiful variety of "Canterbury Bells." The flowers are large and resemble a cup and saucer. Colors are mixed blue, rose, lilac and white. Price, per pkt., 15c.

NEW CAMPANULA, "CUP AND SAUCER." Pkt., 15c.

New Spotted Bell Flower.
(*Campanula Punctata.*)

655. An elegant, new, perfectly hardy perennial, about 1 1/2 feet high. The pendulous bell-shaped flowers are milk white, dotted and striped with red on the inner surface and as large as the well-known Canterbury Bells. A splendid cut flower of elegant and graceful appearance in vases or bouquets. Pkt., 25c.

NEW SPOTTED BELL FLOWER. Pkt., 25c.
Campanula Punctata.

CANDYTUFT.
(*Iberis.*)

Favorite plants of the easiest culture, useful for growing in beds or masses; bloom long and freely. Hardy annuals.

620. **I. Fragrant** (*Pectinata*). Pure white, pinnated foliage; 1 ft. Pkt., 5c.
621. **Crimson.** Very beautiful; 1 ft. Pkt., 5c.
622. **WHITE ROCKET** (*Amara Grandiflora*). Large trusses of pure white flowers; 1 ft. Pkt., 5c.
623. **White Tom Thumb** (*Hybrida Nana*). A new dwarf variety, growing about six inches high branching into a handsome bush, about sixteen inches in diameter. Pkt., 10c.
624. **Fine Mixed.** Comprising all the choicest tall-growing varieties; 1 ft. Pkt., 5c.
625. **C. NEW EMPRESS.** One of the finest varieties of recent introduction. It is intermediate in height between the old Rocket and the newer Tom Thumb sort. The plant is of a very branching habit, and assumes when fully grown and covered with its large trusses of pure white flowers, a very handsome candelabrum-like aspect. Pkt., 10c.

NEW EMPRESS CANDYTUFT. Pkt., 10c.

CARNATION, OR PICOTEE PINK.
(*Dianthus Caryophyllus Flore Pleno.*)

STRIPED CARNATION. Pkt., 15c.

660. **C. Grenadin.** Blooms much earlier than any other Carnation; more floriferous, larger and finer double flowers, which are of a brilliant scarlet color; 1 ft. Pkt., 25c.
661. **Finest German Double, Mixed.** Saved from extra choice named double flowers, 1 1/2 ft. Pkt., 25c.
662. **Fine Double, Mixed.** Comprising the hardiest and best varieties for garden culture; 1 1/2 ft. Pkt., 10c.
663. **C. Marguerite.** See Novelties, page 82. Pkt., 15c.
664. **C. Finest Double Striped.** (See cut.) Pkt., 15c.

"Oh the green things growing, the green things growing,
The faint, sweet smell of the green things growing!
And how many a tender touch they comfort me so much,
With the soft, mute comfort of green things growing."

✦ New Dwarf French Large Flowering Cannas. ✦

This new class of Cannas, introduced by Monsieur Crozy of France, are very dwarf in habit, while their foliage is very luxuriant and varied in color, from the lightest pea-green to the dark rich bronze. But their great merit consists in the form and great size and dazzling brilliancy of their flowers. These colors range through all shades of yellow and orange to the richest crimson, scarlet and vermilion. Many are beautifully spotted, some are striped and flaked. They flower freely from seed the first season if the seed is sown early. Pour scalding water over the seed and then let them soak in warm water near the stove for twenty-four hours before planting. Don't let them be in the scalding water long enough to cook them. Seed started in this way in February will produce blooming plants in July and will bloom continuously till frost and then the roots may be taken up and stored till next spring.

646. **Canna, Mme. Crozy.** One of the most magnificent Cannas ever raised; a very vigorous dwarf grower, with bright green foliage; compact habit, throws up quantities of flower stalks; the blooms are extra large, of bright vermilion red, bordered with gold, and of beautiful Gladiolus form. Pkt., 20c.

647. **C. EMILE LECLAIRE.** Flowers large, bright golden-yellow, mottled and spotted crimson and scarlet. Pea-green foliage. As a cut flower it will be found useful, as its peculiar color gives it the appearance of an orchid. One of the best and most distinct varieties. Roots, 20c. each; pkt., 15c.

648. **C. President Carnot.** A strong grower with upright foliage of fine silky purple; very free in bloom; flower large and round; color a soft crimson, lined and pointed a lighter shade. Pkt., 15c.

649. **C. Little Gypsy.** Very dwarf, beautiful dark foliage; young growth of a purplish brown tint, flowers brilliant cherry color in light airy trusses. Pkt., 15c.

650. **C. Antoine Crozy.** Rich shade of crimson, fine spike; foliage dark green, edged purple. Pkt., 15c.

651. **C. Felix Crousse.** Glaucous green foliage, large coppery red flowers. Price, 20c. each; pkt., 15c.

652. **C. Henry Martin.** Orange scarlet; extra large flowers; foliage dark green. Price, roots, 20c. each; pkt., 15c.

653. **C. Nabob.** Magnificent foliage; slashed and striped purplish red; large crimson-scarlet flowers. Price, 30c. each; pkt., 15c.

654. **C. Francisque Morel.** One of the finest; good grower, free flowering; blooms large, long petalled, bright cherry red. Pkt., 15c.

655. **C. Oriental.** Dark foliage, shaded chocolate; flowers rich scarlet; very showy. Pkt., 15c.

> One packet each of the above ten choice sorts for $1.00, and this would make a bed of which you might well be proud.

615. **C. Large Flowering French Varieties.** Mixed. Pkt., 15c.

OLDER SORTS.

610. **C. Marechal Vaillant.** Foliage rich maroon; large, bright orange flowers; 5 ft. Pkt., 5c.

641. **Tricolor.** Foliage green, red and creamy yellow; bright scarlet flowers; 3 ft. Oz., 75c.; pkt., 5c.

642. **Finest Mixed.** Embracing twenty of the best sorts. Oz., 40c. pkt., 5c.

643. **C. Gigantea.** 8 ft. Pkt., 5c.

CANNA ROOTS.

C. Ehemanni. The most distinct of all Cannas on account of its large oval soft green leaves and carmine-red flowers, which are produced on long flower stems; each of the smaller branches bears about twelve flowers. 20c. each; $2.00 doz.

C. Emile Leclaire. Flowers large, bright golden-yellow, mottled and spotted crimson and scarlet. One of the best and most distinct varieties. Pea-green foliage. 20c. each; $2.00 doz.

C. Noutoni. Is quite distinct from Ehemanni in coloring, being a rich shade of crimson scarlet. The flowers are very large, growing erect instead of drooping. The foliage is of a beautiful bluish green. 20c. each; $2.00 doz.

C. Robusta Perfecta. A most distinct and handsome sort, bearing immense leaves twelve to eighteen inches wide and three feet long, of a bright bronze-red color, and reaching a height of twelve feet. 15c. each; $1.50 doz.

C. Henry Martin. See description above. 20c. each; $2.00 doz.

> One each of above roots prepaid, by mail, for 75c., or three each for $2.00.

COCKSCOMB, QUEEN OF THE DWARFS. Pkt., 15c.

CEDRONELLA.

670. **C. Cana.** An interesting evergreen plant from New Mexico, with fragrant foliage and long spikes of crimson flowers; 2 ft. Hardy perennial. Pkt., 10c.

CELOSIA (Cockscomb).

Interesting and brilliant plants of tropical origin, which never fail to please the grower and attract attention; one of the most satisfactory plants for garden decoration. Half-hardy annuals.

675. **C. Cristata, Dwarf Crimson.** Large, velvet-like combs; 1 ft. Pkt., 5c.
676. **Cristata, Variegata.** Brilliant combs of crimson and gold; 3 ft. Pkt., 5c.
677. **Japonica.** A distinct handsome variety, combs of the most brilliant scarlet and ruffled like lace; 2½ ft. Pkt., 5c.
678. **Glasgow Prize.** Very fine, dwarf variety; brilliant crimson comb, and handsome dark variegated foliage; 1 ft. Pkt., 10c.
679. **Cristata.** Finest mixed. Pkt., 5c.
680. **C. Queen of the Dwarfs.** A very dwarf variety growing only eight inches high, with combs seven to ten inches across of a rich dark rose color, of very even growth. A fine bedding sort. Pkt., 15c.
681. **C. Plumosa.** Of bushy pyramidal growth, each branch being tipped with a spike of bright crimson flowers; very fine. Pkt., 10c.

JOHNSON & STOKES

CENTAUREA (Dusty Miller).

Extensively used for margins, beds and vases. Half-hardy perennials.

685. **Candidissima.** Attractive, silvery, cut leaves. Half-hardy perennials; 1 ft. Pkt., 1c.

686. **Gymnocarpa.** Graceful, finely cut, silvery gray leaves. Half-hardy perennials; 1½ ft. Pkt., 10c.

687. **Cyanus Minor, Mixed** (Blue Bottle or Corn Flower). Beautiful flowers, in bloom all summer; pretty shades of white, blue and deep rose. Hardy annual; 1½ ft. Pkt., 5c.

CENTRANTHUS.

Will grow freely in any garden soil; flowers produced in clusters and blooms freely; hardy annuals.

689. **C. Mixed.** Red and white; 1½ ft. Pkt., 5c.

CHRYSANTHEMUMS.

700. **C. Gladstone.** A new and beautiful English variety, flowers rich crimson, great size and perfect form; profuse bloomer. Hardy annual; 1 ft. Pkt., 10c.

701. **The Sultan.** Flowers are a rich velvet crimson maroon, with gold colored rim about one-quarter inch deep next to the centre; 1½ ft. Hardy annual. Pkt., 10c.

702. **Burridgeanum.** Crimson, with white edge and inner white circle; very pretty; 1 ft. Hardy annual. Pkt., 5c.

703. **Carinatum Tricolor** ("Eclipse." Resembles C. Burridgeanum, but surpasses it greatly by its striking colors of great beauty, which are a pure golden-yellow with a purplish scarlet ring on the ray florets, the disc being a dark brown; 1 ft. Hardy annuals. Pkt., 5c.

704. **Selected, Mixed.** Comprises a full assortment of the prettiest single and double sorts. Hardy annuals. Pkt., 5c.

705. **New Double Japanese and Chinese Mixed.** These superb flowers present many odd and beautiful types, frequently measuring six inches in diameter, with broad petals deeply incurved, varying in color from pure white to pale pink, crimson, maroon and rich orange brown. Pkt., 25c.

706. **LORD BEACONSFIELD.** An exceedingly handsome and wonderfully brilliant variety. The flower is very large and perfect in form; color a rich crimson maroon, edged and striped with gold and having a golden rim surrounding the eye. Pkt., 10c.

707. **C. Coronarium.** Double white and yellow, fine. Pkt., 10c.

708. **C. MAXIMUM.** See cut. This new variety is a grand addition to our collection of choice hardy perennials. Its beautiful snow-white flowers are produced in great abundance the whole season, and as cut flowers they are unexcelled in lasting qualities. Pkt., 10c.

CHRYSANTHEMUM MAXIMUM. Pkt. 10c.

CINERARIA—Continued.

720. **C. Hybrida Grandiflora, Prize, Tall Mixed.** Extra selected seed, unsurpassable in quality and beautiful brilliant colors; 2 ft. Pkt., 10c.

721. **Hybrida Grandiflora, Prize, Tall Mixed.** Produce the same large and brilliant flowers as the above variety, but only grow about 1 ft. high. Pkt., 60c.

CINERARIA (Dusty Miller).

740. **C. Maritima Candidissima.** Large silvery, deeply cut foliage. Pkt., 10c.

741. **Acanthifolia.** Beautifully cut silvery foliage; hardier than the above; 1 ft. Pkt., 10c.

CLARKIA.

An old favorite plant, growing well in any garden soil. Seed can be sown either in September or early spring. Hardy annual.

760. **C. Single and Double, Mixed.** Beautiful snow-white, rosy crimson, and deep rose; 1½ ft. Pkt., 5c.

761. **C. Elegans, Purple King.** Pkt., 5c.

CLEMATIS.

780. **C. Jackman's Large-Flowering Hybrids.** The flowers will average three inches in diameter, ranging through all conceivable shades of purple, violet, porcelain, blue and white. Hardy perennials 10 ft. Pkt., 20c.

781. **Coccinea.** Of slender habit, tubular flower, deep vermilion on outside and yellow within. Hardy perennial; 10 ft. Pkt., 15c.

782. **Virginiana.** Greenish white, fragrant flowers; dies down to the ground in winter, but starts up in spring. Hardy perennial; 20 ft. Pkt., 10c.

782. **Hybrida Double, Mixed.** Possesses all the varied hues of the hybrid tall and dwarf varieties; 2 ft. Pkt., 25c.

783. **Flammula.** A luxuriant climber, with large clusters of small white, sweet-scented flowers; 15 ft. Pkt., 10c.

CLEOME (Spider Flower).

790. **C. Speciosissima.** The stamens of this strange looking, rose-colored flower resemble the legs of a spider. Half-hardy annual; 3 ft. Pkt., 5c.

791. **Cleome Pungens** (Giant Spider Plant). This is a showy, robust growing plant, four to five feet high, producing long curious spikes of flowers of bright rose color with long antennae-like stamens, giving a very graceful cloud-like effect. They are of easy cultivation, blooming even when the plants are small, and continuing until late in the season. Pkt., 10c.

CLIANTHUS (Australian Glory Pea).

800. **C. Dampieri.** A beautiful plant with brilliant, rich scarlet, pea-shaped flowers, with an intense black spot in each centre. Green-house perennial, 4 ft. Pkt., 15c.

CLINTONIA.

820. **C. Elegans.** A pretty blue flower, similar in shape to the Lobelia. Splendid for hanging baskets or rock-work, or damp, shady situations. Hardy annual; 1 ft. Pkt., 10c.

PRIZE DWARF CINERARIA.

CINERARIA (Cape Aster).

Very attractive, free-blooming greenhouse plants, blooming during the winter and spring months. Though perennials, they do better when treated as tender annuals.

*"Scowling and growling will make a man old;
Money and fame at the last are beguiling;
Don't be suspicious and selfish and cold—
Try smiling."*

✧ SUCCESSFUL ✧ FLOWER ✧ SEEDS ✧

COBEA SCANDENS. Pkt., 10c.

COBEA.

810. **C. Scandens.** A beautiful, rapid-growing climber, with handsome foliage and large bell-shaped flowers, green at first, changing to a beautiful, deep violet blue; 20 to 40 ft. Half-hardy perennial. (See cut.) Pkt., 10c.

COLEUS.

860. **C. American Hybrids.** Mixed. Seed saved from the finest hybrid sorts; remarkable for their brilliant and varied foliage. Pkt., 25c.
861. **C. New Hybrids.** Choicest new varieties. Pkt., 50c.

Collinsia.

A pretty, free blooming plant with various colored flowers, white, pink, violet, purple, blue and gray-blue. Hardy annual.
880. **C. Mixed.** 1 ft. Pkt., 5c.

COSMOS HYBRIDUS. Mixed. Pkt., 10c.

COMMELINA.

900. **C. Cœlestis.** An erect plant, producing pretty sky-blue flowers in great profusion. Roots should be preserved like Dahlias; its beauty will increase from year to year; 1½ ft. Half-hardy herbaceous perennial. Pkt. 10c.

CONVOLVULUS *(Morning Glory)*.

The most popular annual in cultivation. The dwarf varieties are very pretty for bedding, hanging baskets and vases. Hardy annual.
920. **C. Tricolor Roseus.** Beautiful rose color, with pure white centre, fringed with purple, shading towards the throat with five broad bands of golden yellow; 1 ft. Pkt., 5c.
921. **Major, Mixed.** Finest colors; 15 ft. Oz., 20c.; pkt., 5c.
922. **Mauritanicus.** A beautiful trailing plant, with rich blue flowers; 1 ft. Pkt., 10c.
923. **New Crimson Violet.** 1 ft. Pkt., 5c.
924. **Minor, Mixed.** All colors, 1 ft. Pkt., 5c.

Cosmos Hybridus. (See Cut.)

930. Plants four to six feet high; literally covered in the autumn with large single flowers. A group in bloom is a gorgeous sight. Colors range through shades of rose, purple, flesh and white. Price, per pkt., 10c.
931. **C. Pearl.** Beautiful snow white. Pkt., 15c.

Cuphea *(Cigar Plant)*.

When planted outside will bloom all summer; on the approach of frost they may be removed to the conservatory, where they will continue to bloom the entire winter. Half-hardy perennial.
940. **C. Hookeriana Grandiflora Superba.** Beautiful vermilion and orange color; 1 ft. Pkt., 10c.
941. **C. Miniata.** Curious flowers of a bright vermilion, with a centre of reddish violet; 1½ ft. Pkt., 10c.
942. **C. Platycentra.** Scarlet. Very pretty species. Pkt., 10c.

CYCLAMEN.

950. **C. Persicum.** Charming bulbous-rooted plants, with beautiful foliage and rich-colored, orchid-like fragrant flowers. If seed is sown early they make flowering bulbs in one season. They require sandy loam; half-hardy perennial; 6 in. Pkt., 25c.
951. **C. Giganteum.** A new large flowering variety; mixed; 8 in. Pkt., 50c.

CYCLAMEN—Continued.
952. **C. G. Album.** Pure white. Pkt., 50c.
953. **C. S. Rubrum.** Red. Pkt., 50c.
954. **C. Mt. Blanc.** See Novelties, page 82. Pkt., 50c.

CYPRESS VINE.

(Ipomæa quamoclit.)

An elegant climbing plant, with beautiful fern-like foliage, and masses of beautiful star-shaped flowers; 15 ft. Half-hardy annuals.
980. **Crimson.** Pkt., 5c.
981. **White.** Pkt., 5c.
982. **Mixed.** Pkt., 5c.
983. **Scarlet Ivy-leaved.** Deeply lobed ivy-like leaves; flowers fiery scarlet. Pkt., 5c.

DAHLIA.

Will bloom the first year from seed if sown not later than March; 2 to 8 ft. Half-hardy perennial.
1000. **D. Large Flowering, Double.** Comprising every known shade of color. Pkt., 10c.
1001. **Single, Mixed.** Saved from the very choicest single varieties. Pkt., 10c.

DATURA.

(Trumpet Flower.)

It is strange that so many of the most beautiful and showy of our annuals are so little known and cultivated, and amongst them, these Trumpet Flowers or Thorn Apples, as they are also called, grow two to three feet high, and form a handsome bush, covered with deliciously fragrant flowers, until late in the fall. They are annuals and easily grown.
1040. **D. Fastuosa Huberiana, Mixed.** Large, double flowers, of various colors. Pkt., 5c.
1042. **D. Fastuosa Alba, fl. pl.** Large, double, pure white handsome flowers. See cut. Pkt., 10c.
1041. **Wrightii** *(Meteloides).* Handsome, white, single flowers of exquisite fragrance. Pkt., 5c.

DATURA FASTUOSA ALBA, FL. PL.
Large pure white Double Datura. Pkt 10c.

NEW DOUBLE DAISY, "GIANT" SNOWBALL. Pkt., 20c.

1081. **Heddewigii Diadematis, Fl. Pl.** (*Double Diadem Japan Pink*). Densely double flowers, three inches in diameter, beautiful tints of crimson, lilac, purple, outer edges fringed with white, 6 in. Hardy annual. Pkt., 10c.
1082. **Scoticus, Fl. Pl.** (*Double Scotch, or Paisley Pinks*). Flowers with fringed edges; mixed colors; 1 ft. Hardy perennial. Pkt., 40c.
1083. **Plumarius, Fl. Pl.** (*Finest Double Garden Pink*). Hardy perennial. Pkt., 15c.
1084. **D. Imperialis.** Double imperial pink; fine. Pkt., 5c.
1085. **D. Laciniatus Flore Pleno** (*Double Fringed Japan Pink*). Large, double, showy flowers, with fringed edges, mixed, various colors and beautifully striped. Pkt., 10c.

DIGITALIS (*Foxglove*).

1130. **D. Mixed.** Long spikes of beautiful thimble-shaped flowers, 3 ft. Hardy perennial. Pkt., 5c.

NEW GIANT AMERICAN COWSLIP (*Dodecanthon Clevelandi*).

1150. A beautiful perennial, native of California. It throws up flower stalks surmounted by beautiful cyclamen-like flowers of the loveliest shade of violet blue, with yellow and black centres. It is perfectly hardy, but does best in partial shade. Pkt., 20c.

DOLICHOS (*Hyacinth Bean*).

1170. **D. Giganteus.** A beautiful climbing plant of free growth, producing clusters of beautiful purple flowers; 20 ft. Tender annual. Oz., 25c., pkt., 5c.
1171. **D. Purpurea.** Pkt., 5c.

DIANTHUS LACINIATUS, FLORE PLENO. Pkt., 10c.

These are very popular and desirable for winter decoration, bouquets, wreaths, etc. They should be cut when they come into full bloom tied into bunches and dried in the shade, with their heads downward.
1240. **Acroclinium Roseum, Fl. Pl.** Bright rose, double; larger than the old sorts. 15 in. Half-hardy annual. Pkt., 5c.
1241. **Ammobium Alatum Grandiflorum.** A leading everlasting; flowers very large and pure white color. Hardy annual. Pkt., 5c.
1242. **Gomphrena Mixed** (*Bachelor's Buttons*). Remarkably handsome flowers, comprising pure white, crimson, orange and variegated colors; 2 ft. Half-hardy annual. Pkt., 5c.

DAISY (*Bellis Perennis*).

1020. **D. Double, Mixed.** Extra quality. Pkt., 10c.
1022. **Longfellow.** Very large, double, dark rose flowers, borne on long stems. Pkt., 15c.
1023. **New "Giant Snowball."** Has unusually large double flowers, having very long stems, render it very valuable for cutting; color, pure white. Pkt., 20c.

DELPHINIUM (*Larkspur*).

1060. **D. Formosum.** Brilliant, rich, blue flowers, with a white centre; 2 ft. Hardy perennial. Pkt., 5c.
1061. **Nudicaule.** Bright scarlet flowers, with clear, yellow petals, 18 in. Hardy perennials. Pkt., 10c.
1063. **Imperiale Flore Pleno** (*Emperor Larkspur*). With beautiful, long spikes of brilliant, dark blue, tricolor and red striped, double flowers; 1½ ft. Hardy annual. Pkt., 10c.
1064. **Finest Mixed Hybrids.** A fine collection of twenty sorts; 2 ft. Hardy annuals. Pkt., 5c.
1065. **Dwarf German Rocket.** Hyacinth-flowered larkspur, mixed. Pkt., 5c.
1066. **D. Elatum.** See Larkspur. Pkt., 5c.
1067. **D. Chinensis.** Blue Larkspur. Pkt., 5c.
1068. **D. Sulphureum.** See Novelties, page 81. Pkt., 15c.

DIANTHUS (*Pinks*).

1080. **D. Chinensis, Fl. Pl.** (*China, or Indian Pink*). Extra large, double, fragrant flowers, mixed; 1 ft. Hardy annual. Pkt., 5c.

HELICHRYSUM. Pkt., 5c.

ERYSIMUM (*Hedge Mustard*).

1160. **E. Perofskianum.** Large clusters of beautiful deep red, very showy orange flowers, resembling a single Wall Flower; 1½ ft. Hardy annual. Pkt., 5c.

ESCHSCHOLTZIA (*California Poppy*).

1180. **E. Californica.** Very large, bright yellow flowers, with rich orange centre; 1½ ft. Hardy annual. Pkt., 5c.
1181. **Crocea, Fl. Pl.** Beautiful double, bright orange, scarlet, shading to salmon red; 1 ft. Hardy biennial. Pkt., 10c.
1182. **Fine Mixed.** Comprises fully a dozen of the finest colors. Pkt., 5c.
1183. **E. Mandarin.** Inner side of the petals rich orange, the outer side brilliant scarlet; when in full bloom the plants of this charming novelty present a gorgeous outline. Pkt., 5c.

EUPATORIUM.

1206. **E. Fraseri.** Snow-white flowers, blooming the first season from seed; 1½ ft. Hardy herbaceous perennial. Pkt., 5c.

EUPHORBIA (*Snow on the Mountain*).

1220. **E. Variegata.** A pretty foliage plant, with white and green variegated bracts; 2 ft. Hardy annual. Pkt., 5c.
1221. **E. Heterophylla.** See Novelties, page 83. Pkt., 20c.

EUTOCA.

1230. **E. Viscida.** Pretty dark blue flowers; will keep fresh for several days if placed in water; 2 ft. Hardy annual. Oz., 25c.; pkt., 5c.

EVERLASTINGS.

1243. **Helipterum Humboldtianum** (*Sanfordi*). Large clusters of bright, golden-yellow flowers, retaining their brilliancy for years; 2½ ft. Hardy annual. Pkt., 5c.
1244. **Helichrysum, Finest Mixed.** Large, beautiful, very double, white, yellow, scarlet; 1½ ft. Hardy annual. Pkt., 5c.
1245. **Rhodanthe, Finest Mixed.** Very rich colors of rose, crimson, purple, carmine and white; 1 ft. Half-hardy annual. Pkt., 5c.
1246. **Xeranthemum.** Leaves silvery, brilliant colors of purple, rose and white flowers, produced on long stems; 2 ft. Hardy annual. Pkt., 10c.

SUCCESSFUL FLOWER SEEDS

FENZLIA.

1378. **F. Dianthiflora.** A very showy profuse flowering little plant. Flowers, rosy lilac with orange centre; 3 in. Hardy annual. Pkt., 10c.

FERNS.

1280. **F. Choice Mixture for Greenhouse Cultivation.** Comprising most of the desirable and handsome sorts for this purpose. Pkt., 15c.

1281. **Hardy Mixture.** Comprising twelve of the most desirable hardy sorts for out-door culture. Pkt., 15c.

HARDY FERNS. Pkt., 15c.

GAILLARDIA.

Very attractive plants, producing a profusion of bloom the entire summer and autumn. Half-hardy annuals.
1305. **G. Picta Lorenziana.** Sulphur, golden, bright yellow, orange claret and amaranth; 1½ ft. Pkt., 10c.
1301. **Hybrida Grandiflora.** Large flowers of rich crimson and yellow; 1½ ft. Pkt., 5c.
1302. **Picta Nana** (*Painted Lady*). Showy crimson, bordered with yellow; 1 ft. Pkt., 5c.

GERANIUM.

A popular and handsome plant, extensively used for bedding; 1 to 3 ft. Half-hardy perennial.
1320. **G. Zonale, Mixed.** Saved from the largest and finest varieties. Pkt., 10c.
1321. **Apple Scented.** Very fragrant; pretty foliage. Pkt., 25c.

GILIA.

1340. **G. Tricolor.** Flowers orange yellow, with a white margin, separated by a circle of deep purple; 1 ft. Hardy annual. Pkt., 5c.

GLAUCIUM (*Horned Poppy*).

1360. **C. Corniculatum** (*Phœniceum*). A very showy plant, with long, graceful, silvery leaves, deeply cut and curled; 1 ft. Half-hardy biennial. Pkt., 5c.

GLOXINIA.

A bulbous-rooted plant, producing in great profusion, during the summer months, large bell-shaped flowers of the richest and most beautiful variety of brilliant colors; the bulbs must be kept warm and dry during the winter; 1 ft.
1380. **Grandiflora, Mixed.** Pkt., 25c.
1381. **Grandiflora Erecta, Mixed.** Rich colored, erect flowers. Pkt., 25c.
1382. **Grandiflora Horizontalis, Mixed.** Rich colored, horizontal flowers. Pkt., 25c.
1383. **Grandiflora Pendula, Mixed.** Rich colored drooping flowers. Pkt., 25c.
1384. **Spotted and Tigered.** Finely spotted and marbled. A fine addition to the varieties. Pkt., 35c.

GLOXINIA DEFIANCE. Pkt., 40c.

1385. **New Scarlet Defiance.** The flowers of this most beautiful sort are large, borne upright and of an intense, glowing, crimson scarlet color not before found among Gloxinias. They come true from seed and will certainly please every lover of this charming plant. Pkt., 40c.

GODETIA.

Profuse flowering plants, worthy of more extended cultivation, bloom well in almost any situation.
1400. **G. Lady Satin Rose.** Large, handsome flowers of carmine crimson, petals tinged with pale blue; 1 ft. Hardy annual (See cut.) Pkt., 5c.
1401. **Bijou.** A new variety, with snow white flowers and a bright carmine spot on each petal; ½ ft. Hardy annual. Pkt., 5c.
1402. **Choice Mixed.** Pkt., 5c.
1403. **Lady Albemarle.** Flowers 3 inches across, crimson and carmine, delicately suffused with lilac. Pkt., 5c.

GRASSES (Ornamental).

1440. **Agrostis Nebulosa.** Pkt., 5c.
1441. **Avena Sterilis** (*Animated Oats*). 2½ ft. Pkt., 5c.
1442. **Briza Maxima** (*Rattlesnake Grass*). 1 ft. Pkt., 5.
1443. **Coix Lacryma** (*Job's Tears*). 2 ft. Pkt., 5c.
1444. **Erianthus Ravennæ.** Very ornamental; 10 ft. Pkt., 5c.
1445. **Gynerium Argenteum** (*Pampas Grass*). 10 ft. (See cut.) Pkt., 10c.
1446. **Hordeum Jubatum** (*Squirrel Tail Grass*). Pkt., 5c.
1447. **Zea Japonica Variegata** (*Variegated Japanese Maize*). Striped gold and white. Pkt., 5c.
1448. **Stipa Peonata** (*Feather Grass*). 2 ft. Pkt., 5c.
1449. **Eragrostis Elegans** (*Love Grass*). 1 ft. Pkt., 5c.
1450. **Eulalia Zebrina** (*Zebra Grass*). 7 ft. Pkt., 5c.

GYSOPHILA.

Free-flowering and elegant plants for rock-work, baskets and borders.
1480. **G. Elegans.** Pretty star-shaped, white and pink flowers; ½ ft. Hardy perennial. Pkt., 5c.
1481. **Paniculata.** Produces numerous panicles of small, white, handsome flowers; fine for bouquets; 2½ ft. Hardy annual. Pkt., 5c.

HEDYSARUM (*French Honeysuckle*).

1500. **H. Coronarium, Mixed.** A very handsome, free-flowering plant, producing beautiful masses of red and white pea-shaped flowers; particularly adapted for borders; 3 ft. Hardy perennial. Pkt., 5c.

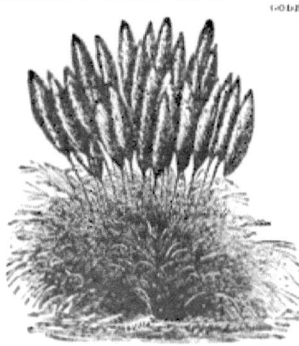

PAMPAS GRASS, GYNERIUM ARGENTEUM. Pkt., 10c.

HORDEUM JUBATUM, SQUIRREL TAIL GRASS. Pkt., 5c.

GODETIA LADY SATIN ROSE. Pkt., 10c.

JOHNSON & STOKES

HELIANTHUS (Sunflower).

A well-known and attractive popular flower of stately growth, well-adapted to serve in unsightly objects.
1540. **H. Californicus Plenissimus.** Extra large, double, very showy, saffron colored flowers; fine; 6 ft. Hardy annual. Pkt., 5c.
1541. **Cucumerifolius** (*Miniature Sunflower*). Of a very pretty branching habit; flowers orange yellow with a black centre; blooming profusely until killed by frost; 3 ft. Hardy annual. (See cut.) Pkt., 5c.
1542. **Globosus Fistulosus** (*Dahlia Sunflower*). Flowers very double and of medium size; 6 ft. Hardy annual. Pkt., 5.
1543. **H. Sulphur Gem.** See Novelties, page 84. Pkt., 10c.

HELIOTROPE.

These are deliciously fragrant flowers, remaining in bloom a long time; fine for pot culture or bedding; 1½ ft. Half-hardy annuals.
1550. **H. Fine Mixed.** A choice assortment of the choicest fragrant varieties. Pkt., 10c.

HELIANTHUS CUCUMERIFOLIUS, MINIATURE SUNFLOWER. Pkt., 5.

HIBISCUS.

The two varieties mentioned below are fine branching plants, free blooming and of the easiest culture.
1560. **H. Africanus** (*H. Trionum*). Very pretty foliage and large cream-colored flowers, with brown centre; 2 ft. Hardy annual. Pkt., 5c.
1561. **Palustris.** Beautiful large pink flowers; 3 ft. Hardy annual. Pkt., 5.

HOLLYHOCK (*Althea Rosea*)

This is one of the oldest inhabitants of our gardens, and now ranks as one of the finest autumn flowers; 6 ft. Hardy perennial.
1562. **H. Double White.** The newest strain of perfectly double, pure white flowers. Pkt., 15c.
1563. **Double Yellow.** Comprising the finest shades of orange, straw and buff. Pkt., 15c.

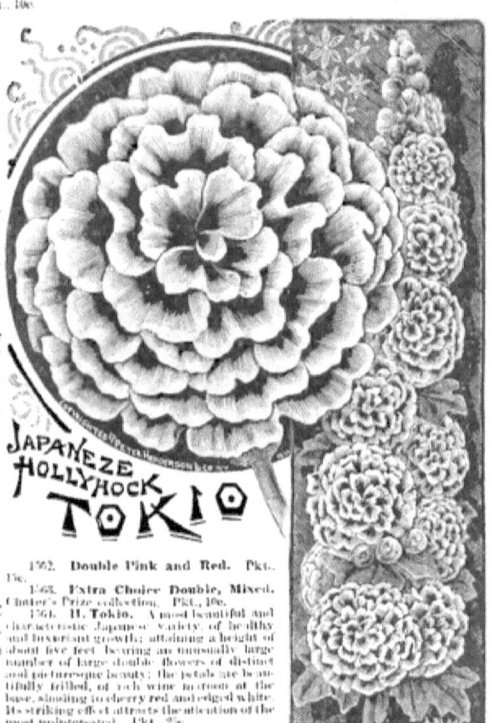

JAPANEZE HOLLYHOCK TOKIO

1562. **Double Pink and Red.** Pkt., 15c.
1563. **Extra Choice Double, Mixed.** Chater's Prize collection. Pkt., 10c.
1564. **H. Tokio.** A most beautiful and characteristic Japanese variety, of healthy and luxuriant growth; attaining a height of about five feet, bearing an unusually large number of large double flowers of distinct and picturesque beauty; the petals are beautifully frilled, of rich wine maroon at the base, shading to cherry red and edged white. Its striking effect attracts the attention of the most uninterested. Pkt., 25c.

HONESTY (*Lunaria*).

1580. **L. Biennis** (*Satin Flower*). Pretty single purple flowers; 2 ft. Hardy biennial. Pkt., 5c.

HUMEA.

1600. **H. Elegans.** When fully grown this is a very attractive, handsome plant, ruby red, grass-like flowers; 8 ft. Half-hardy biennial. Pkt., 10c.

HUMULUS JAPONICUS, or JAPANESE HOP.

1620. A wonderful new annual climber from Japan, growing with great rapidity, and very dense foliage. Color is a lively green. It is undoubtedly one of the best climbers for covering verandas, trellises, etc.; 20 ft. Hardy annual. Pkt., 5c.

HUMULUS JAPONICUS. Pkt., 5c.

*Happiness stands like a maid at your gate;
Why should you think you could find her by roving?
Never was greater mistake than to hate,
Try loving.*—JOHN ESTEN COOKE.

SUCCESSFUL FLOWER SEEDS 95

IMPATIENS SULTANI.

1640. One of the most distinct and beautiful plants of recent introduction for the warm greenhouse or summer bedding; owing to its gorgeous coloring and profuse and continuous flowering it is rapidly becoming popular. The plant is of compact, neat habit of growth, with good constitution, and since a perpetual bloomer. Planted out in the open ground at the end of June, it grows luxuriantly; flowers with the greatest profusion, and produces an admirable effect until cut down by frost. The flowers are of a brilliant rosy-scarlet color, about one and a half inches in diameter. Price, per pkt., 15c.

IPOMŒA.

Very pretty rapid growing plants with handsome, bright colored, trumpet-shaped flowers, excellent for covering old walls, stumps, arbors, etc. Half-hardy annuals.

1660. **I. Bona Nox** (*Evening Glory or Good Night*). Very large; white, fragrant flowers; 10 ft. Pkt., 10c.
1661. **I. Coccinea** (*Star Ipomœa*). Handsome little scarlet flowers; 10 ft. Pkt., 5c.
1662. **I. Huberi, Mixed.** Comprising all the new Japanese hybrids; 10 ft. Pkt., 10c.
1663. **I. Hederacea.** Mixed; very fine. Pkt., 5c.
1664 **I. Noctiflora or Grandiflora Alba** (*White Seeded*). Moonflower. Pkt., 10c; 3 pkts., 25c.
1665. **I. Heavenly Blue.** See Novelties, page 81. Pkt., 15c.

MOONFLOWER—IPOMŒA NOCTIFLORA Pkt. 10c.

IPOMOPSIS (*Standing or Tree Cypress*).

Beautiful free-flowering plants, with fine foliage. Will bloom the first year from seed if sown early.
1680. **I. Elegans.** Dazzling scarlet flowers; 3 ft. Half-hardy biennial. Pkt., 5c.
1681. **I. Superba.** Dazzling orange flowers; 3 ft. Half-hardy biennial. Pkt., 5c.

KAULFUSSIA (*Charieris Heterophylla*).

1700. **K. Mixed.** The flowers resemble single asters. Violet. Hardy annual; 1 ft. Pkt., 5c.

LANTANA.

1720. **L. Hybrida, Mixed.** Desirable greenhouse or bedding plants, embracing every shade, white, pink, orange and purple. Half-hardy perennial; 2 ft. Pkt., 10c.

LATHYRUS.

(*Hardy Sweet Peas.*)
1730. **L. Latifolius.** A handsome, free flowering plant, useful for covering trellises, old stumps, fences, etc. Flowers a beautiful scarlet. Hardy perennial; 5 ft. Pkt., 10c.
1741. **L. Latifolius Albus.** Large clusters of pure white, grand, hardy, low climber. Pkt., 10c.

NEW HARDY SWEET PEA FROM CALIFORNIA (*L. Splendens*).

1742 This is one of the finest novelties offered this season. It bears dense clusters of brilliant deep rose flowers. Dr. Parry, who saw it growing wild in Lower California, describes it as the handsomest flower in all California. (See cut.) Pkt., 15c.

LEPTOSIPHON.

1760. **L. Fine Mixed.** A very pretty plant, well adapted to marginal lines in ribbon beds; ½ ft. Hardy annual. Pkt., 5c.

LINARIA (*Kenilworth Ivy*).

1780. **L. Cymbalaria.** A very handsome, small, neat, trailing plant; admirably suited for baskets. Hardy perennial. 8 ft. Pkt., 10c.

LINUM (*Scarlet Flax*).

1820. **L. Grandiflorum.** A showy bedding plant, with fine foliage, remaining in bloom a long time; 1 ft. Hardy annual. Pkt., 5c.

LOASA.

1830. **L. Aurantiaca.** A rapid growing, free-flowering climber with beautiful orange flowers; 4 ft. Hardy annual. Pkt., 10c.

LATHYRUS "SPLENDENS." Pkt. 15c.

"O swinging nest, by summer winds
Like rustic cradle gently rocking,
How slight the tie that lightly binds
Thy would-be swinging boughs among!
I bend above with loving eyes

"To peep into the downy home,
Then, with a start of quick surprise
Set off across the fields to roam.
Whoa—whoop! There are, as near as can be guessed,
Four hundred thousand hornets in that nest!"
—BURDETTE.

LOBELIA.

Handsome little plants, admirably adapted for borders, vases, pots or hanging-baskets. Half-hardy annuals.

1880. **L. Erinus Crystal Palace Compacta.** (See cut.) A compact, deep blue variety; ½ ft. Pkt., 10c.
1881. **L. Erinus Speciosa Alba Maxima.** Showy white flowers of drooping and spreading habit; ¾ ft. Pkt., 5c.
1882. **L. Cardinalis** (*Cardinal Flower*). A hardy perennial native variety, with spikes of brilliant scarlet flowers, blooming the first season if sown early; a fine border plant; 3 ft. Pkt., 10c.
1883. **L. Gracilis.** Light blue; long, slender trailing stems. Pkt., 5c.
1884. **Mixed Finest Erinus, or Trailing Varieties.** Best for baskets, vases, etc. Pkt., 5c.
1885. **Mixed Erecta Compacta Varieties.** Best for edgings, ribbon beds, etc. Pkt., 10c.

LOPHOSPERMUM.

1886. **L. Scandens.** A highly ornamental climber for the garden or conservatory. Blossoms of a very rich purple and violet color; 10 ft. Half-hardy annual. Pkt., 10c.

LUPINS (*Sun Dials*).

1889. **L. Mixed.** Highly ornamental, varied colored, free flowering, pea-shaped flowers; 2 ft. Hardy annuals. Pkt., 5c.

LYCHNIS.

1890. **L. Chalcedonica.** Brilliant scarlet flowers, blooms the first year. Hardy perennial, 2 ft. Pkt., 5c.
1890. **MANDEVILLA SAVEOLENS.** See Novelties, page 82. Pkt., 5c.

LOBELIA ERINUS CRYSTAL PALACE. Pkt., 10c.

MALOPE.

1920. **M. Grandiflora.** A handsome plant with fine large, dark crimson flowers covering the entire plant the whole season. Half-hardy annual. 1 ft. Pkt., 5c.

MARIGOLD (*Tagetes*).

A very showy and popular plant of easy culture. Half-hardy annuals.
1940. **Gold Striped.** The flowers of this beautiful variety are regularly striped with a golden yellow and exquisite chestnut brown; 1½ ft. Pkt., 10c.
1941. **El Dorado.** Flowers three to four inches in diameter, perfectly and extremely double, and embracing every shade; 1½ ft. (see cut.) Pkt., 10c.
1942. **Dwarf French, Mixed.** Seed saved from the choicest double flowers; 1 ft. Pkt., 10c.
1944. **Large African.** Very double flowers, orange-brown and yellow. Pkt., 5c.

MARVEL OF PERU (*Mirabilis*).

This is the fine old garden plant known as Four O'Clocks. It succeeds well in any garden soil, a very showy and popular flower. Hardy annual.
1960. **M. Mixed.** Beautiful colors; 2 ft. Pkt., 5c.
1961. **New Dwarf White.** Snowy white flowers and fine yellow foliage, 10 in. Pkt., 5c.

MARIGOLD, "EL DORADO." Pkt., 10c.

MAURANDIA.

A very graceful climber for the green-house, parlor, baskets, or outdoor purposes, blooming the first season from seed. Half-hardy perennials.
1980. **M. Alba.** Pure white; 10 ft. Pkt., 10c.
1981. **Barclayana.** Very rich violet or purple; 10 ft. Pkt., 10c.
1982. **Mixed.** The finest colors. Pkt., 10c.

MESEMBRYANTHEMUM.

Dwarf growing, profuse flowering plants of great beauty. Half-hardy annual.
2000. **M. Crystallinum** (*Ice Plant*). Flowers white, with ice-like foliage. Pkt., 5c.
2001. **Tricolor** (*Fig Pink*). Very pretty, rosy pink flowers; ½ ft. Pkt., 5c.

MIGNONETTE.

A well-known and universal garden favorite, and one that requires no extra instructions for growing. Hardy annual.
2020. **M. Sweet scented** (*Reseda Odorata*). 1 ft. Oz., 20c.; pkt., 5c.
2021. **Grandiflora Ameliorata.** Petals of a reddish tint; 1½ ft. Oz., 35c.; pkt., 5c.
2022. **Golden Queen.** Flowers golden-yellow; 1½ ft. Pkt., 10c.
2023. **Parson's White.** Strongly scented, large, well-formed spikes; 1½ ft. Pkt., 10c.
2024. **Machet.** Produces long, broad spikes of deliciously scented red flowers; 1 ft. Pkt., 10c.
2025. **Bird's Mammoth.** Pkt., 15c.
2026. **Hybrid Spiral.** Pure white; 1 ft. Pkt., 10c.
2027. **Giant White Spiral.** This grand mignonette grows two to three feet high, perfectly erect, and the flower spikes of wonderful size and snowy whiteness. Its fragrance is rich and powerful, and will produce much more bloom than any other variety. Seed may be sown in April or May, and it will commence blooming in June. The illustration shows the beauty of the foliage and bloom. Pkt., 10c.

MIMOSA.

2040. **M. Pudica** (*Sensitive Plant*). A curious plant. The leaves will close if touched or shaken, 1 ft. Half-hardy annual. Pkt., 5c.

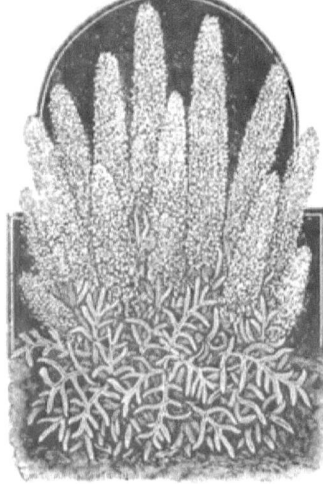

GIANT WHITE SPIRAL MIGNONETTE. Pkt., 10c.

A persistent habit of looking on the bright side will soon become fixed like any other habit and make life a much pleasanter thing for us, and for every one connected with us.

MIMULUS.

(Monkey Flower.)

Showy, profuse flowering plants, comprising numerous varieties, with white, sulphur and yellow grounds, spotted with crimson, scarlet and pink, fine for the green-house, or moist shady situations; half-hardy perennials; blooming the first year from seed if sown early; 1 ft.

2060. **M. Moschatus** *(Musk Plant).* Beautiful yellow flowers; ⅓ ft. Pkt., 10c.
2061. **M. Cardinalis.** Flowers of a brilliant scarlet hue; hardy; 1 ft. Pkt., 10c.
2063. **M. Tigrinus.** The finest tigered and spotted varieties, rivalling the Calceolaria in its brightness; mixed colors. (See cut.) Pkt., 10c.

MINA LOBATA.

2080. **M. Lobata.** The flowers are tube-like, of a bright red color when first formed, changing to an orange yellow; 20 ft. See novelties. Pkt., 15c.

MOMORDICA.

2090. **M. Balsamina** *(Balsam Apple).* The fruit when ripe is used for medicinal purposes. Half-hardy annual; 15 ft. Pkt., 5c.
2091. **M. Charantia** *(Balsam Pear).* Same as the above, excepting that the fruit is longer in shape. Pkt., 5c.

MYOSOTIS *(Forget-Me-Not).*

Popular and beautiful little plants, with neat star-like flowers, blooming the first year from seed. Half-hardy perennials.

2100. **M. Palustris** *(The True Forget-Me-Not).* Beautiful blue flowers; ½ ft. Pkt., 10c.
2101. **Alba.** Pure white; ½ ft. Pkt., 10c.
2102. **Dissitiflora.** Large dark blue flowers, compact and very early; ½ ft. Pkt., 15c.
2103. **NEW FORGET-ME-NOT, "VICTORIA."** Grows perfectly round in shape, five to seven inches high and eight to ten inches in diameter, and is entirely covered with large umbels of flowers of azure blue. This beautiful Forget-me-not is the best of all for edgings and growing in pots for market. Price, per pkt., 15c.

MYRSIPHYLLUM *(Smilax).*

2120. **M. Asparagoides.** Beautiful, delicate, wavy, glossy, deep green foliage. 10 ft. Tender perennial. Oz., 75c.; Pkt., 10c.

NEW DWARF NASTURTIUM, "PEARL." Pkt., 10c.

NASTURTIUM

The dwarf varieties of Nasturtium are among the most useful and beautiful of annuals for bedding, massing, etc., owing to their compact growth, richness of color and profusion of blooming. The tall sorts are admirably adapted for rock-work, covering trellises or rustic work. They flower most profusely when planted in a poor soil, and remain in bloom for a long time; stand heat and drought without the slightest effect. The seed, if picked young, is an excellent substitute for capers. Hardy annual.

TOM THUMB, OR DWARF NASTURTIUMS.

2140. **Scarlet.** Pkt., 5c.
2141. **Yellow.** Pkt., 5c.
2142. **Pearl.** New creamy white. (See cut.) Pkt., 10c.
2143. **Empress of India.** Splendid, very dark leaves and crimson flowers. Pkt., 10c.
2144. **King Theodore.** Bluish green foliage, flowers velvet crimson. Pkt., 5c.
2145. **Lady Bird.** A new and distinct sort, rich golden yellow, each petal barred with a broad vein of bright ruby crimson; very showy and charming. Pkt., 10c.
2146. **Aurora** (Novelty). The ground color of this new dwarf variety is chrome yellow, the upper petals being of a lighter tint; the two lower ones are spotted and veined with purplish carmine; fine. Pkt., 15c.
2147. **Tom Thumb, Mixed.** Oz., 20c.; Pkt., 5c.

LOBB'S NASTURTIUMS *(Tropæolum Lobbianum).*

The leaves and flowers are somewhat smaller than the Tall Nasturtiums, but their greater profusion renders them superior for trellises, arbors, for hanging over vases, rockwork, etc.; the flowers are of unusual brilliancy and richness; they are also splendid for winter decoration in the greenhouse and conservatory. Half-hardy annual; 4 to 6 ft.

2148. **Asa Grey.** (Novelty.) The flowers of this new kind represent the lightest shade hitherto obtained among Nasturtiums. (See cut.) Pkt., 20c.
2149. **Napoleon III.** Yellow striped, rosy scarlet. Pkt., 10c.
2150. **Roi des Noires.** Almost Black. Pkt., 10c.
2151. **Spitfire.** Fiery Red. Pkt., 10c.
2152. **Lobb's Nasturtiums, Mixed.** Pkt., 10c.

TALL NASTURTIUMS.

2153. **Nigro Purpureum.** Very dark maroon. Pkt., 10c.
2154. **Tall Orange.** Oz., 20c.; pkt., 5c.
2155. **Tall Scarlet.** Oz., 20c.; pkt., 5c.
2156. **Tall, Mixed.** Oz., 20c.; pkt., 5c.

VASE OF LOBB'S NASTURTIUM "ASA GREY."

If you "say what you like," you must make up your mind to hear other say what you won't like.

KINGLY PANSIES.
OUR "CROWNED" COLLECTION.

In this collection we have gathered together an assortment of varieties that for size and color and markings stand unrivalled by any offered. They are "Kings" in their respective colors, and, by growing them separately and planting them out in beds of special patterns, the most charming effects may be produced. For bedding purposes they are unrivalled, as they are of a vigorous growth and the immense flowers are held well above the foliage.

2250. P. Imperial German Large Flowering. Embracing fifty choice prize varieties in every known color and marking. Oz., $8.00; 6 pkts., $1.00; 3 pkts., 60c.; pkt., 25c.

2251. Bugnot's Large Stained. A new French variety, flowers of enormous size; the colors are extremely varied. Pkt., 10c; 3 pkts., $1.60.

2252. Giant Trimardeau. Flowers of great size and in an endless variety of beautiful shades. 3 pkts., 60c.; 6 pkts., $1.00; pkt., 25c.

2253. Premium. Seeds saved from first-class named flowers only. A magnificent strain, embracing the most beautiful colors and finest shades. Oz., $5.00; pkt., 15c.

2254. Pure Yellow. Oz., $4.50; pkt., 10c.

2255. Snow Queen. Very large satiny white, yellow centre. Oz., $2.00; pkt., 10c.
2256. Faust. Uniform, coal-black flowers. Pkt., 15c.
2257. Extra Choice English Mixed. Oz., $2.50, pkt., 10c.
2258. King of the Bronzes, ... Pkt., $0.20
2259. King of the Striped, ... .20
2260. King of the Blotched, ... .20
2261. King of the Stained, ... .20
2262. King of the Blacks, ... .20
2263. King of the Pure Whites, ... .20
2264. King of the Golden Yellows, ... .20
2265. King of the Blues, ... .20
2266. Our Eight Kings, 1 pkt. each, ... 1.50
2267. Our Kingly Collection, Mixed, ... .25

NEMOPHILA (Grove Love).
2268. N. Mixed. Flowers bright blue, white margined and spotted. 1 ft. Pkt., 5c.

NIEREMBERGIA.
2269. N. Frutescens. A very pretty, shrubby plant, with white and blue flowers. Half-hardy annual, 1 ft. Pkt., 10c.
2270. N. Gracilis. White and purple, with yellow centre. Pkt., 10c.

NIGELLA.
2271. N. Damascena Nana (Devil in a Bush). Double, blue and white. 1 ft. Pkt., 5c.
2272. N. Hispanica (Love in a Mist). Deep blue, with blood-colored stamens; 1½ ft. Pkt., 5c.

NOLANA.
The plant resembles the Portulaca, and the flower that of the Morning Glory. ½ ft. Hardy annuals.
2273. N. Finest Mixed. Sky blue, white, yellow and purple. Pkt., 5c.

OBELISCARIA.
2274. O. Mixed. A rare plant with showy flowers of rich, velvety crimson, edged with yellow. Hardy annuals, 2½ ft. Pkt., 5c.

KING OF THE STRIPED. Pkt., 20c.

ŒNOTHERA (Evening Primrose, or Sun Drops).
2275. O. Biennis (Grandiflora, or Lamarckiana). Showy, Large, delicately fragrant, pale, yellow flowers; blooms the first season from seed; 3 ft. Hardy biennial. Pkt., 5c.

OXALIS.
2276. O. Rosea. Flowers delicate rose; ½ ft. Pkt., 10c.
2277. Tropæoloides. Flowers deep yellow, foliage dark green, very desirable for borders; ½ ft. Pkt., 10c.
2278. Mixed Varieties. Pkt., 10c.

SUCCESSFUL FLOWER SEEDS

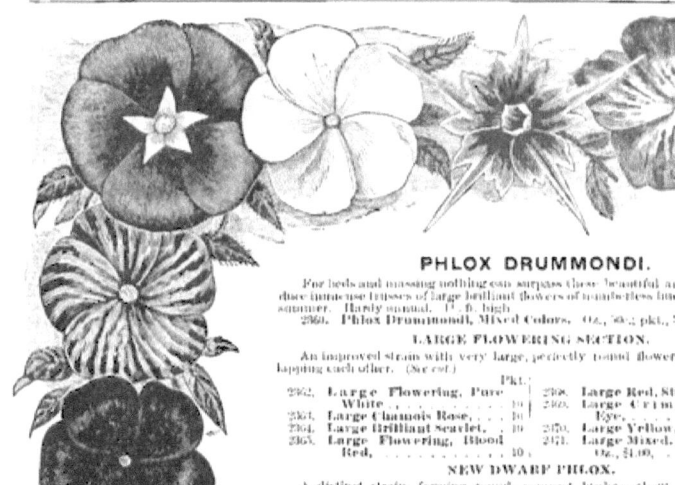

PHLOX DRUMMONDI.

For beds and massing nothing can surpass these beautiful annuals. They produce immense trusses of large brilliant flowers of countless hues throughout the summer. Hardy annual. 1½ ft. high.
2369. **Phlox Drummondi, Mixed Colors.** Oz., 50c; pkt., 5c.

LARGE FLOWERING SECTION.

An improved strain with very large, perfectly round flowers, the petals overlapping each other. (See cut.)

	Pkt.		Pkt.
2362. **Large Flowering, Pure White**	10	2368. **Large Red, Striped White,**	10
2363. **Large Chamois Rose,**	10	2369. **Large Crimson, White Eye,**	10
2364. **Large Brilliant Scarlet,**	10	2370. **Large Yellow,**	10
2365. **Large Flowering, Blood Red,**	10	2371. **Large Mixed, Many colors,** Oz., $1.00,	10

NEW DWARF PHLOX.

A distinct strain, forming round, compact bushes, about six inches high. Splendid for pot culture and ribbon bedding.

	Pkt.		Pkt.
2372. **Dwarf Snowball,** Pure white,	15	2374. **Violet Spotted White,**	15
2373. **Dwarf Fireball,** Fiery scarlet,	15	2375. **Chamois Rose,** Fine,	15
		2376. **Dwarf Sorts, Mixed,**	15

2367. **PHLOX, Star of Quedlinburg.** A very striking novelty of extraordinary character. In the flowers, the centre petals, which are few in number, are much elongated, from four to five times the length of the lateral ones, thus giving the flowers a most distinct and regular star-like appearance. Many colors, mixed. Pkt., 15c; 2 for 25c. (See above.)

HARDY PHLOX.

Magnificent flowering plants for permanent beds and borders, bearing immense heads of large waxy flowers of lovely shades of color. Hardy perennial; 2 ft.
2366. **Hardy Phlox.** Fine mixed varieties. Pkt., 10c.

PENSTEMON.

One of the most effective free-flowering plants for beds or borders. Long spikes of finely-shaped and richly-colored flowers; grows well in any soil. Half-hardy perennial.
2381. **P. Extra Fine Mixed.** 2 ft. Pkt., 5c.

PERILLA.

2320. **P. Nankinensis.** A very fine, dark ornamental-leaved foliage plant, similar to Coleus. Half-hardy annual. 1½ ft. Pkt., 5c.

PETUNIA.

The hybrid sorts are especially fine in mixed borders and beds, while the larger flowering kinds, with their delicate colors and pervading fragrance, are deserving favorites for pot culture.

SINGLE VARIETIES. (For Bedding.)

2340. **P. Dwarf Inimitable.** Dwarf plants, six to eight inches high; flowers cherry red, with a white centre; splendid for edgings, massing, etc. Pkt., 10c.
2341. **P. Striped and Blotched.** Extra strain. Pkt., 10c.
2342. **P. Alba.** White; suitable for cemetery. Pkt., 5c.
2343. **P. Choice Single, Mixed.** ¼ oz., 75c.; pkt., 5c.

SINGLE LARGE FLOWERING SORTS. (For Pot Culture.)

The flowers of this class are from four to six inches in diameter, beautifully marked, veined and spotted.
2345. **P. Grandiflora Venosa.** Large flowering, finest shade of color, beautifully veined. Pkt., 10c.
2346. **P. Grandiflora Fimbriata.** A fine strain with handsomely frilled and fringed flowers, very distinct and pretty. Pkt., 25c.
2347. **P. Yellow-Throated.** The flowers are very large and of perfect form, with a broad, deep yellow throat, veined very much like a Salpiglossis. Pkt., 10c.

PETUNIA, DOUBLE LILIPUT. Pkt., 25c.

DOUBLE FLOWERING SORTS.

The seed of these is obtained by artificial fecundation, and about 30 per cent. of double flowers may be expected.
2350. **P. Dwarf Double Liliput** (*Nana Compacta Multiflora Fl. Pl.*). New double kind, producing bushy plants covered with double flowers, which are partly spotted, blotched and self-colored, making a very pretty plant when in full bloom. (See cut.) Pkt., 25c.
2351. **Flore Pleno.** Best large flowering double in finest mixture. Pkt., 25c.
2352. **Extra Large Flowering, Double Fringed.** This extra choice strain produces about thirty per cent. of splendid double fringed flowers. Pkt., 25c.
2353. **Extra Large Flowering, Double Fringed** (*Lady of the Lake*). This seed will produce about thirty per cent. large, double, pure white fringed flowers. Pkt., 35c.

.˙. JOHNSON .˙. & .˙. STOKES .˙.

✢ POPPIES. ✢

Showy plants, making a gorgeous display of large, brilliant flowers. They are of easy culture; but the seed should be sown where it is to remain, as they will not bear transplanting.

2380. **P. Umbrosum.** Brilliant deep scarlet, marked with four large black spots. Pkt., 5c.
2381. **Victoria Cross.** The centre represents a Maltese cross of silvery white. The large surface of the petals is of a rich vermilion crimson. Pkt., 10c.
2382. **Carnation Flowered, Mixed.** Splendid large double flowers. Oz., 30c.; pkt., 5c.
2383. **New Shirley.** Is perfectly hardy and flowers profusely the first season from seed. The colors are pure, soft and varied, and range from blush white, rose, delicate pink and carmine to a bright, sparkling crimson. (See cut.) Pkt., 10c.
2384. **P. SNOWDRIFT.** This charming new poppy produces pure snowy-white extremely double flowers of perfect form and large size. Pkt., 10c.
2385. **P. Nudicaule.** Perennial. Pkt., 10c.
2386. **P. Orientale.** Large oriental poppy; a stately perennial; 2½ ft. high; with bold showy flowers. Pkt., 10c.
2387. **P. White Swan.** See Novelties, page 84.
2388. **P. Glaucum.** See Novelties, page 84.

PORTULACA.

A popular strong growing plant, sandy soil; neither heat nor drought is too great for it; ½ ft. Hardy annual.

NEW "SHIRLEY" POPPY. Pkt., 10c.

2389. **P. Finest Single, Mixed.** A large variety of the most brilliant colors. Oz., 30c.; pkt., 5c.
2390. **Double Rose Flowered, Mixed.** The most brilliant shades and choice flowers. Pkt., 20c.

PRIMULA (Primrose).

We exercise great care in growing and saving the seed of these most satisfactory and beautiful of house plants; ½ ft. Tender perennial.
2420. **P. Fimbriata Sinensis, Mixed.** Extra choice mixed. Very large, magnificent flowers of the richest and most varied colors. Pkt., 5c.
2421. **Fimbriata Flore Pleno, Mixed.** An exceedingly choice strain of double varieties. Pkt., 50c.
2422. **Fimbriata Sinensis, Fine Mixed.** Very good strain. Pkt., 50c.
2423. **P. Verus** (English Cowslip). Pkt., 10c.

PRIMULA OBCONICA.

2424. A profuse blooming primrose, bearing on long stems heads containing ten to fifteen flowers. It thrives in a cool house and will grow in favor with those desiring plants that will grow easily. The flowers are pure white, shading occasionally to lilac, and have the true primrose fragrance. It is in all respects a lovely flower, and as it becomes better known it will be appreciated at its true worth. Pkt., 25c.

PRIMULA SINENSIS FIMBRIATA. Pkt., 50c.

PYRETHRUM (Feverfew).

2440. **P. Parthenifolium Aureum** (Golden Feather). A highly ornamental golden yellow foliage plant, unexcelled for bedding. Hardy perennual; 1½ ft. Pkt., 10c.
2441. **P. Roseum.** Handsome aster-like flowers, with pink rays and deep yellow centres, foliage fern-like, most beautifully cut. Pkt., 10c.

RICINUS (Castor-Oil Bean).

A tall, majestic, ornamental foliage plant; with leaves of a metallic hue. Half-hardy annuals.
2460. **R. Gibsoni.** Handsome deep red foliage, compact branching habit; 5 ft. Pkt., 5c.
2461. **Sanguineus.** Leaves green, stalks blood-red, showy red fruit; 8 feet. Pkt., 5c.
2462. **Phillippiniensis.** A majestic variety, with beautiful gigantic foliage; 10 ft. Pkt., 5c.
2463. **Mixed.** Many choice sorts. Pkt., 5c.

2464. **RICINUS, "DUCHESS OF EDINBURGH."**
The stem and leaves of this beautiful plant are of a bright metallic bronze; the large branches of the fruit are of a fiery red, and as they are borne up some ten to twelve feet from the ground it gives a tropical effect that is unexcelled, and makes this regal plant one of the finest for decorating the lawn or garden in cultivation. All this can be obtained in one year from the seed. Pkt., 15c.

PRIMULA OBCONICA. Pkt., 25c.

ROCKET.
(*Hesperis Matronalis*.)

2490. **R. Sweet Mixed.** Large clusters of single purple and white flowers that are deliciously fragrant during the evening. Hardy annual; 1½ ft. Pkt., 5c.

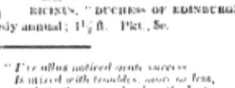
RICINUS, "DUCHESS OF EDINBURGH." Pkt., 15c.

SWEET PEAS.

2700. **Sweet Pea Vesuvius.** The large upper petals show a brilliant carmine rose, shading toward the centre into a deep, glowing purple throat, the whole being sprinkled with crimson dots. Pkt., 5c.
2701. **Scarlet Invincible.** Pkt., 5c.
2702. **Butterfly.** Pure white, laced with lavender blue. Pkt., 5c.
2703. **White.** Pure white. Pkt., 5c.
2704. **Striped.** Very handsome. Pkt., 5c.
2705. **Adonis.** Bright rosy carmine. Pkt., 5c.
2706. **Lady Bird.** New beautiful blue. Pkt., 5c.
2709. **Princess Beatrice.** Carmine rose, slightly shaded. Pkt., 5c.
2710. **Painted Lady.** Pink and white. Pkt., 5c.
2711. **Queen of the Isles.** Very beautiful. Pkt., 10c.
2712. **Miss Blanch Ferry.** Pink and white, very large and very early; continuous bloomer and one of the finest. Pkt., 10c.
2713. **Boreatton.** A very fine dark pea, with bold, stout flowers; rich bronze-crimson with wings of crimson-purple, shaded rose. The finest sweet pea extant. Pkt., 15c.
2714. **Orange Prince.** Orange-pink flushed scarlet, wings bright rose, veined pink; choice. Pkt., 10c.
2705. **Everlasting Peas, Mixed** (*Lathyrus Latifolius*). 5 ft. Pkt., 10c.
2706. **Mixture of Sweet Peas.** All colors, both standard and new varieties; splendid, mixed. Oz., 20c.; pkt., 5c.

SALPIGLOSSIS (*Velvet Flower*).

2500. **S. Fine Mixed.** Sky blue and scarlet flowers, very beautifully penciled. Hardy annual; 1½ ft. Pkt., 10c.
2501. **SALPIGLOSSIS GRANDIFLORA.** The large flowering Salpiglossis is one of the most beautiful of flowering annuals, the flowers large, of many beautiful colors and exquisitely veined and laced. They remain long in bloom, and in rich coloring they vie with orchids. Pkt., 15c.

SALVIA.

A very ornamental free-flowering plant, remaining in bloom until killed by frost.
2520. **S. Splendens** (*Scarlet Sage*). Large spikes of vivid scarlet flowers; 2 ft. Pkt., 5c.
2521. **Patens.** Superb deep blue flowers; 2 ft. Pkt., 20c.

SANVITALIA.

2540. **S. Procumbens Flore Pleno.** Very pretty trailing plants, excellent for rock-work or edgings. Flowers of a brilliant golden-yellow. Hardy annual; ½ ft. Pkt., 10c.

SAPONARIA.

2560. **S. Calabrica.** Charming little plants, producing a profusion of rich, deep pink flowers. Hardy annual; ½ ft. Pkt., 5c.

SCABIOSA.

A handsome border plant, bearing a profusion of beautiful fragrant flowers; very handsome for table bouquets. Hardy annuals.
2580. **S. Candidissima Alba Plena.** Pure white, double flowers; 2 ft. Pkt., 5c.
2581. **Dwarf, Mixed.** White, red and purple flowers; 1 ft. Pkt., 5c.

SCHIZANTHUS.

2600. **S. Papilionaceous** (*Butterfly Flower*). A showy variety, with curiously spotted dark violet, yellow and crimson flowers. Half-hardy annual; 1½ ft. Pkt., 5c.
2601. **Fine Mixed.** A large variety of choice sorts. Pkt., 5c.

SEDUM (*Stone Crop*).

2620. **S. Coeruleum.** Remarkably pretty succulent plants, growing readily upon rocks, walls and roofs of houses; ¼ ft. Pkt., 10c.

SILENE.

A beautiful genus of free flowering plants, with bright attractive flowers. Hardy annual; 1 ft.
2640. **S. Armeria, Mixed.** Red, white and rose. Pkt., 5c.
2641. **Pendula Flore Pleno.** Charming rose-colored flowers. Pkt., 15c.

SMILAX. See *Myrsiphyllum*.

SALPIGLOSSIS GRANDIFLORA. Pkt., 15c.

STOCKS, TEN-WEEKS.

2660. **S. Blood Red.** Pkt., 10c.
2661. **Crimson.** Pkt., 10c.
2662. **White.** Pkt., 10c.
2663. **Blue.** Pkt., 10c.
2664. **Dwarf Large Flowering German Double Blood-Red.** Blue, crimson and blue. Each, pkt.; 10c.
2665. **Extra Choice Mixture.** Very double flowers. Pkt., 10c.
2666. **Dwarf Wallflower-Leaved German, Mixed.** Very fine, large double. Pkt., 15c.
2667. **Snowflake.** A fine new variety, with extremely large and double, pure white flowers. Pkt., 15c.

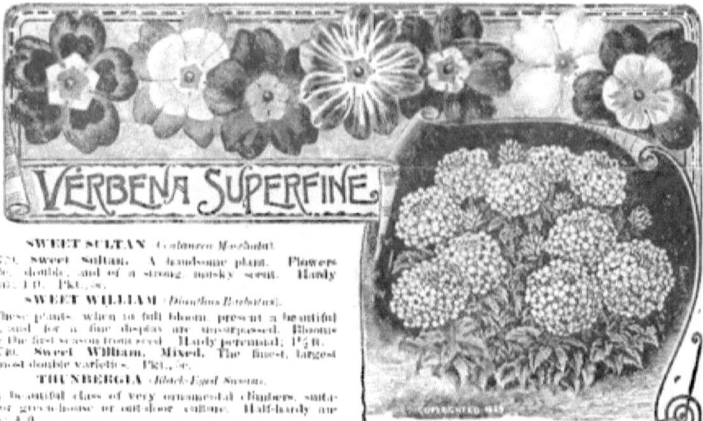

SWEET SULTAN (*Calanza Maschata*)

Sweet Sultan. A handsome plant. Flowers purple, double, and of a strong musky scent. Hardy annual; 1 ft. Pkt., 5c.

SWEET WILLIAM (*Dianthus Barbatus*)

These plants, when in full bloom, present a beautiful sight, and for a fine display are unsurpassed. Bloom freely the first season from seed. Hardy perennial; 1½ ft.
Sweet William, Mixed. The finest, largest and most double varieties. Pkt., 5c.

THUNBERGIA (*Black-Eyed Susan*)

A beautiful class of very ornamental climbers, suitable for greenhouse or outdoor culture. Half-hardy annuals; 4 ft.
T. Alba Oculata. White, dark eye. Pkt., 5c.
T. Aurantiaca. Orange, dark eye. Pkt., 5c.
T. Bakeri. Pure white. Pkt., 5c.
T. Finest Mixed. Choice shades. Pkt., 5c.
T. Alata. Buff, dark eye. Pkt., 5c.

TORENIA

Very pretty summer plants for hanging baskets or borders. Half-hardy annuals; ¾ ft.
T. Fournieri. Sky-blue, with a bright yellow throat. Pkt., 5c.
T. Bailloni. Golden yellow flowers, with a brownish red throat. Pkt., 5c.

TROPÆOLUM

Very elegant and profuse blooming climbers, for indoor or outdoor culture. Half-hardy annuals.
T. Peregrinum. *Canary Bird Flower*. Yellow; 10 ft. Pkt., 5c.
T. Lobbianum. Brilliant mixed varieties; 6 ft. Pkt., 5c.

VERBENA

Well-known plants of great beauty and variety, with beautiful dazzling, self-colored, striped and variegated flowers. Half-hardy perennials; 1 ft.
V. Hybrida, Striped. Very brilliant shades. Pkt., 5c.
V. Candidissima. Large trusses of the purest white flowers. Pkt., 15c.
V. Coccinea. Brilliant scarlet. Pkt., 15c.
V. New Mammoth. Very large flowering, many of the flowers being the size of a silver quarter. Pkt., 25c.

WILD FLOWER GARDEN. Large pkt., 10c., oz. 50c.

VERBENA—Continued.

Choicest Mixed. Selected from the newest and finest named varieties. Pkt., 15c.
Fine Mixed. All good varieties. Pkt., 10c.

VINCA.

Beautiful free flowering plants, suitable for house culture or bedding purposes, blooming the first year from seed. Half-hardy perennials; 1½ ft.
V. Rosea. Rose, with dark eye. Pkt., 10c.
V. Alba. White with crimson eye. Pkt., 10c.
V. Alba Pura. Pure white, exquisite. Pkt., 10c.

VIOLET (*Viola Odorata*).

A great favorite, much in demand, on account of its abundant and fragrant bloom. Hardy perennial; ½ ft.
V. Single White. Sweet scented. Pkt., 10c.
V. Single Blue. Sweet scented. Pkt., 10c.
V. Mixed. Pkt., 10c.

VIRGINIA STOCK.

A beautiful free-flowering plant for beds, baskets, or edgings. Hardy annuals; ½ ft.
Virginia Stock. Fine red and white, mixed. Pkt., 5c.

WALL FLOWER (*Cheiranthus Cheri*).

A handsome popular plant with massive spikes of fragrant flowers. Hardy perennial; 2 ft.
Wall Flower, Double Mixed. Yellow, brown and purple flowers. Pkt., 10c.
Single Mixed. Showy colors. Pkt., 5c.

WHITLAVIA.

W. Grandiflora. A pretty and charming plant, with delicate and handsome foliage, and bright blue and white bell-shaped flowers. Hardy annual; ¾ ft. Pkt., 5c.

ZINNIA (*Youth and Old Age*).

The Zinnia is one of our most showy plants, so easy of cultivation and handsome that it will always be popular. Hardy annual; 1½ ft.
Z. Elegans Flore Pleno. Dazzling scarlet, yellow, orange; rose, lilac, crimson and white. Pkt., 5c.
Haageana Fl. Pl. Deep orange yellow, retaining its color when dried. Pkt., 10c.
Z. DOUBLE STRIPED ZEBRA. A superb strain of this very popular flower, the petals being distinctly striped. They run through all shades known to the Zinnia, such as orange, crimson, pink, yellow, rose, violet and white. They are very compact in growth, and are far superior to those usually grown. Pkt., 10c.
Double Pure White. Pkt., 10c.
Z. Pigmy. See Novelties, page 83.

A WILD FLOWER GARDEN.

A mixture of many varieties of beautiful, easy-growing, hardy flowers, producing a constant and varied bloom the whole season, for sowing in shrubbery, under trees, and in beds on which no care will be bestowed, or even for sowing in exposed situations, where wildness is preferred to order and precision. The mixture comprises, Mignonette, Candytuft, Larkspurs, Marigolds, Poppies, Foxgloves, and many other garden favorites, which will flower successively and yield an abundance of bloom. Large pkt., 10c., ½ oz., 25c., oz., 50c.

SUMMER FLOWERING BULBS.

The cultivation of flowers from *Bulbs* and *Dormant Roots* commends itself to the amateur as being simpler than culture from seed and as being more sure in its results. They soon make a gorgeous display, flower the first summer and bloom and multiply season after season. Prices include prepayment by mail.

MILLA BIFLORA.

One of the finest bulbs recently introduced; flowers pure waxy-white, very fragrant, borne on stalks about eighteen inches high; the petals are very thick and firm and flowers last well in water. It blooms with wonderful freedom and is already a favorite florists' flower. Each, 15c.; 10 for $1.00.

BESSERA ELEGANS.

Long, narrow, grass-like leaves and tender flower stalks, one foot high, carrying a loose umbel of flowers, each a scarlet bell marked with white lines, stamens with light blue anthers. A wonderfully free bloomer. Each, 15c.; doz., $1.25.

AMARYLLIS.

The Amaryllis is one of the noblest and grandest families of flowering bulbs. They can be kept in pots the year round or planted in the open ground, as may be desired.

A. Atamasco (*Zephyranthes Rosea*). A most beautiful summer flowering bulb, growing one foot high and bearing flowers from two to three inches across, of the most exquisite shade of rosy pink; groups of one or two dozen bulbs in sunny flower beds are in continuous bloom during the summer months. 10c. each; $1.00 per doz.

A. Atamasco Sulphurea. A beautiful yellow variety of the above; very rare. 20c. each; $2.00 per doz.

A. Belladonna. This splendid species is perfectly hardy, with lovely violet and white flowers. Plant the bulb six to eight inches deep in sand with good fibrous loam pressed around it and do not disturb for years. After they become established they will give grand masses of bloom. 25c. each; 5 for $1.00.

Amaryllis Belladonna Spectabilis Bicolor. The finest of all the Belladonna lilies, and bearing flowers larger than the type on stalks one and one-half to two feet high. The colors are of a deep silvery pubescent rose, and often striped or marbled in bright carmine. The perfume is delicious. They frequently begin to bloom as soon as planted. In mild localities this Amaryllis is perfectly hardy if planted from five to six inches deep. It enjoys a light, sandy, well drained soil. 40c. each; 3 for $1.00.

AMARYLLIS BELLADONNA SPECTABILIS. 40c. each.

CYCLOBOTHRA FLAVA.

Flowers golden yellow, with four black dots in the inside of the petals; bell-shape, 10c. each; 10 for 60c.

BLACKBERRY LILY.

(*Pardanthus Sinensis*.)

The fruit of this is exactly like a blackberry. Dried for winter, they make a beautiful ornament. Perfectly hardy. Pretty flowers succeeded by these beautiful berries. 10c. each; $1.00 per doz.

CALADIUM ESCULENTUM. 20c.

CALADIUMS.

C. Esculentum (Elephant's Ears). A very effective plant and suitable for either a single plant on the lawn, masses in beds, or for margins of water; it is very distinct, apron-like leaves often attaining the length of three feet by twenty inches wide. Bulbs can be stored in dry sand in winter, and kept from year to year. 20c. each; $2.00 per doz.

CINNAMON VINE.

A beautiful, rapid growing summer climber, with clean glossy foliage and spikes of delicious cinnamon-scented flowers, perfectly hardy, the stem dying down in winter, but growing with great rapidity in the spring. Insects do not trouble it. Bulblets, 6 for 10c., or 50c. per doz. Roots, 10c. each; $1.00 per doz., all post-paid.

CINNAMON VINE. 10c. each.

BLACKBERRY LILY. 10c. each.

MADEIRA OR MIGNONETTE VINE.

A rapid, luxuriant summer climber, with thick, waxy foliage and fragrant flowers. Price, 5c. each; 50c. per doz.

APIOS TUBEROSA.

Hardy bulb of the same family as the Wisteria "Glycine," and sometimes called the Tuberous-Rooted Wisteria, which it resembles. Curious bloomer, lovely clusters of rich maroon flowers. 8c. each; 7 for 50c.; 15 for $1.00.

HYACINTHUS CANDICANS

A coarse but showy flower. The bulbs are cheap and can be effectually used for borders and among shrubbery. 10c. each; 75c. per doz.

TUBEROUS-ROOTED BEGONIAS.

The Tuberous-Rooted Begonias are not grown to the extent they should be, as they are the handsomest of our summer flowering bulbs and make grand bedding plants, flowering magnificently in the open garden under the full rays of our hot summer sun. They bloom continuously like the geraniums but have a far finer range of color than this popular flower. The bulbs can be taken up after frost and kept over winter in a dry, warm place. POST-PAID.

Single varieties in finest mixtures,   Per each, $1.50 per dozen.
"   separate colors, crimson, pink, white, yellow and orange, 20c.   2.00 " "
Double flowering kinds, splendid,   40c   4.00 " "

MONTBRETIAS.

A very pretty Gladiolus-like class of bulbs, free blooming and easy of cultivation. The sorts we offer succeed well in any sunny spot, in fairly rich, well drained soil; must be taken up in the fall and wintered like a Gladiolus. They are in full glory a month after all tender plants are killed by frost.

M. Crocosmiæflora. Large flowers on spikes twelve to twenty-four inches long, bright orange, dotted purple. Each, 10c.; doz., 75c.

M. Potsii. Flowers funnel-shaped, bright orange red with spotted throat. Each, 10c.; 3 for 25c.; doz., 75c.

M. Rosea. Like the above except that the flowers are a beautiful rose color. Each, 15c.; 4 for 50c.; doz., $1.25.

OXALIS (Summer Blooming).

Valuable for edging the borders of walks or flower beds. When planted two inches apart they soon produce an unbroken row of beautiful foliage and pretty flowers. They are also excellent for pot culture. Varieties, **Dieppi** and **Lasiandra**, doz., 10c.; 100, 75c.

SINGLE TUBEROUS-ROOTED BEGONIA.
Half natural size.

TIGRIDIAS (Shell Flower).

These are extremely beautiful, and should be in a very garden. Planted in the open ground in May they commence blooming early in July, and produce an abundance of gorgeous flowers until October. Late in autumn the bulbs should be lifted, dried and stored in the cellar, like Gladioli. They are one of the easiest plants in the world to cultivate and always bloom abundantly.

Tigridia Grandiflora Alba. Its flowers are large, of a clear, pearly-white color, marked at the base of each division with large spots of a reddish-brown on a yellowish ground, forming a fine contrast with the white of the petals. 10c. each; 6 for 50c., or 15 for $1.00.

Tigridia Conchiflora. Fine yellow, spotted crimson. 7c. each; 4 for 25c., or 18 for $1.00.

Tigridia Grandiflora. Very large, bright crimson, centre variegated with yellow. 7c. each; 4 for 25c.; 9 for 50c., 18 for $1.00.

IRIS (Flower-de-Luce).

This beautiful genus of plants obtained its title of Iris—which is the Greek name for the rainbow—from the ancients, as the most appropriate because of the varied hues and tints of the flowers. Robust growing, flowering in midsummer, varying in shades of white, maroon, deep blue, yellow, carmine and violet, beautifully veined and mottled. They are perfectly hardy and when once planted will increase in size and beauty every year.

I. Kaempferi. These Japanese Iris often have flowers ten inches in diameter; bloom in July; prefer a moist, sunny situation. All colors, mixed, 20c. each; doz., $2.00.

I. Germanica. These rival the orchid in variety of coloring, shape and shading. Perfectly hardy and adapted to all situations. Price, 15c. each; $1.50 per doz.

I. "Florentina." Pure white, very free-flowering, deliciously sweet-scented. 15c. each; $1.50 per doz.

MONTBRETIA ROSEA. 15c. each.

One Bulb of each variety for 20c., or six bulbs of each variety for $1.00, post-paid.

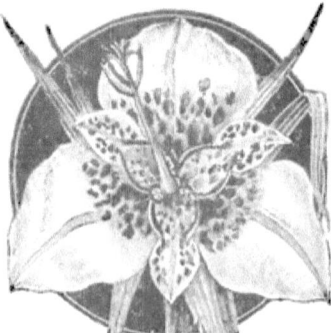

TIGRIDIA GRANDIFLORA ALBA. 10c. each.

✤ THE IRIS. ✤

*Thou art the Iris, fair among
the fairest,
Who, armed with golden rod,
And winged with the celestial
azure, bearest
The message of some God.*

*Oh, Flower-de-Luce bloom on,
and let the river
Linger to kiss thy feet!
Oh, flower of song, bloom on,
and make forever
The world more fair and
sweet.*

IRIS KAEMPFERI. 20c. each.

SUMMER ∴ FLOWERING ∴ BULBS ∴

HERBACEOUS PAEONIES.

Magnificent hardy plants, almost rivalling the Rose in brilliancy of color and perfection of bloom. They thrive in almost any soil or situation, and when planted in large clumps on the lawn make a magnificent display of flower and foliage. Some of the varieties are very fragrant. They are perfectly hardy, require little or no care, and produce larger and finer blooms when well established.

PRICE. Strong Flowering Roots, by mail, post-paid:

Shades of pink and crimson, 30c. each; $3.00 per doz.

Shades of white and light, 35c. each; $3.50 per doz.

When sent by express, 5c. less each and 50c. less per doz.

TUBEROSES.

Double Italian. One of the most delightfully fragrant and beautiful of the summer-flowering bulbs, throwing up tall spikes of double white flowers three feet high, which remain in bloom a long period. For flowering in the open border plant about the first of May.

Postpaid, 5c. each; 50c. per doz.

Express, 4c. each; 40c. per doz.; $3.00 per 100.

Pearl. The value of this sort consists in its flowers being of larger size, very double and imbricated; of dwarf habit, growing only from eighteen inches to two feet in height.

Postpaid, 5c. each; 50c. per doz.

Express, 4c. each; 40c. per doz.; $2.50 per 100.

HERBACEOUS PAEONIES.
GLADIOLUS.

This magnificent family contains hundreds of varieties, comprising all imaginable colors, shades and variegations, from the most gorgeous and dazzling to the softest and most delicate shades. They deserve to be grown in every garden, no matter how large or small. There is nothing in the floral kingdom so easy of culture and so sure to succeed as the "Gladiolus."

(In Separate Colors.)

	Post-paid, Each.	Doz.	Exp. 100.
Shades of red, mixed,	3c.	25c.	$1.75
Shades of pink,	6c.	50c.	3.25
Shades of buff and salmon,	8c.	65c.	4.25
Shades of yellow,	5c.	40c.	2.75
Shades of white and light,	6c.	55c.	3.75
All kinds, mixed,	3c.	30c.	2.00

New California Strain. Very large flowers of a fine assortment of colors. Strong growers. 10c. each; $1.00 per doz.

NEW GLADIOLUS, SNOW WHITE. *(See cut.)*

The finest White Gladiolus ever offered. The entire flower is a perfect paper white, with a slight cream shade in lower half of the lower petals. For withstanding dews, rains and hot sunshine, without changing color, we have never seen its equal. 25c. each; $2.50 per doz.

TRITOMA.

PEARL TUBEROSE.

TRITOMA.
(Flame Flower.)

A splendid summer and autumn flowering plant, with stately flower scapes and magnificent terminal dense spikes of rich orange-red tubular flowers, familiarly known from its glowing colors as the Red-hot Poker. Perfectly hardy and produces a fine effect when planted among shrubbery. 20c. each; 3 for 50c.; $1.75 per doz.

GLADIOLUS SNOW WHITE. 25c. each.

JOHNSON & STOKES

LILIUM AURATUM.

✦ ✦ LILIES. ✦ ✦

Lilies should be planted six inches deep and about twelve inches apart; cover at the approach of winter with dry leaves or manure, three or four inches deep. Plant as early in the season as possible and put them in earth as soon as received.

LILIUM AURATUM.

The Golden-Banded Lily of Japan. This queen of Lilies has immense blooms, measuring nearly a foot across. The large white petals are thickly spotted with rich, chocolate crimson and have a bright golden-yellow band through the centre of each. (See cut.) Price, 25c. each; 6 for $1.35; $2.50 per doz., postpaid.

Lilium Harrisi. The well-known Bermuda Easter Lily. Pure white. 25c. each; $2.50 per doz.

Lilium Longiflorum. Snow white, trumpet-shaped flowers. 20c. each; $2.00 per doz.

Lilium Batemanni. Flowers rich apricot color. 25c. each; $2.50 per doz.

Lilium Candidum (*Lily of the Annunciation*). Pure white petals, with lemon-yellow anthers. Perfectly hardy. 15c. each; $1.25 per doz.

Lilium Martagon (*Turk's Cap*). 15c. each; $1.50 per doz.

Lilium Superbum. A native lily growing six to eight feet high; flowers orange red. 15c. each; $1.25 per doz.

Lilium Tenuifolium. The Coral Lily of Siberia. Scarlet; a perfect little gem. 25c. each; 5 for $1.00.

Lilium Tigrinum. The old Tiger Lily. 10c. each; $1.00 per doz.

Lilium Tigrinum. Flore Pleno Double Tiger Lily. 15c. each; $1.25 per doz.

Lilium Wallacei. A magnificent Japanese variety; flowers clear buff, spotted maroon. 15c. each; $1.25 per doz.

Lilium Speciosum Album Præcox. Pure white, with a slight rose tint at end of petals; one of the most beautiful of the entire list. 30c. each; 4 for $1.00.

Lilium Rubrum. Rose spotted crimson. 15c. each; $1.50 per doz.

> **Special Lily Offer.**
> We will send one each of the above beautiful Lilies for only $2.00, all charges prepaid.

✦ ✦ PINK SPIDER LILY. ✦ ✦

Our well-known White Spider Lily has been so popular (see below), that we know a pink variety will create a sensation among flower lovers. As shown in our illustration, a clump of bulbs produces a large number of spikes of the most delicate flowers, varying in their colors from pinkish salmon to pink, vermilion and scarlet, the petals being beautifully undulated, and by artificial light sparkling like jewels; an ornament indeed for the finest parlor. Bulbs, 35c. each; 3 for $1.00.

WHITE SPIDER LILY (*Pancratium Caribæum*).

A native blooming bulb, bearing pure white fragrant flowers, of easy culture and sure to please. Price, 25c. each; $2.50 per doz.

THE CHINESE SACRED LILY.

These bulbs are very large, and each one sends up from five to eight spikes, which bear clusters of large, perfect, waxy white blossoms, with a yellow centre as shown in our illustration. They have a powerful and delicious fragrance, which is not excelled by any flower, and grow well in pots of soil, but the most popular way of blooming them is the Chinese method, as follows: Fill a bowl or some similar vessel with pebbles, in which place the bulb, setting it about one-half its depth, so that it will be held firmly, then fill with water to the top of the pebbles and place in a warm sunny window. The bulb will at once commence a rapid growth and bloom in four to five weeks. Price by mail, 25c. each, or 5 for $1.00, postpaid.

NEW BLACK CALLA

(*Arum Sanctum*).

Arum Sanctum is a most remarkable plant from the Holy Land, bearing enormous sweet-scented flowers in the shape of a Calla, but fourteen to eighteen inches long and four inches broad, of a brilliant dark purple color, the spadix being jet black and ten inches long. Each, $1.25.

CHINESE SACRED LILY. 25c. each.

SPOTTED LEAF CALLA (*Richardia Alba Maculata*).

This Calla resembles the White Calla, but is of a somewhat smaller habit. The leaves are of a glossy deep green, with numerous white spots, making it very ornamental at all times, even when not in bloom. It makes a splendid plant for border or beds. Price, first size, dry roots, each, 15c.; doz., $1.50.

CALLA ETHIOPICA. The old favorite pure white Calla. Let the plants rest during the summer by turning the pots on their sides. Repot in September in fresh soil. Thus treated the plants will bloom two or three times each year. First size, each, 25c.; doz., $2.50; one root each of the Callas, first size, for 35c.

LILY OF THE VALLEY. No garden is complete without a few clumps of these fragrant flowers which are such universal favorites as to need no description. Pips, per doz., 40c.; per 100, $2.50.

PINK SPIDER LILY. 35c.

FRUIT TREES AND PLANTS.

Great care has been exercised in making the following selection of Fruit Trees and Plants. Many by thorough trial and severe tests having established for themselves reputations for great hardiness, freedom from disease and uniform productiveness of large and luscious fruits, while those of more recent introduction, by their many points of excellence, give promise of decided merit, so that any article from the list may be ordered with an assurance that it will succeed over a wide territory and adapt itself to almost any fruit section of the United States.

TREES AND PLANTS BY MAIL.

We make a specialty of medium size, well-rooted trees and plants by mail, post-paid, which in many ways are more desirable than larger trees. They can be transplanted with more certainty of success, make better growth and handsomer trees. Though when preferred we send larger trees and plants by express at same price at purchaser's expense.

APPLES.

The following six varieties have proven hardy, vigorous and productive, and will succeed in all sections. Ripening in the order named, they cover the entire season.

PRICES. Mail or express, 25c. each; $2.50 per doz.; or one each of the following six apples, by mail or express, for $1.00.

Yellow Transparent. The earliest apple known; medium to large, rich, transparent, handsome yellow, juicy and excellent.

Parry White. Medium size, clear transparent, tender, crisp, juicy, very handsome, excellent.

Red Beitigheimer. Of German origin. Very large, beautiful purple, crimson red. Very fine quality.

Dickinson. Large, striped red, juicy, mild sub-acid. Good, young and abundant bearer.

Delaware Winter. Vigorous and productive. Large, deep red, sub-acid. Rich and good. Season, December to June.

● ● PEARS ● ●

THE IDAHO PEAR.

The Idaho Pear originated at or near the latitude of Quebec. It has survived winters when the thermometer ranged from fifteen to thirty degrees below zero. Very productive of fruit of largest size, weighing from sixteen to twenty-three ounces; flavor pleasant—equal to Bartlett; flesh entirely free from gritty texture; core exceedingly small and often without seed; later than Bartlett, and good shipper, having carried two thousand miles in good condition. Price, mail or express, $1.00 each; 3 for $2.00; or 1 each Japan, Golden Russet and Idaho for $1.00.

PEARS—Continued.

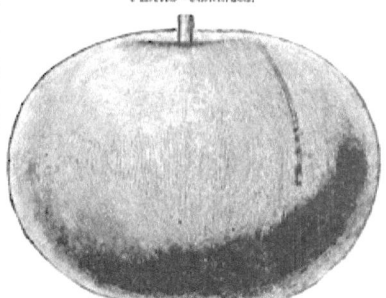

JAPAN GOLDEN RUSSET PEAR.

The above cut represents Japan Golden Russet Pear, of medium size. It is a variety of rare value introduced from Japan. Of very vigorous growth, so that it requires intense cold to injure it, and assures an enormous crop of fruit, which it seldom fails to produce at two years of age. It thrives in the hot, dry climates and parched soils of the South, where the ordinary varieties cannot exist. Nor has it ever been affected by blight or other disease. Fruit of beautiful golden-yellow, very handsome, perfect shape, pleasant, crisp and juicy. Unsurpassed for canning or cooking. Price, mail or express, $1.00 each; 3 for $2.00.

Bartlett. The most popular summer pear, good grower, heavy bearer, fruit large, yellow and excellent.

Le Conte. Very vigorous grower, with handsome foliage, making beautiful lawn tree; fruit large, greenish-yellow, smooth, juicy, very productive, ripening immediately after Bartlett.

KIEFFER. Large, yellow with red cheek, very handsome and excellent for canning as well as a good table fruit. Tree a vigorous grower, enormously productive and free from blight. Price, mail or express, the above three varieties for 40c. each, or the 3 for $1.00.

Lawson, Clapp, Howell, B. D'Anjou, Seckle and Lawrence, at same rates.

JAPAN PLUMS.

Since the introduction of Japan varieties we can plant plums with confidence of success. They are vigorous growers, come into bearing generally at two years of age, resist the curculio and produce enormous crops.

ABUNDANCE. Strong, upright grower; prodigious bearer of handsome luscious fruit.

SATSUMA. Vigorous grower, enormously productive, very large, handsome and excellent.

KELSEY is also a vigorous grower and an abundant bearer, fruit very large, beautiful and luscious.

Price, mail or express, 40c. each, or the 3 for $1.00.

THE TRIFOLIATE ORANGE.

A NEW HARDY ORANGE. (CITRUS TRIFOLIATA).

This is the most hardy of the orange family, and will stand our Northern climate with little or no protection, and is also desirable for pot culture. In the parks of both New York and Philadelphia it is growing luxuriantly, and blooming and fruiting profusely. Think of it, friends, you can have an orange tree growing, blooming and fruiting on your lawn or yard. It is a dwarf, of a low, symmetrical growth, with beautiful trifoliate, glossy green leaves, and abundance of large, white sweet-scented blossoms, larger and finer than any other variety of orange blossoms, and borne almost continuously. The fruit is small, bright orange-red in color, having a peculiar flavor, of no value for eating, though for refreshing drink it is equal to lime juice or lemonade. It blooms very profusely in spring and early summer, but after the fruit begins to form, blossoms are not plentiful. We predict for this tree a great future. Strong, young, thrifty trees, by mail or express, 25c. each; $2.50 per doz.

MULBERRIES.

DOWNING. Ever-bearing, not only makes a handsome lawn tree, but produces delicious berries, beginning to fruit at four and five years of age, continues in bearing three to four months of the year, making it very desirable. Price, by mail or express, each, 50c.

The foliage of mulberries is valuable for silkworms while the fruit makes excellent chicken feed as well as fine table dessert. The late Henry Ward Beecher said he regarded it as an indispensable addition to every fruit garden, and that he would rather have a Downing Mulberry tree than a strawberry bed.

THE JAPAN MAMMOTH CHESTNUT is among the most valuable introductions from Japan. It is quite distinct from the European varieties, being hardier. Nuts much larger and of superior flavor and sweetness. Commence bearing very young, usually at two to three years of age, producing nuts four to six inches around and running three to seven in a burr. Price, mail or express, 50c. each; 3 for $1.00.

STRAWBERRIES.

At rates per dozen will be mailed free. At 100 rates add 25c. per 100 to cover postage, expenses, etc.

LOVETT'S EARLY. Supposed to be a cross between Crescent and Wilson, ripening earlier, more prolific and larger than either, equalling in firmness the Wilson. Excellent conical form, uniform in size and shape, of superior quality, and bright crimson color. Blossom, perfect; plant, vigorous and healthy. Price, mail, $1.00 per doz.; express, $4.00 per 100.

MICHEL'S EARLY. Strong grower, good foliage, very productive, and has proven to be much larger and several days earlier than Crescent. Price, mail, 50c. per doz.; express, $3.00 per 100; $20.00 per 1000.

BUBACH. A wonderful berry in vigor of plant and yield of fruit of large size. Exceedingly productive, ripens early and is very valuable. Price, mail, 40c. per doz.; express, $1.00 per 100; $5.00 per 1000.

PARRY. A seedling of Jersey Queen, which it resembles. A perfect flower, very productive, good grower; fruit, large, handsome, and excellent quality. Price, mail, 40c. per doz.; express, 75c. per 100; $5.00 per 1000.

SHARPLESS. Strong, vigorous grower, very large, good quality and very popular. Price, mail, 40c. per doz.; express, 60c. per 100; $3.00 per 1000.

GANDY. The best late strawberry. Extremely vigorous and robust. Plant very productive, large size, good quality, firm and very late. Price, mail, 50c. per doz.; express, $1.00 per 100; $5.00 per 1000. Collection No. 1 —By mail, 1 Lovett Early and 6 each of the other five varieties for $1.00.

RASPBERRIES AND BLACKBERRIES

Will be sent, postage free, by mail at rates per dozen; by mail, at rates per 100, add 40c. per 100 to cover postage, expenses, etc.

THOMPSON'S E. PROLIFIC. A very early bright raspberry of good quality. Vigorous grower with good, healthy foliage; succeeds admirably at the South, and endures a temperature of twenty-two degrees below zero without injury; very fine, early and prolific and of good size. Price, mail, 10c. each; 3 for 25c.; 12 for 90c.; express, $4.00 per 100; $25.00 per 1000.

GOLDEN QUEEN. The best yellow raspberry. Very large, exquisite beauty, very good quality, hardy and very productive; very strong grower and succeeds well in the South and Pacific Coast, as well as in colder climates. Price, mail, 10c. each; 3 for 25c.; 12 for 90c.; express, $3.00 per 100; $25.00 per 1000.

PROGRESS (Pioneer). Black Raspberry. Very early, jet black, good quality, ripening with Souhegan, stronger grower and more prolific; very valuable market variety; extremely hardy. Price, mail, 10c. each; 3 for 25c.; 12 for 75c.; express, $1.50 per 100; $12.50 per 1000; Hansell, Cuthbert, Souhegan, Ohio and Gregg, price, mail, 10c. each; 3 for 25c.; 12 for 75c.; express, $1.50 per 100; $12.50 per 1000.

JAPAN WALNUT.

This is a native of mountains of northern Japan and is extremely hardy. Very vigorous growers, handsome symmetrical form, mature early, bear young and are much more productive than the English walnut, and having an abundance of fibrous roots, transplant as safely as an apple tree. The nuts grow in clusters of fifteen or twenty. The meat is sweet and of very best quality, flavor like butternut, but less oily and much superior. Price, mail or express, 50c. each; 1 for $1.00.

SMALL FRUITS AND PLANTS

BLACKBERRIES.

EARLY HARVEST. The earliest known variety. Strong grower, upright, enormously productive and good quality. Price, mail, 10c. each; 3 for 25c.; 12 for 75c.; express, $1.50 per 100; $12.50 per 1000.

WILSON Jr. The largest known variety, ripening immediately after E. Harvest. Very productive and good quality. By its low, trailing habit of growth it is easily protected in winter and well adapted on that account to cold climates. Price, mail, 10c. each; 3 for 25c.; 12 for 75c.; express, $2.00 per 100; $15.00 per 1000.

LUCRETIA (Dewberry). As early as Early Harvest and as large as Wilson. Shiny jet black, melting and delicious quality, devoid of core. Plant is entirely hardy, healthy, strong grower, and very productive. Price, mail, 10c. each; 3 for 25c.; 12 for 75c.; express, $2.00 per 100; $15.00 per 1000.

WILSON JR.

CURRANTS.

CHERRY. The most popular market sort. Bunch and berry very large, bright red; bush, healthy, vigorous and productive. Price, mail or express, 10c. each; 3 for 25c.; 12 for $1.00.

FAY'S PROLIFIC. The best red currant. Strong grower, wonderfully productive and comes to bearing young; fruit large, bright red, and good quality. Price, mail or express, 25c. each; 3 for 50c.; 12 for $1.50.

WHITE GRAPE. The largest and best white currant. Bunch, large; berries, large, handsome, transluscent and excellent quality. Strong grower and very productive. Price, mail or express, 10c. each; 3 for 25c.; 12 for $1.00.

GOOSEBERRIES.

INDUSTRY GOOSEBERRY.

INDUSTRY. An English variety that succeeds admirably in the United States. Very productive and free from mildew. Berries very large, dark red color, and delicious quality. Price, mail or express, 25c. each; 5 for $1.00.

DOWNING. An American variety of very large size. Productive, free from mildew, excellent quality. Price, mail or express, 10c. each; 4 for 50c.; 9 for $1.00.

GRAPES.

MOORE'S EARLY. A seedling of Concord, ripening ten days earlier, much larger and better quality; vine strong, healthy grower, free from rot or mildew. Price, mail or express, 25c. each; 5 for $1.00.

CONCORD. The most popular black grape. Strong grower and productive. Price, mail or express, 20c. each; 5 for $1.00.

NIAGARA. Very vigorous and productive, bunch very large and handsome; greenish-white, turning to pale amber; good quality. Price, mail or express, 25c. each; 5 for $1.00.

LADY WASHINGTON. Very vigorous grower, clusters enormous size, greenish amber; very productive; late. Price, mail or express, 25c. each; 5 for $1.00.

WYOMING RED. Very healthy grower and enormously productive. Berries medium size, ripening early and resembling Delaware in appearance. Price, mail or express, 25c. each; 5 for $1.00.

BRIGHTON. Free grower and productive; large loose bunch, dark wine-red; delicious quality. Price, 25c. each; 5 for $1.00. Grape collection.—By mail or express, one each above six varieties grapes for $1.00.

FRUIT SEEDS.

Remit for postage 8 cents per pound, or 1½ cents per quart, when ordered to be sent by mail.

Peach Pits. Pure Southern, natural, or seedling. Qt., 15c.; lb., $2.50. **Apple Seed.** Qt., 35c.; bush., $6.00. **Apricot Pits.** Oz., 10c.; lb., 50c. **Plum Pits.** Qt., 50c.; bush., $10.00. **Pear Seeds.** French imported, oz., 15c.; lb., $1.50. **Quince Seed.** Oz., 15c.; lb., $1.50. **Mulberry.** White or black. Oz., 20c.; lb., $2.00.

THE JAPANESE WINEBERRY.

THE JAPANESE WINEBERRY.

There have been few novelties introduced to this country that are more interesting or beautiful in their way than the Japanese Raspberry, brought out last year under the name of Wineberry. It originated from seed sent home by Prof. Georgeson, late of the Imperial College of Agriculture, Tokio, Japan, and gathered by him from a plant growing in a wild state on the mountains of that country. The canes of this interesting plant are large, robust and entirely hardy here; they are thickly covered with purplish red hairs, which extend along the stem to the extremity. The leaves are large, tough, dark green above and silvery gray beneath. Each berry is at first tightly enveloped by the large calyx, forming a sort of burr, which is also covered with purplish red hairs so thickly as to present the appearance of a moss rosebud. These gradually open and turn back, exposing the fruit in all its beauty. The berries are of medium size as compared with our raspberries, but of a beautiful, translucent appearance, running through all the shades of amber to crimson as they ripen. There is a freshness and brilliancy about them impossible to describe, and we know of nothing in the way of raspberries so attractive. A bush in full fruiting is a sight not readily to be forgotten and a decided ornament to the garden. In quality it is good, with a rich and sprightly flavor, but decidedly brisk sub-acid. When cooked it is simply grand, surpassing by far, when canned, the huckleberry and all other small fruits. Season of ripening early in July. Price, mail or express, strong, well-rooted plants, 25c. each; $2.50 per doz.

HOLT'S MAMMOTH SAGE.

We have grown and fully tested this valuable new variety for several years past and offer the plants to our customers with the greatest confidence in its merits. The plant is of very large, strong growth, single plants covering a circular space of nine feet in circumference in one season. It is perfectly hardy and a decided improvement on the ordinary sage, a single plant producing eight to ten times as much, from being much larger. It is also stronger in flavor and superior in quality, never running to seed. Price, 3 plants for 25c.; 7 for 50c.; 15 for $1.00, by mail, post-paid; $5.00 per 100 by express.

Special $1.00 Plant Collections.

Free by Mail.

For $1.00 we will send, free by mail, any one of the following Collections of Plants.
PLEASE ORDER COLLECTIONS BY NUMBER.

CHRYSANTHEMUMS.
(The Queen of Autumn.)

Collection No. 1. One plant each of
Mrs. Alpheus Hardy, White "Ostrich Plume Chrysanthemum."
Gloriosum. The best early yellow.
Princess. Very large; light pink; fine for cut flowers.
L. Canning. White; late; one of the finest.
Mandarin. Deep Indian red colored; beautiful.
Golden Beauty. A beauty; fine golden-yellow.
E. H. Fitler. Yellow, streaked with red; magnificent.
Volunteer. Light pink, striped white; very early.

Collection No. 2. One each of the following:
Mrs. Irving Clark. Pearly white; large and fine.
L. B. Bird. Largest size; pink; whorled.
Pure Gold. Fine yellow.
T. C. Price. Cream-colored; incurved; very double.
Golden Fleece. Beautiful clear lemon; very early.
White Bedder. Pure white; early flowering.
White Cap. Reddish violet color; very double.
Lord Tennyson. Light lemon color; early.

No. 3. Twelve choice Chrysanthemums, our selection. These will be fine varieties, many of them of the more recent introduction, or we will mail five varieties for 75c.

CARNATIONS.

Collection No. 4.
L. L. Lamborn. Large, pure white.
Grace Wilder. Fine pink.
Mrs. Ferdinand Mangold. Strong grower; salmon pink.
Hinzie's White. Creamy white; finely fringed.
Portia. Fine scarlet; a constant bloomer.
Sunrise. Variegated orange and scarlet.
Constance. New bright scarlet; very fine.
Anna Webb. Crimson maroon; beautifully fringed.
Buttercup. Pure yellow penciled scarlet.
Duke of Orange. Orange edged and striped with carmine.
Or any 4 for 50c.

No. 5. Collection of Carnation Novelties.
Angelus. Clear pink flower; ideal in shape.
Golden Gate. A clear yellow; free bloomer.
Nellie Bly. Variegated red and white in finely divided lines; flowers large and half double.
American Flag. Large flowers white, striped scarlet.
Aurora. Pure pink flowers, very large with fine odor. Winner of silver cup at the Madison Square flower show New York, November, 1891.

We can quote you special prices on large quantities of any of the above Carnations.

No. 6. Ten fine Everblooming Roses. A Gem Collection.
No. 7. Twelve choice Bedding Plants.
No. 8. Ten Basket Plants for hanging baskets, including one Manetta Vine.
No. 9. Ten Fuchsias. Fine assortment, including "Storm King."
No. 10. Ten good Geraniums, including one "Gem" and one "Chrysanthum."
No. 11. Four Manetta Vines, two Moon Vines and one Hardy Passion Vine.
No. 12. Eight Verbenas. Finest mammoth.
No. 13. Eight Snapdragons. Assorted.
No. 14. Fifteen Pansies. Large flowering.
No. 15. Eight Double Petunias. A magnificent collection.
No. 16. Ten Single Petunias. Blotched and striped.
No. 17. Six Moon Vines, including one hardy day-blooming Moonflower.
No. 18. Eight Violets. Sweet-scented, double and single, white and blue.

No. 20. Six Cannas. Thick leaved varieties; tall and tropical looking.
No. 21. Six Cannas. Large flowering; dwarf French varieties.
No. 22. Eight Dahlias. Single varieties, assorted.
No. 23. Eight Dahlias. Double varieties, assorted.
No. 24. Eight Dahlias. Assorted single and double, including Mrs. Hawkins.
No. 25. Twelve Coleus. Choice Colors.
No. 26. Four Hardy Passion Vines and one Hardy Ivy.
No. 27. Twelve Ageratums. New white and blue.
No. 28. Six Fine Hardy Perennials, including Hardy Phlox.
No. 29. Six Choice Hardy Shrubs.
No. 30. SPECIAL $1.00 BARGAIN COLLECTION. These are collections made up from our surplus stock and will represent several times the money's worth as in growing a large assortment we leave at times a surplus of many things and rather than throw out we offer them at a low price. Send $1.00 and see what you get.

SPECIAL!

Unless where specified on plant orders will be filled for less than $1.00, but customers may have the collections; thus half No. 7 and half No. 12 may be sent for $1.00, but no further division will be made.

PREMIUMS. Two collections will be sent for $1.75; three collections for $2.50; four collections for $3.00; six collections for $4.00, or of 3d collections for $5.00.

.:. GARDEN .:. TOOLS .:. AND .:. SPRAYING .:. APPARATUS .:.

"PLANET JR." GARDEN TOOLS.

NEW HILL DROPPING DRILL

Has two carrying wheels, fifteen inches high and six inches apart. Has a rubber double screw agitator and a two-quart hopper. It sows in drills or drops in hills, as desired, either four, six, eight or twelve inches apart, and can be altered from one to the other in an instant. Does not sow when going backward or turning at end of row, and is altogether the most practical and accurate seed sower ever offered. Price, ... $11.00.

NEW COMBINED HILL DROPPING AND FERTILIZER DRILL.

This is the same as the New Hill Dropping Seed Drill, except that it has a fertilizer sowing attachment. It works in a most perfect and regular manner, sowing any desired quantity, and is so arranged that the fertilizer can be placed either above or below the seed, covering it lightly. This machine is a perfect and invaluable tool for every market gardener, onion and strawberry grower.
Price, complete, ... $16.00.

New "Planet Jr." Combined Hill Dropping and Fertilizer Drill.

Our Price, $16.00.

"PLANET JR." COMBINED DRILL.
Our Net Price, $10.00
(List Price, $12.00.)

THE "PLANET JR." No. 2 DRILL holds two and one-half quarts. Is the old reliable drill, equally as good as the new, except that it does not drop in hills. Price, $7.50.

THE "PLANET JR." COMBINED DRILL, WHEEL HOE, CULTIVATOR AND PLOW. This most popular tool is suitable for either the farm or garden. As a drill, it is exactly similar and equal to the No. 2, except for size. It holds one quart. As a plow, it opens furrows, covers them, hills, plows to and from, etc. As a hoe, it works safely and closely to and from both sides of the row at once, when plants are small, between rows as plants grow larger, working all rows from eight to sixteen inches wide at one passage. Price, $10.00.

"PLANET JR." DOUBLE-WHEEL HOE, CULTIVATOR, RAKE AND PLOW COMBINED. Has the invaluable feature of tending both sides of the row at once. The wheels can be set four, seven or ten inches apart. It has a pair of plows, two pairs of cultivator teeth, a pair of rakes and a pair of leaf lifters, making it capable of every variety of gardeners' work. Price, $7.00. Onion set gatherer, extra, $1.25.

"PLANET JR." SINGLE WHEEL HOE is considerably lighter than the double, and is supplied with one pair of hoes, three reversible cultivator teeth, two narrow and one broad, a large garden plow and a pair of rakes. It is capable of a great variety of combinations and is admirably adapted to the use of small gardens. Price, $5.50.

"PLANET JUNIOR" DOUBLE-WHEEL HOE.
OUR NET PRICE, - $7.00
(List Price, $8.00.)

Complete "Planet Jr." Catalogue Describing Horse Hoes and Hand Machines, also complete Repair Lists, sent on Application.

SPRAYING PUMPS.

The practice of spraying orchards and vineyards with a solution of copper and Paris green has become so universal and has been found to be so beneficial to the growing crops of fruit that we have provided for our customers, four pumps, that we believe have no superiors on the market. Circulars with full directions and description sent on application.

OUR "GEM" BRASS PUMP. We only recommend this when a very limited amount of work is to be done. Price, $3.00.

"SOUTHERN QUEEN" ORCHARD SPRAYER" is an excellent pump to be fastened on a barrel and placed in a wagon. Will do splendid work. Price (with vermorel nozzle, but not including barrel), $7.00. (See cut.)

THE PERFECTION FORCE PUMP is a larger pump than the "Southern Queen." It has ten feet of discharge hose with a spray nozzle. It also has three feet of return hose, so that at every stroke a small part of the liquid is redischarged into the barrel, which keeps the poison and water well mixed. Weight, 35lbs. Price (not including barrel), $9.80.

"DOUBLE EMPIRE" PUMP. Is a large powerful pump, throwing two streams at once over the tallest orchards. Price (with two vermorel nozzles, but not including barrels), $12.50.

"GARFIELD KNAPSACK SPRAYER." (See cut.) Is to be carried on the shoulders, and is a copper tank holding five gallons. The pump is made entirely of brass and copper and cannot corrode or rust. Price, complete, $11.00.

Send for Special Spraying Outfit Circulars.

Paris green or London purple, is generally used in about the proportion of one pound to two hundred gallons of water for spraying apple, plum and other trees. For spraying currant and gooseberry bushes to kill the currant worm, white hellebore is generally used, a tablespoonful to a pail of water. For grapes use Bordeaux mixture; for hop lice use kerosene emulsion.

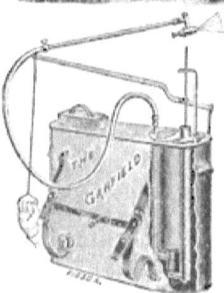

OUR KNAPSACK SPRAYER FOR VINEYARDS AND POTATO FIELDS.
Price, $11.00.

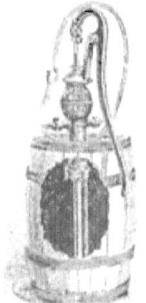

OUR GEM HAND SPRAYER.
Price (not including barrel), $7.00.

JOHNSON & STOKES

POULTRY SUPPLIES.

HAMMONTON INCUBATORS.

No. 1, 150 eggs, complete	$17 00
No. 2, 300 " "	25 00
PRESSY BROODERS	8 00

Special Catalogue of above mailed on application.

PREPARED MEAT, a choice sample of beef scraps.

25 lbs., $1.50; 100 lbs., $2.50; 500 lbs.	$12 00
Per ton, 200 lbs.	12 00
OYSTER SHELL, crushed, 100 lbs.	1 00
500 lbs., $4.50; per ton	12 00
DESICCATED FISH, 50 lb. bag	2 75
100 lbs., $2.75; 500 lbs.	12 75
CRACKED POULTRY BONE, 100 lbs., $2.50; 500	11 00
lbs., $12.00; ton	41 00
SUNFLOWER SEED, mammoth Russian, per bush.	2 00
ANIMAL MEAL, a combined meat and meal food, 100 lbs.	2 25
POULTRY MARKERS, by mail	30
GAPE WORM EXTRACTORS, by mail	50
WILSON'S BONE MILLS	5 00
MALLORY'S BONE MILLS	3 00
MANN'S GREEN BONE MILL	20 00
NECESSITY CLOVER CUTTER, for cutting hay and clover for fowls and other stock. A very excellent machine	8 00
LITTLE GIANT CLOVER CUTTER. When a limited amount of clover is to be cut this will be found all that is necessary	3 00

POULTRY MARKER.

This little instrument is for marking young and old chickens and all kinds of fowl. It is invaluable to breeders and farmers, as the markings will enable them to recognize their own fowl at a glance. Price, by mail, 30c.

POULTRY MARKER.

Gape Worm Extractor.

A little instrument for extracting the small worms from the little chicks. It does it well. One chick saved pays the price of the instrument. Price, by mail, postpaid, 50c.

GAPE WORM EXTRACTOR.

Send for Complete Poultry Supply Circular.

CHICK MANNA.

The Chick Manna comprises a variety of such food that is adapted to the wants of the little chicks when first hatched, and by continuing feeding for two weeks will tend to lay a strong, healthy foundation and prevent scouring and the other annoying ills they are heir to. Chicks fed on Manna from the start will loudly relish it. After feeding two weeks other food may be given, but should contain a part of Manna for at least a few days longer. 1 lb., by mail, 25c.; 5 lbs., by express, 90c.; 10 lb. box in bulk, $1.20.

An Invaluable Food for Little Chicks.

Wholesale agents wanted for "Chick Manna," the finest food for young chicks known.

H. D. Chew, Glassboro, N. J., writes, Nov. 20, 1894.—"Chick Manna" is a first-class food for little chicks. After I commenced feeding it I had no bother with them dying with scours, shall want a lot more in about two days, as soon as my first hatch of six hundred and forty eggs comes off.

AGATHA POULTRY FOOD. The best food on the market. 5 lb. bag	$0 30
10 lb. bag, 65c.; 20 lb. bag	1 20
MADOC GAPE CURE, sure cure (by mail 50c.)	35
ROUP PREPARATION, ½ lb., (by mail 30c.)	25
" 1 lb., (by mail 55c.)	40
CAPONIZING SETS (by mail $3.00)	
POULTRY NETTING, all sizes, 2-inch mesh, per square foot	2½c.
DRINKING FOUNTAINS, earthenware, 2 qt., doz.	2 50
" " 4 qt.	4 50
" " 8 qt.	6 00
CLIMAX, " " galvanized iron, 1 gal.	1 00
2 gal., $1.25; 3 gal.	

CURES POULTRY CHOLERA.

It is a positive preventive and cure for gapes and poultry cholera, and a most excellent medicine for young turkeys that have been exposed to weather; also a most excellent medicine for horses, cattle, sheep and hogs. It is not a food, but an honest medicine at an honest price. Price, per package, by mail, 40c.; per doz., by express, $2.50.

COOPER'S SHEEP DIPPING POWDER.

Cures Scab, Kills Ticks, Improves the Wool. Used on Ninety Million Sheep Annually.

Every sheep owner should dip his sheep a month or two after shearing to keep them clean and prevent disease. This practice is adopted in many countries, and Scab, Ticks, Lice, etc., are thereby rendered comparatively scarce. Feeders will market their sheep more profitably if they dip a month or so before selling. The animals fatten quicker and the wool is given a nice appearance. Cold water alone required.

Sold in cases of 100 lbs. to make 1000 gallons of dip at $16 00	
½ packages	100	7 00
" "	25	1 50

☞ Copy of Sheepman's "Guide to Dipping" Sent Free.

DANA'S STOCK LABELS.

For Marking, Numbering and Registering Cattle, Sheep, Swine, Goats, Colts, Etc.

This method consists in attaching a label to the animal's ear, as represented in the cut. These labels are made of iron wire rolled flat, washed with tin and stamped with numbers and any name ordered. Then they are bent into link shape and left open as seen in the cut in the label at the left. It is attached to the ear by passing it through a hole punched in the ear and lapping around the edge of the ear, then pressing the long hooked end to even with the short end.

Cattle Labels stamped with your name (if not more than thirteen letters), and on the reverse side the number from one upward, 75c. per doz.; $5.00 per 100; cattle punches, $1.75.

Sheep and Hog Labels, stamped with name (if not more than ten letters), and on the opposite side consecutive numbers and so otherwise ordered, 40c. per doz.; $3.00 per 100; punches, $1.00.

These are all too heavy to be sent by mail. They must be sent by express at purchaser's expense.

We invite your perusal of the following pages, which we have devoted to our Live Stock Department. To our old customers, we need only say that we have added fresh prize-taking blood to all of our pens and yards, and you need not be afraid of in-breeding by purchasing of us again. To those who have never bought Live Stock of us, we would add that we guarantee the safe arrival of all shipments, and that they will be of the **finest and choicest thoroughbred stock** of this and other countries; fully up to representation, and well worth the price asked, which is as low as such high-class stock can be bred for.

EGGS FOR HATCHING. We guarantee all eggs fresh and true to name. We can ship eggs **only by express**, to any State. We cannot guarantee any certain number to hatch, as this depends on so many causes over which we have no control, but our system of packing is so perfect that excellent hatches are the rule, no matter how great the distance.

NO LIVE STOCK OR EGGS SENT C. O. D. Cash must accompany all orders.

SHIPMENTS. Always give us your Express and Post-Office plainly, and we will notify you by telegraph or mail in advance of all shipments. Express agents feed and water, and collect express charges at destination.

Bred by Johnson & Stokes

GOLDEN PRINCE AND PRINCESS

OUR PRIZE GOLDEN WYANDOTTES.

Although we have been breeding the Golden Wyandottes but two years at "Trebreh," their large size, fine shape, rich plumage, beautiful markings and high-bred carriage have enthroned them as the prime favorites of our yards, their remarkable beauty making them the admiration of every beholder. They are the most popular new breed this country has produced and are already looked upon with great favor in England and on the Continent. They are a cross of the deservedly-popular Silver Laced Wyandottes made with the Winnebagos as the top cross. They are extremely hardy and more active foragers than most of the heavier breeds. As both summer and winter layers they are unrivalled, even surpassing the Leghorns. It is also rare indeed to find an infertile Golden Wyandotte egg, while the chicks, when hatched are remarkable for their high degree of vigor and "gimp," being quickly on their feet, foraging for food in the liveliest manner and showing by their strong, rapid growth abundant evidence of thrift and early maturity. **Prices:** Single cockerel, $1.50 to $5.00; pair mated for breeding, $8.00; trio, $12.00. **Eggs for Hatching:** per setting of 13, $3.00; per 2 settings of 26, $5.00.

BREEDING PEN OF PRIZE WHITE WYANDOTTES
OWNED BY JOHNSON & STOKES

We know of no fowl possessing so many points of superiority for the poultry raiser or practical farmer as the White Wyandotte. For beauty, style and fine form they have no equal. Their plumage being a pure snow white, with legs, beaks and skin a rich yellow. As a market or table fowl they have no superior. They have a close-fitting, medium-sized rose-comb, and thus are not troubled by the frost, as the Minorcas and Leghorns. They mature quickly, commence laying very early and continue through the season uninterruptedly. They are good foragers and make the kindest mothers. The birds we are breeding are the best that careful selection and money could secure, breeding so remarkably true that out of several hundred bred the past two seasons not one bird showed a black feather.

PRICES:—Single cock or cockerel, $4.00 to $4.50; pair mated for breeding, $7.00; trio, cock and 2 hens, $10.00. Eggs for Hatching, from our best prize stock, per setting of 13, $2.50; per 26, $4.75.

MAMMOTH BRONZE TURKEYS.

It is well to remember that it costs no more to raise good stock than it does poor. The common Turkey gobler at maturity weighs from eighteen to twenty-five pounds—the Mammoth Bronze from thirty-five to forty pounds. When the result is so much better the slight difference in first cost is not to be considered. Our strain of these Mammoth Bronze Turkeys has no superior in this country. Their plumage is a beautiful metallic bronze. Yearling goblers weigh from thirty-five to forty pounds each, and yearling hens eighteen to twenty-six pounds each. Our young goblers, at six months old, frequently weigh twenty to twenty-five pounds each. Prices: trio, tom and two hens, mated for breeding, $16.00; pair, mated, $12.00; single tom or hen, $7.00 to $8.00. Eggs for hatching, $3.00 for 8; $5.75 for 12.

As Turkeys do not lay until late in the spring we are sometimes obliged to hold orders for a time.

IMPERIAL PEKIN DUCKS.

The largest, finest, heaviest and most profitable breed of ducks in existence. In color they are creamy-white, loose, fine feathers, erect carriage, large size, plump bodies and are nearly as large as geese. Orange legs and yellow bills; mature early and can be marketed young. Prolific layers, easily confined, and need only water enough for drinking purposes. Prices: drake, $3.50 to $4.50; pair, $7.00; trio, $9.00. Eggs for hatching, $1.25 for 6; $2.25 for 12.

PRIZE MAMMOTH BRONZE TURKEY.

Imported Indian Games.

A Pair of our Prize Birds, "Trebreh" and Mate.

INDIAN GAMES have met with a greater "boom" from all the best Poultry Journals of the country than any other new breed ever introduced, and have created the greatest sensation in the poultry kingdom ever experienced. The illustration above gives an idea of the male and female, but no picture can portray the wonderful plumage and grand physical development of these birds. They are par excellence the table fowls of the century. Beautiful yellow skin and legs, deep full breast, without prominence of the keel bone, they are fit for the table of a king. The hens are good layers of large, brown eggs, and make the best of mothers. Indian Games are very tame, can be thoroughly domesticated and make the very best of fowls for the poultry farmer as well as the fancier. Our yards are without question as fine as any in the world, the birds being noted for their great size. Elegant double lacing; free from the objectionable white feathers. Our stock comes from the champion breeder in England, John Fmyn, who at the present time owns the champion cock in England, having refused $125.00 for the bird. Many of our fowls from pen headed by this cock. Eggs that will hatch prize birds, $3.00 per setting of 13. Prices of Birds by letter on application.

BARRED PLYMOUTH ROCKS.

Our strains of this popular and very profitable farmers' fowl are very fine. They are yellow-legged, hardy and easily reared. They commence laying very early, and feather early; meat yellow and juicy; good mothers. Prices: trio, $9.00; pair, $6.50; cockerel, $3.50 to $4.50. Eggs for hatching, $2.00 for 13, or $3.75 for 26.

WHITE PLYMOUTH ROCKS.

This new breed is a sport from the Barred Plymouth Rock, and promises to become even more popular than their "colored cousins." They breed truer to color than any of the new white breeds with probably the exception of White Wyandottes. Their large size, stately carriage and snow-white plumage are the admiration of all. They are sure to be in great demand, and all who secure good breeding stock will find it a profitable investment. The stock from which we are breeding we obtained at high cost, direct from the originator in Maine. Prices: White Plymouth Rocks, single cockerel, $4.00 to $5.00 each; pair, cockerel and hen, $7.00; trio, $10.00. Eggs for Hatching, $2.50 per setting of 13; $4.75 for 26.

PARTRIDGE COCHINS.

The best of the Cochins, and like all Asiatic breeds are the best of winter layers. They are the largest and hardiest of all fowls and in great demand by farmers for crossing with barn-yard fowls, to increase, size, hardiness and early maturity and there are none better for the purpose. Cocks, $4.00 to $6.00; pair, $7.00; trio, $10.00. Eggs, $2.50 per setting of 13; $4.00 for 26.

POULTRY PRICE-LIST.

Below we give a list of prices of fowls and eggs, kept by us at all times. If any variety is wanted not included in this list, write us, as our extensive acquaintance with poultry raisers enables us to procure almost any breed.

	Good Cockerel.	Extra Selected Cockerel.	Per Trio.	Eggs. Per 13.	Eggs. Per 26.
White Wyandottes,	$4 00	$5 50	$10 00	$2 50	$4 75
Golden Wyandottes,	4 50	6 00	12 00	3 00	5 50
Laced Wyandottes,	4 00	5 00	10 00	2 50	4 50
White Plymouth Rocks,	4 00	5 00	10 00	2 50	4 75
Barred Plymouth Rocks,	3 50	4 50	9 00	2 00	3 75
Indian Games,				5 00	10 00
Black Minorcas,	4 00	5 00	10 00	2 50	4 75
Black Spanish,	3 50	5 00	9 00	2 50	4 50
Silver Spangled Hamburgs,	3 50	5 00	9 00	2 50	4 50
Langshans,	3 50	5 00	9 00	2 50	4 50
Houdans,	3 50	5 00	9 00	2 00	3 75
Light Brahmas,	4 00	5 00	9 00	2 00	3 75
Dark Brahmas,	4 00	5 00	9 00	2 00	3 75
White Leghorns,	3 50	5 00	9 00	2 00	3 75
Brown Leghorns,	3 50	5 00	9 00	2 00	3 75
B. B. Red Games,	3 50	5 00	9 00	2 50	4 50
Golden Polish,	3 50	5 00	9 00	2 50	4 50
Buff Cochins,	4 00	6 00	10 00	2 50	4 50
White Cochins,	4 00	6 00	10 00	2 50	4 50
Partridge Cochins,	4 00	6 00	10 00	2 50	4 50
				Per 6.	Per 12
Mam. Bronze Turkeys,	7 00	8 00	16 00	3 00	5 75
Pekin Ducks,	3 50	4 50	9 00	1 25	2 25

Rough-Coated
Scotch Collie Shepherd Dogs.

A DOG THAT EVERY FARMER NEEDS.

The pure-bred Scotch Collie Shepherd Dog takes as naturally to driving stock as the Pointer and Setter to hunting birds. They are of a kind and affectionate disposition, and become strongly attached to their master's family. They are very watchful and always on the alert, while their intelligence is really marvellous. At one year old they are able to perform full duty, herding sheep, cattle, swine and other kinds of stock, attending them all day when necessary, keeping them together and where they belong, and driving off strange dogs and intruders. They learn to know their master's animals from others in a very short time, and a well-trained dog will gather them together, drive them home, and put each into its right stall. They can easily be taught to attend poultry, and are declared enemies of all species of vermin that infest the poultry-yard, and can be made most useful in a hundred different ways. They have a dainty carriage and fine style, profuse silky hair, bushy tail carried low, ears small and semi-erect, head long and sharp, chest deep with plenty of lung room. In general form lithe, symmetrical and graceful; altogether a handsome dog, and in sagacity he excels all others of the dog family.

IF FARMERS KNEW a Collie's usefulness in guarding his property, his assistance in the care of his cattle and sheep, his faithful, gentle and affectionate guardian and playmate of his children, they would not be without him at almost any cost.

At our "Harmony Grove" Kennels, at West Grove, Chester County, Pa., we have some of the finest stock ever imported into this country. We give below a short synopsis of our dogs with abridged pedigrees.

STUD DOGS.

Imported **DONCASTER LAD**, A. K. C.'S Book, No. 1818, is a large magnificent sable. A most intelligent face, semi-erect ears, very heavy coat and thick under coat, with a beautiful mane and frill. Sired by champion the Squire, No. 15767, Ex Truth. The Squire by Champion Charlemagne, No. 1604 and Truth by Champion Rutland, No. 1847. He is kind and gentle as a kitten. He has won seventeen prizes in England and Scotland.

Imported **Leonard**, A. K. C.'S Book, No. 20760, is a full golden sable. Sired by the celebrated Metchly Wonder, No. 2502, out of Peggy H, No. 1266. This beautiful dog is a full brother to the noted Christopher, who it is said became to this country at the fabulous price of $5000. He is the highest price ever paid for a Scotch Collie.

Imported **Don Juan II**, A. K. C.'S Book, No. 1812, is a large dark sable. Very intelligent face, long head and wonderfully active and alert. The engraving on the opposite page, taken direct from a photograph, speaks for itself. Sired by Doncaster Lad (see pedigree above), out of Princess Nigra. She by Champion Valiant by the Champion Rutland. So in Don Juan II it will be seen we have a combination of extra fine stock.

Clyde 5d, A. K. C.'S Book, No. 1509. A large handsome black and tan.

Logan, A. K. C.'S Book, No. 1567. Black and tan with white on fringe.

Gladstone, A. K. C.'S Book, No. 1568. Handsome black and tan.

Cloud's Galen, A. K. C.'S Book, No. 1517. Black and tan.

Chiltand, A. K. C.'S Book, No. 17588. Black and tan and white.

BREEDING BITCHES.

Imported **Drumlin Jessica**, A. K. C.'S Book, No. 1815, is a magnificent sable, with long pointed head and all the good points you could ask for in a perfect Collie. Sired by Champion Dublin Scot, No. 1661, Ex Jenny Lind No. 1692. Has won seven prizes.

Imported **Drumlin Tab**, A. K. C.'S Book, No. 1846. Another beautiful sable. Beautifully marked, very intelligent face and an excellent disposition. Sired by Marcy Trefoil, who was sold recently for $1500.

Imported **Drumlin Mona**, A. K. C.'S Book No. 1844. A black and tan with white feet and breast. Full of life and fire and perfect in form. Magnificent feet and legs and can run like a deer. She won second prize at Dublin against twenty-three dogs and bitches.

Imported **Nymph**, A. K. C.'S Book, No. 1847. A fine rich sable. Sired by Lothian Chief, No. 4047, out of imported Lass O'Glenluig, No. 1467.

Lady Glenburnie, No. 2664. A fine rich sable. Sired by Lothian Chief, No. 4047, out of imported Lass O'Glenluig, No. 1467.

Among others of our brood bitches space not allowing full pedigree, we would mention:

Beauty, No. 1331; **Beauty 2d**, No. 1356; **Darling**, No. 1365; **Bessie Startle**, No. 1393; **Clifton**, No. 1472; **Silva**, No. 1499; **Faithful Nell**, No. 1573; **Flora Bell**, No. 1545; **Minnie Garfield**, No. 1571; **Mollie Noble**, No. 1584; **Yarrow 3d**, No. 1586; **Nellie of Kennett**, No. 1459; **Kildoon**, No. 1349; **Lucy**, No. 1367; **Jennie LaCombe**, No. 1399.

PRICES: First-class puppies ten to twelve weeks old, $10.00 each, and $17.50 per pair, no akin. These are for first-class dogs in every respect, but for extra choice puppies bred directly from our imported stock and registered in the American Kennel Club stud-book, we charge $15.00 to $25.00 each, or $30.00 to $45.00 per pair.

✦ A FEW TESTIMONIALS. ✦

W. M. INGRAM, Nocona, Tex., Nov. 10, 1890, writes: The two Collie pups that I received from your house last February have done well. They have killed all the rats and vermin about the place and are fine workers on all sorts of stock. Are very biddable—always on the alert, and without the privilege of replacing them, would not take $100 for the pair.

Peter Johnson, Milton Fla. Nov. 1, 1890, writes: The Collie puppies I got from you have given perfect satisfaction. Would not take $100 each for them and he so I could not replace them.

W. SAM L. GOOLSBY, Emporia Va., Oct. 29, 1890, writes: The Collie pup is one of the finest dogs I have ever seen. He herds my cattle every day and has more intelligence than an ordinary man. I would not take $200 for him. He is very large and beautiful and the pet of the family.

F. H. BETTS, Tecumseh Neb., Nov. 11, 1890, writes: The Collie I bought from you last spring is a fine one and she is full of work.

E. Locke, Choccolocco Ala., Oct. 31, 1890, writes: The pair of Scotch Collie puppies from the first took the whole family by storm—so intelligent, affectionate and docile. They have a warm spot in all our hearts. $500 would not buy them to-day.

> "HEV A DOG, MISS? THEY'RE BETTER FRIENDS NOR ANY HUMAN. SHE MEANS MORE SENSE WI' HER BARK NOR HALF THE CHAPS CAN PUT INTO THEIR TALK FROM BREAKFAST TO SUNDOWN. LOR'S, IT'S A FINE THING TO HEV A DUMB BRUTE FOND ON YOU; IT'LL STICK TO YOU AN' MAKE NO JAW."
> — "THE MILL ON THE FLOSS."

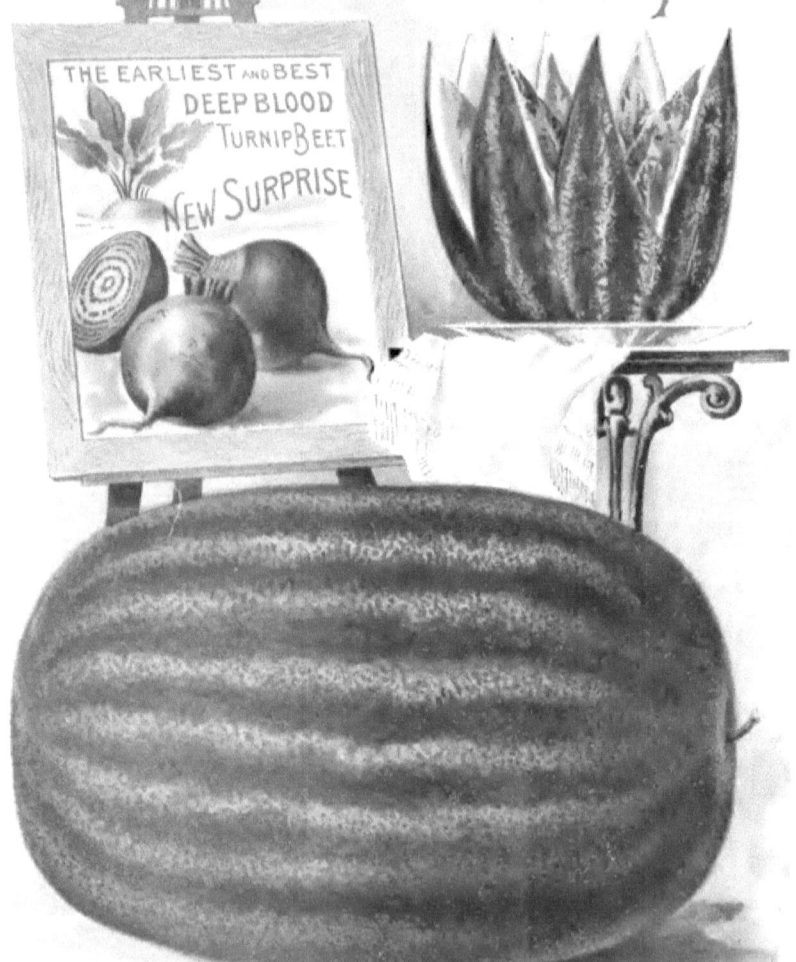

www.ingramcontent.com/pod-product-compliance
Lightning Source LLC
Chambersburg PA
CBHW020118170426
43199CB00009B/558